INNOVATION

GOVERNANCE

INNOVATION
GOVERNANCE

How Top Management Organizes and Mobilizes for Innovation

Jean-Philippe Deschamps and

Beebe Nelson

To Peter wonderful colleague in the writing game
Beebe

JB JOSSEY-BASS™
A Wiley Brand

This edition first published 2014
© 2014 John Wiley & Sons, Ltd

Under the Jossey-Bass imprint, Jossey-Bass, 989 Market Street, San Francisco CA 94103-1741, USA
www.josseybass.com

Registered office
John Wiley & Sons Ltd, The Atrium, Southern Gate, Chichester, West Sussex, PO19 8SQ,
United Kingdom

For details of our global editorial offices, for customer services and for information about
how to apply for permission to reuse the copyright material in this book please see our
website at www.wiley.com.

Wiley publishes in a variety of print and electronic formats and by print-on-demand. Some
material included with standard print versions of this book may not be included in e-books
or in print-on-demand. If this book refers to media such as a CD or DVD that is not
included in the version you purchased, you may download this material at http://
booksupport.wiley.com. For more information about Wiley products, visit www.wiley.com.

Library of Congress Cataloging-in-Publication Data

Deschamps, Jean-Philippe.
  Innovation governance : how top management organizes and mobilizes for innovation /
Jean-Philippe Deschamps and Beebe Nelson.
    pages cm
  Includes bibliographical references and index.
  ISBN 978-1-118-58864-2 (paperback)
    1. Technological innovations—Management.   2. Diffusion of innovations—
Management.   3. New products.   4. Corporate culture.   5. Organizational
behavior.   I. Nelson, Beebe.   II. Title.
  HD45.D367 2014
  658.4'063—dc23   2013045070

A catalogue record for this book is available from the British Library.

ISBN 978-1-118-58864-2 (paperback) ISBN 978-1-118-58857-4(ebk)
ISBN 978-1-118-58858-1 (ebk)

Cover design: Dan Jubb

Set in 11.5/13.5pt Bembo Std by Toppan Best-set Premedia Limited, Hong Kong
Printed in Great Britain by TJ International Ltd, Padstow, Cornwall, UK

CONTENTS

FOREWORD

INNOVATION

Many volumes of books and articles have been written on this subject, yet most organizations acknowledge they are not truly innovative in spite of concentrated efforts to become so. Back in 1997 HBS Professor Clayton Christensen wrote his seminal book, *The Innovator's Dilemma*, that described in lucid terms why organizations fail to innovate. Businesses, including my own, Medtronic, took his admonitions to heart, yet most established companies have been unable to move the needle on their efforts to become more innovative. I continue to be amazed at the number of outstanding companies whose leaders talk the innovation talk but fail to create innovative organizations or to come up with innovative business ideas.

In my experience, most companies fail to innovate for five fundamental reasons:

1. Lack of direct engagement of the CEO and clarity around leadership of innovation
2. Absence of a sound, well-established innovation process

3. Failure to distinguish clearly between science, product engineering, and innovation
4. Risk aversion and low tolerance for failure
5. Unwillingness to support innovation budgets during near-term performance shortfalls

World-class innovation expert Jean-Philippe Deschamps and his co-author, Beebe Nelson, have examined the larger scope of innovation and have discovered why companies fail to innovate. In their view two things are sorely lacking in organizations: leadership and governance. In his 2008 book, *Innovation Leaders*, Deschamps addressed the vital question of why innovation leaders are sorely lacking in most established organizations. He also addressed the question of what can be done to develop more innovation leaders who rise to the top of large organizations.

In *Innovation Governance*, Deschamps and Nelson scale new heights in taking the question of innovation leadership to a higher plane by focusing on the core reason for failure: lack of a well-established system for governing innovation. They challenge the reader to ask, why don't all companies who are striving to be innovative have a well-established system of governing their efforts and clear ground rules for carrying them out?

While scholars and practitioners like myself have argued for decades about whether the key is the innovation process or its leaders, Deschamps and Nelson neatly combine the two in their concept of innovation governance. However, their solution is not prescriptive. Rather than advocating a single governance model, they instead explore the full range of innovation governance approaches. Their 3×3 matrix model produces nine ways of thinking about the type of governance system you wish to establish for your company.

To provide depth and context to each of the nine models, Deschamps and Nelson examine the innovation structures of the world's leading companies and how they govern their innovation. By avoiding the one-size-fits-all approach so common in most treatises on innovation, they challenge innovation leaders to create their own approaches that will work best in their cultures and align with their business models and strategies.

MY EXPERIENCES IN LEADING INNOVATION

Throughout my career I have seen innovation as the key to creating value for your customers, motivating your employees, and building growing businesses – all the necessary elements for creating lasting value for your owners and investors. In my early years in business my role models of innovation leaders were Hewlett-Packard founders David Packard and Bill Hewlett, Merck's Roy Vagelos, Louis Lehr of 3M and Medtronic founder Earl Bakken. In recent years, newer innovation role models have emerged, such as Dan Vasella of Novartis, Arthur Levinson of Genentech, eBay's Meg Whitman (now CEO of Hewlett-Packard), Apple's Steve Jobs and Google's Eric Schmidt.

I have never considered myself an innovator who invents products. Rather, I have tried to be a leader who leads and stimulates the innovation process to ensure the real innovators get the encouragement, support, mentoring, and focus they need to produce great innovations. Surprisingly, many CEOs and senior leaders of established companies who are eager for their companies to innovate nevertheless take actions repeatedly that prevent an innovative culture from emerging. For example, during budget season they are prone to trim back budgets for innovation projects rather than protect them, or they stand passively by as their business heads do so in order to meet pre-established targets or protect short-term product upgrades. Or they may be quite critical of innovations that do not materialize, often punishing the innovators who took the risks on their behalf. Other leaders fully fund their research and development budgets, but never engage the innovators themselves. Nor do they understand their own cultures well enough to know why they are not producing any genuine breakthrough products.

My first general management role dates back to 1969. My goal was to create the consumer microwave oven business for Litton Industries, a challenge I found highly stimulating. At the time consumers didn't even know what microwaves were. If they did, most were afraid of potential radiation, as we weren't that far removed from stories of Hiroshima and Nagasaki. At Litton we used innovation in our products and marketing to turn the microwave oven from a popcorn popper to a widely used device that has become standard in most homes. Since neither consumers nor appliance sales people, most of whom were men, understood how to use the product, we hired 2,000 part-time home economists to work at retail, conducting cooking classes and demonstrations.

Sadly, when I moved to Honeywell in 1978, my successor at Litton focused almost entirely on getting product costs down and innovation dried up. In my Honeywell years, innovation became more difficult. This company of superb engineers focused primarily on generating better products and processes, not breakthrough innovations. The ring laser gyroscope that guides all aircraft today was a notable exception.

Joining Medtronic in 1989, I saw the opportunity to harness and expand innovation in a highly creative company that was using medical technology to restore millions of people to full life and health. Medtronic was filled with remarkable innovators and exceptional innovation leaders, yet the company's recent history had been characterized more by missed opportunities and notable failures in innovation. Win Wallin, my predecessor as CEO of Medtronic, revived the process by focusing on the implantable defibrillator, whose inventor had been rejected by Medtronic. However, a system for governing innovation had not yet been established within this predominantly functional organization.

To create the innovation governance system at Medtronic, we started with our board of directors. Between 1990 and 1996 Wallin and I took significant steps to add pioneering medical doctors and technologists to the Medtronic board, who ensured that the company's emphasis stayed laser-focused on innovation. The board established a technology and quality committee, which provided oversight, ideas and guidance to management. The T&Q Committee, as it was known, was very helpful in pointing out emerging technologies that management may have overlooked and examining the viability of technologies we were pursuing. The board wanted to ensure that the company never again overlooked an important medical technology as it had with the implantable defibrillator.

From a management standpoint, it was clear that Medtronic's innovation was not well organized, leading to haphazard results. To bring some clarity to the governance process, I decided to bifurcate the organization between established businesses organized around strategic business units (SBUs) and an innovation function that included new ventures, research projects, and external alliances. The existing businesses were run by chief operating officer Art Collins, who later became my successor. The innovative work was championed by vice chairman Glen Nelson, MD. Nelson was a brilliant physician with a keen interest in medical technology who was recruited from a pioneering health maintenance organization. The company's largest business, cardiac rhythm management (pacemakers and defibrillators), was led by an exceptionally strong innovation leader, Bob Griffin. Griffin had a long history within the company of championing breakthrough innovations, often reprogramming funds to keep them alive. For the next decade Nelson and Griffin drove Medtronic's innovation while Collins skillfully managed the SBUs. Both Nelson and Griffin were masters at scouring the world for new medical technologies being created by courageous physicians and entrepreneurs that we could bring into Medtronic.

During this period Medtronic innovators were successful in using medical technology to create breakthrough innovations that addressed a wide range of complex diseases like sudden cardiac arrest, Parkinson's, atherosclerosis, heart failure, spinal disease, diabetes, and incontinence. All they needed from our top executive team was funding, focus, and a high level of engagement with their innovations. Not infrequently, Nelson, Griffin and I had to make organizational interventions to prevent the SBU leaders from shooting down their ideas before they had been developed or refusing to transfer the talent to them that were needed to make their innovation projects successful.

I recall one especially tense meeting involving a novel idea for minimally invasive cardiac surgery, also known as "beating heart" surgery. Since Medtronic sold one-third of all the heart bypass systems in the world, this invention was very threatening to our core business, whose leaders adamantly opposed going ahead with the venture. To bolster their case, they brought in several of the world's leading cardiac surgeons who opposed any designs that did not give them full visual access to the heart on bypass. In the end we proceeded with the new procedure, which today accounts for more than 20% of the world's bypass procedures and results in better outcomes at lower cost for patients. My assumption was that if we did not go ahead, a more innovative company would perfect the procedure and overtake Medtronic in the market.

In terms of metrics, Wallin established corporate goal in 1986 of growing revenues and profits by 15% per annum. To achieve this growth in markets expanding at only 6-8%, we recognized we had to create entirely new markets through innovation. Thus, we established a second primary goal that 67% of our revenues would come from products introduced in the past 24 months. This goal was especially challenging when compared with 3M or Hewlett-Packard, which had announced goals of 25% of revenues coming from products introduced in the past five years. The 67% was achieved every year from 1990 through 2006, when the innovation process slowed down. Realizing such an aggressive goal meant that Medtronic had to employ rigorous processes for product innovations complemented by separate processes for more speculative research into new medical therapies.

In analyzing the actual results during those years, it becomes clear that product innovations were responsible for the bulk of Medtronic's increase in market capitalization between 1985 and 2001 from $400 million to $60 billion. In the past decade the Medtronic's innovation culture has atrophied as Nelson and Griffin retired, and attention shifted away from new medical technologies to improving existing products with lower risk profiles.

Currently, Medtronic's system of innovation governance is being revived by new CEO Omar Ishrak, who has a clear mandate from the Medtronic board of directors. Ishrak, who was born in Bangladesh, is a pioneer in the process of reverse innovation – bringing innovations from emerging markets to developed markets. He gained notoriety for the invention of low cost ultra sound systems in Asia that enabled General Electric to capture the leading position in the United States and Europe. As CEO of Medtronic, he is focusing not only on product innovation, but also on business model innovation as a vehicle to expand Medtronic's opportunities in emerging markets. Ishrak has established a rigorous innovation governance system led by Medtronic's head of business development with regular reports to the board's T&Q Committee.

A RIGOROUS SYSTEM OF INNOVATION GOVERNANCE CHAMPIONED BY INNOVATION LEADERS

In their examination of the nine types of innovation governance models, Deschamps and Nelson offer convincing evidence that a variety of innovation governance models can be effective. Their insightful case studies, drawn from their work with some of the world's most innovative companies – IBM, Corning, Nestlé, DSM, Tetra-Pak, and Michelin – are not only revealing but inspiring. Their arguments on behalf of establishing an effective system of innovation governance are compelling and irrefutable.

This brings us back to the original question, why don't all companies who have a desire to be innovative adopt clear processes for governing their innovation? The answer, in my view, is leadership. To be successful, companies must be led by leaders – the CEO, top executives and board of directors – who are deeply and irrevocably committed to innovation as their path to success. Just making innovation one of many priorities or passive support for innovation are the best ways to ensure that their company will never become a great innovator.

As Deschamps and Nelson make abundantly clear, building and sustaining an innovative organization requires clearly established processes for governing innovation run by innovation leaders that are willing to devote substantial portions of their time and their political capital to the innovation process. They must be backed by a board of directors who is equally committed to innovation. These were the ingredients that made us successful at Medtronic. The same ingredients have led to the astounding long-term success of such innovation giants as 3M, IBM, Apple and Google.

In my experience sustaining innovation requires *both* innovation leaders and a rigorous system of innovation governance. One without the other is insufficient. Innovation governance without leadership from the top will ultimately wither as the immediate takes precedence over the important. Innovation leaders without a well-established governance process are too dependent on individuals and vulnerable to losing focus when those leaders move on, as we saw in the Medtronic case.

To reiterate Deschamps' and Nelson's fundamental conclusion, "The mission of innovation leaders is to steer and support innovators. Governing innovation means making sure that innovators have as smooth a path as possible, that their commitment and hard work payoff as much and as often as possible." Their advice is well worth heeding for every organization who wants to become innovative.

Bill George
Professor, Harvard Business School
and former Chair & CEO of Medtronic

PREFACE: WHY SHOULD WE PAY ATTENTION TO INNOVATION GOVERNANCE?

Innovation has always been with us, as companies have had to keep innovating to survive and grow. As a consequence, innovation management has been a much discussed topic over the past 30 years, both in management literature and in practice. Scholars, consultants, and company practitioners have studied it and argued at length about what companies need to do to become effective innovators. But we believe the challenge is now leaving the narrow realm of specialists to become a broader and vital general management topic. Indeed, relentless technological progress and global competition over the past decade have put innovation at the forefront of most top management agendas. In short, innovation is no longer a "nice-to-have" capability that needs to be developed, notably in R&D. It is increasingly becoming a core competence of corporations because of its many strategic effects, its disruptive character, and its complex cross-functional and multidisciplinary processes. As such it deserves top management attention.

Today's innovation focus tends to be on building a comprehensive market-oriented capability by systematically addressing all the pieces of the puzzle, with a strong focus on process elements and cultural aspects. In most companies all these elements have been somehow identified and assembled. Process management has been introduced. So has strategic portfolio management. Everyone agrees that an innovation-friendly culture and climate are essential. Customer management is also recognized, and managers are now spending a lot of effort in clarifying the "fuzzy front end" of innovation. Companies with a strong orientation toward either bottom-up or top-down innovation are trying to balance their focus. In short, management teams generally know what to do, at least in theory, to make their company effective, and yet many are not managing to turn their company into sustained innovators. Something is obviously missing! In some companies, it may be a lack of will or consistency in addressing innovation imperatives. In others, resources may be scarce. In yet others, management systems may be inadequate. In most cases, however, the missing element seems to be a holistic approach to innovation, considering it as an integrated system and implementing all aspects simultaneously while remaining open to unexpected environmental and market changes.

In our experience, the main cause of these obstacles is a dearth of innovation leadership at the top. Often, the problem is caused by a lack of continuity in leadership, especially given the acceleration of changes in top management. CEO tenures are getting shorter and many companies are experiencing the impact of mergers, acquisitions, and reorganizations due to globalization, not to mention a succession of economic crises requiring constant restructuring. The book *Innovation Leaders* addressed this aspect by characterizing the key traits of innovation leaders and highlighting the importance of aligning leadership styles with specific innovation strategies. But individual leadership or leadership among a small group of managers does not suffice. Organizational leadership is needed. Companies need to embed innovation into a comprehensive corporate governance system. This means that business leaders need to identify and address all the fundamental questions regarding the deployment of innovation. They must propose a set of values and policies on innovation, review their formal allocation of responsibilities for innovation, and put in place adequate supporting mechanisms. Equally importantly, they need a diagnostic system to help them decide whether their chosen approach will lead to their desired objective.

In many ways, innovation has joined the list of the big corporate issues that landed on the top management agenda and required a coordinated corporate response. Total quality management reached that level in the 1970s and 1980s; lean manufacturing practices followed in the 1980s and 1990s; and sustainability and environmental management have become hot issues in the last decade. In all cases, management has had to recognize that these challenges transcended functional boundaries and needed to be addressed in a coordinated way at a high level. This meant establishing a set of overarching values, a range of concrete policies and initiatives to support these values, a pyramid of measurements, and an auditing process to follow progress at the top level and communicate results. Last but not least, it meant assigning oversight responsibilities, also at a high level. In short, these big scale issues triggered the need for a real governance mechanism, at board and top management levels. In this book, we suggest that the same is now true for innovation. Innovation governance is turning into a new corporate imperative.

Innovation governance provides a frame for all activities related to innovation. It is akin to a company's innovation constitution. As a constitution, it has four broad roles.

First, it sets out all legitimacy aspects by defining and limiting the roles of the various players in innovation, and notably (1) who is really in charge and owns the whole innovation process; (2) who is responsible for what part of this process; and (3) what legitimizes the allocation of responsibilities.

Second, it establishes overarching goals for effectiveness and efficiency in utilizing resources and achieving results in terms of growth and competitiveness, and it specifies who decides on resource allocation.

Third, it proposes methods for handling conflict resolution, for example across functions and/or between business units and functions, and it specifies how complexity and ambiguity will be managed.

Fourth and finally, it pledges to guarantee the delivery of specific benefits to the various stakeholders – customers, employees, shareholders, and communities.

Innovation governance has to be consistent across the organization but adaptable to different parts of the process. It also needs to be future-proof, i.e. to adapt to new market, technological, and other external trends. In short, as a constitution, it needs to be amended from time to time to fit closely with the company's changing environment.

This book has been written by experienced innovation management practitioners to help you rethink your innovation governance system, i.e. to enable you to change the way you allocate overall responsibilities for innovation in your company. It aims to guide you in establishing mechanisms that will ensure continuity of leadership in spite of changes in your company's management and environment. It illustrates the main models of governance proposed with real examples from companies, highlighting some of the challenges and success factors behind each model. It is neither an academic book nor a prescriptive "recipe-type" book. It aims to trigger reflections in the top management team on a topic that has seldom been addressed explicitly, even in highly innovative companies. It ought to enable you to consider whether there are more effective models for allocating responsibilities for innovation than the ones you are using today, and it will guide you on how to implement them successfully.

In summary, this book aims to provide a holistic and systemic approach to (1) understanding what innovation governance is, what it means, and what it entails; (2) recognizing possible governance models and their advantages/disadvantages; (3) assessing and improving current innovation governance policies and activities; and (4) advising on behavioral aspects that will help management make its governance effective. It will look at the innovation governance challenge from the perspective of both the board of directors – i.e. how should the board exercise its governance duties in the field of innovation? – and top management – i.e. how can senior leaders contribute effectively to the governance of innovation in their company given their own models of leadership?

In Part I, we shall start our innovation governance journey by characterizing the challenge. This means first clarifying the concept of innovation governance. Chapter 1 will do so by defining innovation governance as a form of organizational leadership at the corporate level that provides an overall frame for innovation. We shall describe the scope of innovation governance by listing the questions that it addresses, both on the content side of innovation and on the process dimensions. We shall recommend that management ensures a high level of congruence between these various governance aspects and that they are regularly reviewed and updated as the company goes through various phases in its development.

Talking about governance raises the question of the role of the board of directors in "governing" innovation. Chapter 2 will address this question by recommending that the board be proactive and include an innovation aspect in each of its statutory governance missions. For example, the board should ask management to audit the company's innovation effectiveness regularly and to communicate its planned innovation strategy. It should require management to establish and monitor a set of key performance indicators regarding innovation and to regularly review the strategic risks linked with innovation. Finally, the board should ensure that new appointees – particularly in the CEO position – have the experience and talent to support the corporation's innovation focus.

Governing innovation is primarily a responsibility of the top management team. Chapter 3 will list six areas where management initiatives are expected: (1) setting the frame for innovation, in terms of vision, mission, and values; (2) specifying how the company will identify, create, and capture value from innovation; (3) establishing priorities and allocating resources for innovation as part of an explicit innovation strategy and plan; (4) assigning primary and secondary responsibilities for innovation and setting up supporting mechanisms; (5) identifying and addressing current obstacles in the company's organizational system, as well as sources of resistance within the structure; and (6) monitoring and evaluating results continuously.

Our journey will continue in Part II with an exploration of different organizational models for assigning both overall and support responsibilities for innovation.

Chapter 4 will explain what we mean by innovation governance model and why it is important to reflect on possible models before choosing one. Indeed, companies often need more than one model; they combine innovation governance models by choosing a primary model for allocating overall responsibility for innovation and selecting one or several secondary models to support the primary model. These models go beyond merely allocating innovation responsibilities – they convey a general management philosophy, since they define the level of involvement of the CEO and his/her top aides and the company's preference for centralized or decentralized innovation responsibilities.

Chapter 5 will describe a number of models in use today, as well as examining how widely they are used. In some models, overall responsibility is entrusted to a single leader, whether solely dedicated to the task or not. In others, it is allocated collectively to several managers. In yet other models, the overall mission to steer innovation is entrusted to a permanent organizational mechanism. Surprisingly, some companies have even opted not to assign innovation responsibilities to any specific individual or group. Besides these primary governance mechanisms, most companies have established additional mechanisms to support innovation. Many of them are simple replicas of the main models, focusing on a specific part of the company or its processes. We will recommend that the choice of model be based on a systematic review of alternatives and their pros and cons.

Chapter 6 will raise the question of the perceived effectiveness or ineffectiveness of the various models – and the probable reasons – based on the results of a survey that we conducted. Indeed, companies express a rather mixed general assessment of their overall level of satisfaction with the innovation governance models they have put in place, definitely reflecting the need for a rethink! In fact, their level of satisfaction varies significantly according to the models they have chosen. In short, some models seem more effective than others, although no model scores better than 70% on effectiveness. We shall try to understand why all these governance models are deemed unsatisfactory in some cases and, for many, even in a majority of cases.

In Part III, we shall attempt to learn from the field and see how specific companies have chosen to organize for and lead innovation. We will highlight (1) how these companies have evolved and come to their current governance system; (2) the mission and characteristics of their system and the mechanisms they use to leverage their efforts; (3) what challenges they have to address and how they see their governance model and priorities evolving over time; and (4) what lessons, if any, they have learned from their experience.

Chapters 7 and 8 will focus on companies that have chosen to lead from the top. In some cases, as exemplified by IBM, the CEO has assumed direct responsibility for innovation; in other cases, like Corning, it has been assigned to a subset of the top management team. We will highlight how the leaders of these companies are personally engaged and promote an innovation agenda, and what supporting models they use in their task.

Chapters 9 and 10 will focus on companies that have appointed an individual innovation champion. In some cases the champion combines overall responsibility for innovation with his/her functional job. This is frequently the case when the mission has been assigned to the chief technology or chief research officer – what we call the CTO or CRO model. The example of Nestlé illustrates this model at the highest level since the CTO is a member of the company's executive board. In some cases, the responsibility is seen as sufficiently important to be assigned to a fully dedicated leader. DSM, the Dutch life sciences and materials sciences company, has appointed a chief innovation officer reporting to the CEO.

Chapter 11 will describe the experience of a company with another form of governance system, in which responsibility is allocated to a group of managers who take on the mission collectively. What we call the board model – which generally involves a high-level, cross-functional innovation steering group – belongs in this category. The global packaging company Tetra Pak illustrates the board model and its evolution into a number of high-level councils.

Part IV will lead us to focus on concrete steps that leadership teams can take to design or upgrade their own governance system and make it work effectively.

Chapter 12 will describe how to start when building a new governance system. It will follow the example of Michelin, a large and innovative multinational, on its journey of rethinking the way it manages innovation and building a new innovation governance system from scratch. It will describe the steps the company is taking and the challenges it is facing.

Chapter 13 will propose a number of conditions that a governance system must meet to be effective. These imperatives deal with its scope, its management, its relationship with the organization, its transparency, and its capability to evolve over time as the company strategy and market conditions change.

Chapter 14 will stress the importance of aligning individual and collective leadership models to match these imperatives and challenges. This assumes that corporate leaders are able to identify their own model of leadership and understand the leadership and behavioral requirements of the different governance models. The ultimate objective is to build management teams combining different personalities and leadership styles in order to make governance effective.

To complement these recommendations, the appendix will list examples of concrete initiatives that a company can launch as part of its governance system. These specific actions deal with a number of areas, such as diagnostics and continuous improvement; innovation vision and strategy; innovation process and its management; organization and infrastructure; competences and attitudes; climate and culture; and, finally, allocation of innovation responsibilities.

Our ultimate objective is to stimulate members of the C-suite to go deeper than they otherwise might in identifying and allocating the levers of innovation under their direct guidance.

ACKNOWLEDGMENTS

This book has its roots in our long careers as innovation management practitioners, consultants, facilitators, and scholars. For over 20 years, the International Association for Product Development (IAPD) has provided a venue where leading innovators could gather for discussion, learning, and experimentation in the field of innovation. In the early 1990s, the IAPD began exploring new product development processes and practices, which inspired Beebe to co-author the book *New Product Development for Dummies* (Wiley Publishing Inc., 2007) together with Robin Karol. As time went on, IAPD became a leader in discovering the new frontiers of innovation. Our experience with this group of leading innovators – Beebe as co-director and then director, Jean-Philippe as the lead academic at a number of IAPD workshops – helped us to recognize that, once the early questions were resolved, the need for high-level oversight and leadership became increasingly urgent for sustained innovation performance. We observed significant differences between companies in the level of management commitment to innovation as well as in the way they allocated responsibilities for innovation and created innovation-enhancing mechanisms. This led us to recognize that, alongside individual innovation leadership – the topic of Jean-Philippe's latest book *Innovation Leaders* (Jossey-Bass, 2008) – companies need to deploy an organizational form of innovation leadership, or what we describe in this book as *innovation governance*.

One of the first examples of innovation governance in action that we studied was at DSM, the Dutch life sciences and materials sciences company. Rob van Leen, DSM's chief innovation officer, agreed to open his Innovation Center to us and respond to our questions. This research resulted in an IMD case study, *DSM: Mobilizing the Organization to Grow through Innovation*, written in 2009 by Jean-Philippe together with IMD research associate Daria Tolstoy (IMD-3-2111). We would like to thank Rob van Leen for being so supportive and for encouraging us to pursue our investigations on this important topic. Chapter 10 highlights DSM's current innovation governance system.

Conscious of the need to document and assess the various organizational models of governance we had observed in our practice, Jean-Philippe initiated a research survey that IMD's learning technologies specialist, Alberto Brigneti, helped structure and put online. We thank him for his assistance. This survey provided a first glimpse of the way companies allocate their innovation management responsibilities. The results of this survey, which are summarized in Chapters 5 and 6, were presented by Jean-Philippe and discussed in an executive roundtable on innovation governance organized by Beebe at IAPD for its members. The meeting was held at Harley-Davidson in Milwaukee, WI, in September 2009. At the roundtable, several of the companies whose stories are the focus of chapters in this book offered their models of innovation governance as examples of how leading innovators are structuring this newly recognized task. We owe a great debt to these companies, which included DSM, Corning, and IBM, as well as to Sikorsky and Medrad which also presented their models, and to the companies that joined in the discussion – Harley-Davidson, Caterpillar, Eli Lilly, Herman Miller, and Shell.

Jean-Philippe, meanwhile, started discussing innovation leadership and governance issues at management development seminars held at IMD business school in Lausanne, Switzerland. The program directors of these seminars – Professor Ralf Seifert for Mastering the Technology Enterprise; Professor Leif Sjoblom for the Advanced Executive Development Program; and particularly Professor Bill

Fischer and MIT Professor Charlie Fine for Driving Strategic Innovation – keenly supported Jean-Philippe's teaching experiments on this new innovation governance topic. So did Professor David Robertson, who shared his experience with governance issues in a number of companies. Their support proved invaluable and encouraged him to initiate this book-writing project, which Beebe joined without hesitation.

Wiley's executive commissioning editor, Rosemary Nixon, and her staff, as well as her US Jossey-Bass colleague, Kathe Sweeney, accepted our book project with enthusiasm. We thank them for their continued support and confidence.

The project started with an intense two-day workshop together with Beebe and IMD Professor of Leadership and Management Development, Preston Bottger. Preston helped us define and frame some of the essential concepts of innovation governance. We owe a great deal to him for generously sharing with us some of his leadership development experience. His insights have helped us to define innovation governance in Chapter 1 and pay attention to the importance of clarifying one's own model of leadership, as summarized in Chapter 14.

We would like also to express our gratitude to innovation and management thinkers who have shared some of their concepts: Bob Tomasko in Chapters 2 and 14; MIT Professor Charlie Fine in Chapter 3; and innovation bloggers Paul Hobcraft and Jeffrey Phillips in Chapter 5. They have been and remain an invaluable source of inspiration for us.

This book would not have been possible without the enthusiastic support of busy executives and innovators who took the time to talk with us and help us build their stories to provide inspiration and examples for their innovation peers. As always, the credit goes to all those whose generous help allowed us to draw what we hope will be an extremely useful picture of how the task of governing innovation can be accomplished in a variety of companies. Any mistakes that may remain in our interpretation of their governance system are wholly ours.

In particular, we would like to thank Brigitte Laurent at Solvay for her insights in Chapters 3 and 5; Paul Aspinwall, a frequent participant and speaker at IAPD workshops, and Greg Golden for their help on IBM in Chapter 7; and Bruce Kirk, also a frequent speaker and participant at the IAPD, for his help on Corning in Chapter 8.

Our research has also allowed us to delve deeply into the governance system of several multinational companies that have generously given us access to their CEO and C-suite officers. These high-level contacts confirmed us in our belief that nothing can replace senior leaders' firm and personal commitment to innovation.

At Nestlé, covered in Chapter 9, our gratitude goes to CEO, Paul Bulcke; CTO, Werner Bauer; executive vice president in charge of all strategic business units, Patrice Bula; head of Nestlé's Research Center, Thomas Beck; and head of the System Technology Center, Alfred Yoakim. We also appreciate the efforts of assistant vice president for corporate affairs, Ferhat Soygenis, in helping us edit Chapter 9. Finally we wish to express our appreciation to Professor Kamran Kashani who wrote the IMD case *Innovation and Renovation: The Nespresso Story* from which large excerpts are reproduced.

At DSM, the subject of Chapter 10, we would like to thank CEO Feike Sijbesma and, once again, Rob van Leen, for his willingness to update us on DSM's innovation governance system.

At Tetra Pak, described in Chapter 11, we are indebted to a number of people for their wholehearted support of this book project: CEO, Dennis Jönsson; CTO, Michael Grosse; senior technologist, Stefan Andersson; and one of Tetra Pak's first innovation advocates, Richard Tonkin.

At Michelin, covered in Chapter 12, our gratitude goes to CEO, Jean-Dominique Senard, who was willing to share his views on and hopes for his brand new innovation governance system, knowing full well that it was still a work in progress. We were guided in our investigation by Michelin's CTO, Terry Gettys; head of sustainable business development, Patrick Oliva; former head of research, Philippe Denimal; and organization development specialist, Pascal Thibault. We thank them all sincerely for their openness and support.

The job of co-authoring a book is always fraught with difficulty. We are therefore hugely grateful to IMD senior editor

Lindsay McTeague whose patience and tact enabled us to realize what was needed to align styles and create a readable book. Her calm and reassuring attitude as she professionally edited our text helped us to overcome several moments of confusion and classic author despair.

Last but not least, we very much appreciate the warm encouragement and support from our spouses, Danièle Deschamps and Duncan Nelson, during these long solitary research and writing phases.

PART I

ADDRESSING THE INNOVATION GOVERNANCE CHALLENGE

CHAPTER 1

WHAT IS INNOVATION GOVERNANCE?

When business leaders hear the word "governance," they may naturally think of corporate governance, "the system by which companies are directed and controlled."[1] "It involves regulatory and market mechanisms, and the roles and relationships between a company's management, its board, its shareholders and other stakeholders, and the goals for which the corporation is governed."[2]

But what does the concept of *innovation governance* conjure up? Does it belong to the broader governance mission of the board of directors? Is innovation a sufficiently important challenge to be "governed," i.e. directed and controlled at a high level? In many companies immersed in today's global product and service competition, the answer is definitely yes. And innovation governance is not just a mission of the board, as we shall see in Chapter 2. It is clearly also a duty of the top management team, as we will emphasize in Chapter 3 and the rest of this book.

But before we try to define it, let us first briefly review current managerial responses to the governance challenge in respect of innovation, i.e. reflect on the way companies effectively stimulate, steer, and sustain a complex cross-functional and multidisciplinary activity like innovation.

THE INNOVATION MANAGEMENT CHALLENGE

Most large corporations are organized around three axes – business units, regional operations, and functions – which management knows how to steer and control effectively. In addition, these corporations have generally gone further by allocating specific responsibilities and setting up dedicated mechanisms to manage cross-functional processes – a fourth dimension – for example, for new product development. Innovation does indeed consist of several cross-functional processes. But there is more to it than processes. Innovation deals with *hard* business issues like growth strategy, technological investments, project portfolios, and the creation of new businesses. It also includes *softer* challenges, like promoting creativity and discipline, stimulating entrepreneurship, encouraging risk taking, promoting teamwork, fostering learning and change, and facilitating networking and communications. In short, it requires a special type of organizational culture. Like customer focus, innovation is a mindset that should pervade the whole organization.

The scope of innovation is so broad that few companies appear to have thought carefully enough about what it takes now and will take in the future to stimulate, steer, and sustain innovation in an integrated way, across all its aspects. Many companies do not have an overall frame that integrates all these hard and soft innovation aspects under proactive top management supervision. Management today needs a holistic system that sets and aligns goals, defines policies and values, prioritizes processes, allocates resources, and assigns roles, responsibilities and decision-making authority to key players. And that system has to originate from the C-suite. This is the task we call *innovation governance*. The word "governance" is appropriate here because stimulating, steering, and sustaining innovation is a mission that cannot be delegated to any single function or to lower levels of an organization. It remains a top management responsibility and preserve.

Of course, the CEO personally or the C-suite collectively can decide to take on the innovation challenge directly, as a top management responsibility, and thus "govern" innovation proactively as a group. This often happens in start-ups – especially technology-based ones – that grow big. But in our experience, this level of top management ownership and direct involvement in innovation is rare in large and traditional corporations. In many cases, in spite of all the risks that it creates – including lack of integration, short termism, and strategic myopia – management has delegated the responsibility for innovation to different individuals or groups, for example to marketing for improvements to existing product lines, or to R&D for exploring new technologies.

Ad hoc organizational solutions to the governance challenge may work well for some aspects, typically those dealing with process management issues and extensions of current businesses and activities. But many such solutions fail to meet other aspects of the innovation challenge, for example those dealing with the sustained creation of radically new growth businesses or simply with culture change.

Given the newness of the term and of the concept behind it, we should first define what innovation governance really means and determine its scope.

DEFINING INNOVATION GOVERNANCE

In a recent management development seminar at IMD business school in Lausanne, Switzerland, on the theme of innovation governance, the participants – all senior managers vastly experienced in the field of innovation – proposed the following list of innovation governance responsibilities:

- defining roles and ways of working around the innovation process;
- defining decision power lines and commitments on innovation;
- defining key responsibilities of the main players;
- establishing the set of values underpinning all innovation efforts;
- making decisions that define expectations;
- defining how to measure innovation;
- making decisions on innovation budgets;

- orchestrating, balancing, and prioritizing innovation activities across divisions;
- establishing management routines regarding communications and decisions.

This list provides a good first description of the scope of innovation governance but it is worth going further and introducing a structure to capture the various facets of innovation governance.

There are two complementary ways to define innovation governance. The first is to equate it to a collective form of *organizational leadership* with regard to innovation. The second is to compare it to a corporate *innovation constitution*.

Innovation Governance: An Organizational Form of Innovation Leadership

At the start of the Driving Strategic Innovation executive development program, which IMD offers jointly with MIT, we like to frame innovation in a broad leadership perspective by introducing Jay Galbraith's organizational star model.[3] It consists of five elements:

- strategy (including vision, market direction, competitive advantage, and differentiated offerings);
- structure (including power and authority, reporting relationships, and organizational roles);
- processes (including integrative roles, lateral connections, and idea and knowledge flow);
- rewards (including goals, scorecards and metrics, values and behaviors, and compensation); and
- people (including staffing and selection, performance feedback and learning, and development).

It is the role of leaders, we believe, to reflect on each of these five dimensions in order to make them conducive to innovation, and to ensure that they are internally congruent. In other words, each element has a direct impact on the company's ability to innovate, and a single misalignment – for example if management punishes risk taking and failures in its performance evaluation and reward system – can ruin the company's efforts.

This framework reminds managers that innovation has a broad organizational leadership aspect that goes beyond the traditional emphasis on culture and processes. It thrives when leaders adopt a comprehensive perspective and understand how each part of the system influences overall performance; it fails if one of the elements is missing or counterproductive.

Building on this broad organizational leadership perspective, we can define the scope of innovation governance as a combination of five concrete missions for management (refer to Figure 1.1). In the rest of this section we will address each of these missions and reflect on how they define and impact on governing innovation.

Innovation governance starts with a management commitment to promote many types of innovations, i.e. to encourage everyone in the organization to consider opportunities for innovation in all aspects of the company's offerings and in all its internal and external processes. This first governance mission is so critical that we will explore it in more detail later in this chapter.

Besides this missionary call for breadth in perspective, the innovation governance duties of management are fourfold.

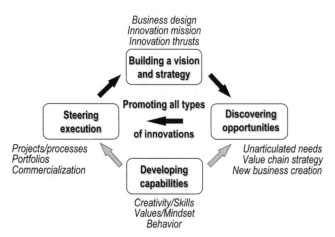

Figure 1.1: The Scope of Innovation Governance

Building a Mission, Vision, and Strategy for Innovation

As part of this first innovation governance element, management should reflect on and explicitly address three fundamental questions:

- *Why innovate?* What benefits can we expect from innovation, or what penalties might we incur if we fail to innovate?
- *Where to innovate?* In what areas should we focus our innovation efforts to implement or reinforce our business strategy?
- *How much to innovate?* How much risk can we bear in our innovation drive, and how many resources are we ready to commit to it?

Unwillingness to Resource Projects?

A large company that serves the medical industry had grown primarily by acquisition. The executive team decided to launch a growth by innovation strategy and appointed a director of innovation. After several years, despite devoting resources to finding innovation opportunities, the group portfolio management team had canceled every suggested project because it was not willing to resource projects that would not build upon existing product lines and pay off in the short term.

It is critical that management make its expectations explicit regarding *why*, *where*, and *how much*, and that these expectations are widely known in the company. Some companies waste scarce resources pursuing opportunities that, in the end, are sidelined or canceled, not because further research shows them to be less likely to succeed, but because management does not adhere to its own guidelines. Management must also make explicit its own willingness to pursue different levels of innovation. Too often, for example, management pays lip service to radical innovation, but fails to fund the projects that emerge from early stage innovation initiatives.

It is imperative that management also take the time to reflect on these questions. Different members of the management team are likely to have different mental models or implicit assumptions about innovation, often stemming from their own experiences. Unless they have the opportunity to reflect together, to discover where they agree and disagree, their actions and decisions are likely to contradict the mission and strategy as they have been defined.

Discovering Opportunities for Innovation

One critical capability to be developed as part of the company's innovation strategy is "foresight," or the ability to track weak signals and sense emerging trends in the market, in customer behavior and preference models, and in technologies. Building foresight is a complex process which requires launching efforts to collect market/customer, competitive, and technological intelligence. It requires a company-wide attitude of openness and curiosity and, possibly, the establishment of small specialist departments to constantly scan the environment for weak signals of change and emerging trends, particularly from outside one's own industry.

Many large R&D departments have set up such a capability, appointing a number of technology gate-keepers to follow the progress of new technologies. In recent years, product management and commercial managers have also begun to dedicate valuable resources to long-term market and competitor intelligence activities.

> **Myopia in Smartphones?**
> The past decline of Nokia and RIM (Blackberry) in smartphones can be attributed, at least in part, to their inability to spot – or their unwillingness to follow – a radical change in the market. Both sold their smartphones primarily to the professional segment of managers and neglected the consumer market, which Apple targeted first with its iPod Touch® and later with its iPhone, followed by Samsung and other Android phone manufacturers. Equipped with a user-friendly touch screen and a growing number of applications, these phones became an attractive alternative to the competent but dull professional smartphones of Nokia and RIM. Professional users quickly convinced their IT department to buy the new fun and "app-rich" smartphones, leaving the two former leaders in a difficult catch-up mode.

These activities include gathering ethnographic information about customers and their wants and needs (in particular so-called latent needs, of which the customer is unaware), building groups of industry "thought leaders," and participating in conferences and other gatherings where it is possible to rub shoulders with technologists and customers. However, many companies run the risk of myopia, failing to sense new opportunities or failing to commit to them once they have been uncovered. Product managers may be tempted to look narrowly at the boundaries of their competitive arena and stick to the paradigm on which they built their business. Marketing managers' perspective is often more operational than strategic, which leaves them boxed in as they try to use incremental improvements to compete in the same markets. R&D can certainly become stuck in a commitment to its own technology and ignore potential disruptive changes. The examples of Nokia and RIM highlight the potentially dramatic consequences of such myopia.

The challenge is to establish appropriate boundaries to frame the search for intelligence. If the scope of the search is too narrow, as the examples of Unilever (see box), Nokia, and RIM show, there is a risk of myopia. If it is too broad, then the company may become lost in an endless search for irrelevant trends.

It is therefore important to stress the role of top management, as part of its innovation governance mission, in ensuring that the organization remains in a mode of constant alert to external trends that could disrupt the com-

---

Foresight Lacking at Unilever?

A former head of research at Dutch food giant Unilever recalled that one of the major trends that impacted the profitability of his company in the past – the microwave oven revolution – took the company by surprise because it had emerged outside the food industry. By triggering a trend toward ready-meals and fatless cooking, it noticeably reduced purchases of margarine, one of Unilever's most profitable product lines. He claimed that no one in marketing had anticipated the development of the new cooking technology and its impact on margarine, since product managers were too busy scanning the development of other fat categories, like butter and oil.

pany's activities and/or create new opportunities. Besides accepting the costs linked to this search for intelligence – some see it as an unnecessary overhead – leaders need to adopt an attitude of extreme openness to external changes, as well as humility to challenge the company's implicit beliefs. Andy Grove, the legendary former CEO of Intel, called it necessary management "paranoia."[4]

Steering the Execution of Innovation Projects

Of all the innovation governance elements, steering the execution of innovation projects is probably the one that has received the broadest recognition. It was the first innovation issue to be recognized. In the 1980s and 1990s, companies and the academic community began to pay attention to two critical execution activities: (1) optimizing the project pipeline, which includes project resourcing and ensuring that the collection of projects in the pipeline fulfills the innovation strategy; and (2) steering the execution of innovation projects by multifunctional teams by designing and implementing phase/review processes. These processes are designed to manage the tasks as well as the critical decisions of developing a new offering. They make it possible to start a project, while delaying the decision to invest significant resources until enough information has been gathered to be able to judge the likelihood of success. The logic of the phase/review process makes it possible to begin attractive but risky projects with low initial investments. As often happens when addressing complex and systemic issues, it was first seen as a simple linear process – from idea to commercialization. As understanding of the linear process grew, companies and consultants and academics were able to appreciate more subtle aspects, so execution now includes many more factors.

In steering the execution of innovation projects, management should address three new questions, which will be explored in more detail later in this chapter:

- *How to innovate more effectively?* What approaches should we adopt to meet our innovation objectives and how can we mobilize our organization behind this challenge?

- *With whom to innovate?* What are the purpose, scope, and process of an effective open innovation strategy and approach?
- *Who should be responsible?* Who should be the owners of our innovation efforts, and what organizational models will we choose to steer innovation?

The role of governance with respect to execution is to ensure that the necessary processes exist and are being used optimally. Many companies have appointed process owners, who are responsible for implementing and improving processes. Corning, for example, uses a kind of ethnographic methodology to assess how well a process is working for those whose work is framed by it, in order to make sure that improvements are targeted and necessary.

There is, however, a problem that has become more severe in recent years. Now that companies do not need to design processes from scratch, there is a temptation to over-perfect them. Processes should of course be improved when necessary – but management should guard against over-engineering processes, spending more time on them than what they can do for the market warrants.

Developing Innovation-enhancing Capabilities

Innovation-minded leaders are generally aware of the need to enlist as many of their staff as possible in focused innovation management development programs. Of course, innovation requires a range of hard skills, such as new technological competencies or advanced commercial proficiency. These are generally offered as part of the company's traditional training programs. They are needed in most circumstances, but they are not sufficient. At least four other categories of softer skills essential for innovation also need to be developed:

- Customer sensing – understanding customers' evolving hierarchy of preferences and subtle patterns of adoption. What used to be called "the fuzzy front end of innovation" is now more widely referred to as just "the front end of innovation," and there are many excellent processes to guide the search. These techniques, which must be learned by a broad range of people, include mapping technologies, ethnographic customer research, and so on.

- Idea and concept evaluation and validation – being able to screen and rank ideas and preconcepts generated through an ideation process against the company's strategic criteria. Here again, processes and tools to accomplish this are widely available and can be shared with a broad range of managers.
- Team management – creating a culture and processes that foster collaboration within projects and across functions and levels. This type of training is essential at the beginning of important projects to help team members to bond and encourage them to cooperate with one another while maintaining a healthy confrontation of ideas.
- A to Z project and venture management – including knowing how to reduce the range of technical and market uncertainties as a project progresses, and how to assess the changing value of the project in terms of its fit with strategy, with the proposed portfolio of new offerings, and with offerings already in the market.

Besides ensuring that such skills are being nurtured, innovation governance also promotes critical innovation-enhancing values and behaviors. The range of values to be promoted is long and well known, since they are constantly repeated in the management literature:

- user orientation and customer intimacy;
- curiosity; openness to the external world and to ideas from all over;
- risk taking, tolerance of failure, and learning from failures;
- teamwork and collaboration across all hierarchies and organizational units;
- entrepreneurship and a bias toward a "just-do-it" attitude;
- experimentation and a tendency to build prototypes very early;
- professionalism in project management; respecting timing and budgets; and
- speed and a sense of urgency.

The role of top management and particularly the CEO in this area is critical, since concrete examples – and not just exhortations – must always come from the top. It takes a lot of repeated efforts, in words and deeds, to propagate these values across the organization and make them stick.

Innovation Governance: A Corporate Constitution on Innovation

Alongside organizational leadership, the second way of defining innovation governance is to think of it as a corporate innovation constitution. In many ways, innovation governance provides a frame for all innovation activities by defining the roles, powers, and limits of the various players, and organizing the functioning of all innovation-related processes. A form of constitution is indeed necessary for an activity that cuts across most organizational units and is not subject to a hierarchical pyramid. Innovation is highly dependent on people's motivation, behavior, and interrelationships. When a company sets up a proper innovation governance system, like a constitution, it is trying to contain individual and functional interests, such as power-hungry moves, and to broaden the scope of everyone's thinking in favor of corporate interests. Of course, the bigger the company and the more complex the organization, the more important this type of constitution becomes.

Concretely, as the innovation constitution of the company, governance articles must cover four different and complementary elements:

- They should establish rules of legitimacy by defining (1) who owns what; (2) who does what; (3) who is responsible for what; and (4) what legitimizes the allocation of responsibilities. This means assigning responsibilities for various parts of the overall process, identifying decision-making authorities, and showing the extent to which all parts and players fit within an overall model of innovation.
- They should state what management sees as a desirable level of efficiency and effectiveness in the utilization of resources and achieving results. This can include targets for growth and

competitiveness, financial boundaries in attaining them, and concrete performance measures to be monitored by management to check whether goals are being attained.

- They should propose methods for conflict resolution. Despite the existence of clear rules regarding responsibilities and decision-making authorities, conflicts are bound to appear, particularly when innovation activities interfere with normal line responsibilities in terms of resource allocation or priorities. This is why management has to intervene on some occasions, without depriving the various functional players of their allocated responsibilities.

- They should state how the company intends to protect the interests of various stakeholders – customers, users, suppliers, employees, communities – other beneficiaries and/or potential victims of the company's innovation activities. For example, agrochemicals manufacturers could include in their innovation constitution firm principles regarding long-term environmental protection and commit publicly to adhere to them, irrespective of profit or growth objectives.

WHAT DOES INNOVATION GOVERNANCE ENTAIL IN PRACTICE?

Leaving broad principles behind, the rest of this chapter will focus on two practical questions: (1) how broadly should we define and promote innovation? and (2) what specific questions does innovation governance address, with regard to both the *content* and the *process* sides of all innovation activities taking place in the company?

How Broadly Should We Define and Promote Innovation?

As we suggested earlier, one of the key roles of management in governing innovation is to ensure that the term itself is defined broadly, something that is often overlooked. At IMD, when we contacted our clients' management development specialists to market a new program – Managing the Innovation Process – these HR officers automatically directed us to their R&D colleagues, as if innovation was the exclusive preserve of technical functions. This reflects a general belief that innovation deals with new products and new technology, and thus primarily involves R&D. We had to fight this prejudice to attract managers from other functions to our seminars and convince them that there is much more to innovation than R&D. This is why it is so important to stress that one of the key tasks in innovation governance is promoting and steering all aspects of innovation, not just new products.

Defining and promoting innovation broadly means at least four things for senior managers. It involves:

- looking at all types of innovations and enriching projects through multiple innovations;
- encouraging a series of incremental innovations, but also seeking breakthroughs to achieve a balanced innovation portfolio;
- paying attention to all the subprocesses within innovation, broadly defined; and
- combining and balancing management-led top-down innovation and spontaneous bottom-up innovation.

Looking at All Types of Innovations and Enriching Projects through Multiple Innovations

Left to their own devices, most business leaders might be tempted to stay within their comfort zone and focus their innovation efforts on only a few areas, typically new technologies, new products, and manufacturing processes, since these correspond to their main functional emphasis. It is top management's responsibility, as part of its governance mission, to make its businesses think more broadly and stimulate them to explore opportunities in a number of other areas.

Many well-accepted innovation typologies can be used for this purpose. The one we prefer is adapted from an original model promoted by the Doblin Group.[5] It points at innovation opportunities across the value chain.

- Innovating on the company's business models, e.g.
  - reorganizing the business to restructure the value chain;
  - introducing new revenue sources and/or a new and different revenue model;
  - creating new sourcing partnerships.
- Innovating on processes, e.g.
  - building an advantage in enabling processes;
  - innovating on the company's core process.
- Innovating on the company's offering, e.g.
  - pioneering a new product or system concept;
  - launching a new technology with a better quality/price performance;
  - focusing on new product features and attributes;
  - building and offering new product platforms to others;
  - extending the offering with new service products.
- Innovating on the company's way to go to market, e.g.
  - building new distribution channels;
  - repositioning the brand creatively;
  - focusing on activities that enhance the customer experience.

Once everyone in the organization is aware of this typology, management needs to encourage teams to search for combined innovations, i.e. to try to uncover and work on other relevant innovation categories. Many products or services that have sustained a strong market position over the past decades – think of Apple's iPod/iTunes, P&G's Pringles potato chips, and IKEA's furniture business – are the result

> **Innovation Matrix at Lego**
>
> Managers at Danish toy manufacturer Lego use an innovation matrix adapted from the Doblin Group model. It consists of eight different types of innovations: core processes; enabling processes; product offering; platform; messaging; customer interaction; sales channel; and business model. This matrix was used by the development team of its Mindstorm NXT® product to map out a series of reinforcing complementary innovations.

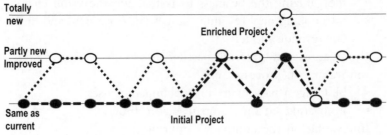

Looking for opportunities to "enrich" projects

Figure 1.2:   Innovation-type Scorecard

of combined initial innovations. They all embodied innovations in product concepts, of course, but they also brought together new approaches in business organization, business models, processes, services, and marketing. The power of combined innovations is so potent in creating a sustainable competitive advantage that some companies, like Lego, expressly demand it.[6]

It is therefore good practice for management to insert a mandatory innovation-type scorecard in a company's project review system. This scorecard reminds project teams and the reviewers that they are expected to explore the introduction of relevant new approaches in their new undertakings.

Figure 1.2 shows the innovation scorecard of an actual project plan, before and after review by management. The initial plan was rejected as too conventional and, after extensive discussions, brainstorming and feasibility studies, the more ambitious project plan was approved. This type of approach requires that project review committees include managers with a broad perspective on innovation.

Management must be aware, of course, that the more innovations that are introduced in a given project path, the riskier the project becomes. It must therefore balance its ambitions to maintain an acceptable project risk profile.

Encouraging a Series of Incremental Innovations, but also Seeking Breakthroughs to Achieve a Balanced Innovation Portfolio

Although a few companies seem to have adopted a permanent breakthrough culture – this was certainly the case with Apple under Steve Jobs and it is still valid for Google – most companies tend to favor incremental innovations over more radical ones. This often reflects business managers' perception that taking undue risk on a project will attract management's attention and, ultimately, disapproval. Although risk taking is encouraged and failures are *officially* accepted – at least in principle – in companies' innovation credos, they may not be totally forgotten when the time comes to review individual performance.

Yet sustained innovators tend to be found among companies that combine a stream of incremental innovations with an occasional breakthrough that creates a new market space. A good example is Toyota, with its *kaizen* approach to traditional product improvements combined with its pioneering development of hybrid vehicle technology. Encouraging a search for radical innovation opportunities in the hope of achieving a breakthrough is therefore part of top management's innovation governance mission. Concretely, this means that risky breakthrough projects must be provided with a different management supervision, team, budget, and process path from incremental ones.

As the Tetra Pak example illustrates, one of the most effective ways to promote breakthrough projects is for management to play

---

Tetra Pak's Level 1 Projects

Members of the group leadership team (GLT) at Tetra Pak, the Swedish carton packaging giant, have a specific process to manage radical innovations, which they call "level 1" projects, in addition to their standard new product development process. Every "level 1" project has to be led by a business manager and is coached personally by a member of the GLT. Management expressly indicates that it expects a high mortality rate from these projects and it does not hesitate to stop many of them mid-course when prospects look unfavorable.

a direct role in initiating them and thereafter in sponsoring and supervising them.

By sponsoring high-risk projects while the rest of the company pursues incremental innovation projects, management can transmit important messages to the organization:

- Why management is pursuing these projects, i.e. what are the objectives and potential contributions of the projects?
- What failure rate, hence yield, management considers as "normal" given these projects' level of risk.
- How management intends to manage and supervise these projects to guarantee maximum control, risk containment, and transparency.
- How these projects will be turned into an ongoing operation if/when successful, and to what unit they will be allocated.

Paying Attention to All the Subprocesses within Innovation, Broadly Defined

Management must also make clear that innovation extends well beyond the traditional project-related processes that companies often refer to as NPD (new product development). Indeed, innovation starts well before and ends well after the NPD process. The book *Innovation Leaders*[7] suggested that management should adopt a broad look at innovation by paying attention to and structuring its eight constituent *i-processes*. Four of these relate to the upstream part of innovation, i.e. the creative *Invention* phase:

- *Immersion:* As we have stressed above, immersion in the market using practices like visiting customers is critical for identifying unarticulated customer needs. For R&D it is important to explore existing and emerging technologies to uncover potential sources of improvement, innovation, and/or disruption.
- *Imagination:* This process is rarely formalized. Yet, innovation always starts with imagining a solution to an untapped customer need or market opportunity. Imagination is a process of concrete visioning or "realistic dream making."

- _Ideation:_ This is generally where a company's NPD process starts. It is the creative part of the innovation process as ideas are collected or generated, clustered, screened, and ranked before being converted into preconcepts and validated.
- _Initiation:_ This process tends to be visible to all because, once a business case has been approved, a formal project is created with an official brief and budget, a project leader and a team, and often a review mechanism.

The other four processes deal with the disciplined _Implementation_ phase:

- _Incubation:_ This process is often under management scrutiny because it is concrete: real work starts for the cross-functional project team with product design and prototype building and testing, and the project proceeds across a range of formal review gates.
- _Industrialization:_ This process receives even more management attention since it generally starts with a formal go/no-go decision and continues with a range of investments in tooling and manufacturing equipment before the production phase starts.
- _Introduction:_ Although critical for success, this process is not always considered as an integral part of the innovation process. Yet it starts and proceeds in parallel with product development up to the roll-out phase and thus needs to be fully integrated.
- _Integration:_ This process (integration of the company's offering into its customers' operations to make them successful) is also part of innovation. It tends to be fully integrated only in those industries that depend on the strength of their technical service or application engineering.

As we have suggested, companies often see the NPD process as starting with ideation and ending with industrialization, which is a rather narrow perspective. So, as part of their governance duties, senior managers need to insist on the first two processes – immersion and imagination – which create the context within which innovation will take place, and the last two – introduction and integration – which will shape market success. They must ensure that these processes are reasonably mapped and understood and that adequate tools are developed to assist in their implementation.

Combining and Balancing Management-led Top-down Innovation and Spontaneous Bottom-up Innovation

Thinking about innovation broadly raises the question of its origin or mode of occurrence. Innovation can indeed be a spontaneous bottom-up phenomenon, driven by the creativity and entrepreneurial spirit of a company's staff. But it can also result from a visionary and ambition-led top-down initiative introduced by management. The two modes of occurrence are, of course, not mutually exclusive. In fact, they are very complementary.

> **Post-it Notes: Typical Bottom-up Innovation**
>
> In his introduction to *New Product Development for Dummies* Dr Geoffrey Nicholson, retired 3M vice president, writes: "I can tell you from my experience in championing Post-it Notes that we had to have passion and courage. We were told several times by management to kill the program." It is often the role of the top level sponsor to challenge his or her peers in order to preserve a suitably aggressive appetite for innovation.

Some companies have a strong tradition of bottom-up innovation. They rely on initiatives from their staff and give them the necessary freedom to come up with new ideas and concepts, which may lead to new business opportunities. In these companies, management sees its role as promoting and supporting front-end innovators, shielding them from possible "idea killers." It also focuses its intervention on filtering ideas and funding the best ones. Archetypal innovators like 3M and Google probably exemplify bottom-up innovation at its best. Their management has set up systems and rules to support it, notably giving individuals the freedom to work on their own ideas (15% of their time at 3M and 20% at Google). Creating these innovation-enhancing systems and rules to encourage bottom-up innovation is an important part of innovation governance duties.

But relying on bottom-up innovation alone may be insufficient, particularly when circumstances or opportunities require the launch of major costly or complex innovation initiatives in a top-down mode. This type of management-inspired innovation is often found in Asian companies, particularly in technology-intensive industries requiring significant R&D and capital investments. It requires the ability to build and share a vision; a talent for mobilizing the organization behind that vision; and determination to persevere in spite of possible initial problems.

So, understanding the conditions under which bottom-up and top-down innovation will prosper, determining the right balance between them, and adopting management attitudes that will facilitate the two innovation modes are essential elements of innovation governance.

What Specific Questions Does Innovation Governance Address?

Questions Dealing with the Content of Innovation Efforts

As mentioned earlier in this chapter, to review whether their company has adopted a comprehensive innovation governance system, leaders need to start with three distinct types of questions about the content of innovation: Why innovate? Where to look for innovation? And how much to innovate? Good innovation governance starts with providing clear answers to these three questions.

Why innovate?

This basic question may seem mundane or unnecessary, particularly to senior managers with a strong innovation commitment, but is it in fact *that* obvious? Does everyone in the organization have the same clear understanding of the mission, purpose, and objectives of innovation for the company? In short, does everyone know – and share – the reasons why innovation is necessary and how this imperative relates to the corporate vision and objectives?

Answers to the *why* question vary from company to company, and for the same company from time to time depending on economic, competitive, and environmental circumstances. For example, companies in a strategic stalemate position, with few opportunities to compete effectively, may look at innovation as a way to generate a totally new business model, and hence to grow profitably. Others may expect innovation to reinforce their current businesses to win a sustainable advantage. Still others will see innovation as a powerful means to build a winning brand reputation and attract and motivate top talent. There are, indeed, many reasons to innovate.

In summary, it is not a vain exercise for the top management team to spend some time, for example in a management retreat, addressing the why question. In fact, it is critically important to iron out differences in perception among the members of the C-suite. As we have said above, executives can have differing assumptions and mental models about innovation. To make the company's position explicit, and to ensure that management will be consistent, managers must create a culture in which frank and open dialogue is a regular practice and the resulting position is communicated clearly to the rest of the organization. This should be the starting point for all innovation governance missions.

Where to look for innovation?

Defining the real purpose and objective of innovation leads naturally to the next question: Where should we focus our efforts and what should our priorities be? Of course, innovation is needed in all business areas, and management should promote a wide open scope for the company's innovation activities. But in some instances, innovation needs to be focused. It will better serve the business if it boosts what really matters for the success of the company.

Useful questions are: What does our strategy call for? Do we need more and better new products? Are we mainly looking for lower costs? Are we searching for better service and attractive customer solutions? Do we need to develop more robust business models? Are we ready to build new ventures that will expand the scope of the business? Management cannot escape the responsibility of determining priorities for innovation, and these may change with economic and competitive circumstances. In a real business crunch requiring drastic restructuring, management may want to change the focus of innovation activities from, for example, new product proliferation to product line rationalization and cost cutting.

Clearly defining and broadcasting the focus and priorities of innovation – where and on what we shall innovate – is therefore a second vital element of innovation governance.

How much to innovate?

There are two very different types of how much questions. The first deals with the issue of innovation funding, while the second refers to the intensity or ambitiousness of our innovation efforts and our innovation risk portfolio.

Determining the desired level of innovation is important from a funding point of view. Breakthrough innovations should not be pursued unless management is ready to commit the necessary resources to implement them fully and market them aggressively. It is not uncommon to see companies having to shelve promising radically new product or service concepts simply through lack of resources, given the current demands of their existing business. Such situations could be

---

Innovating to Cut Costs, not Jobs

In the 2008 economic and business crisis, a socially responsible European company benefited by launching a specific innovation drive that mobilized its entire staff. Management's objective, which was supported by the company's union representatives, was to unleash operational savings opportunities to achieve some of its cost-cutting objectives while minimizing job cuts. This helped to maintain employee morale and prepare the company for an economic upturn.

Shelving an Innovation for Lack of Funds

A leading automotive components manufacturer found itself unable to fund a very large investment for the production and launch of a radical innovation. Its proponents had not reckoned with the fact that all the company's investment capacity had been committed to supporting the company's aggressive development in China. The radical new product had to be shelved, at least temporarily!

avoided if management expressed clearly from the start its innovation expectations and investment constraints, a definite part of its
innovation governance mission.

Defining how much innovation we want is also important in
determining the risk we are ready to bear to meet our objective
– be it building a revolutionary new market category or developing an advantage over competitors – and the sustainability of the
anticipated reward. In other words, are we searching for breakthroughs and hence accepting a high level of uncertainty? Or do
we instead favor a more prudent approach by encouraging a series
of incremental innovation moves? Or do we expect both and, if
so, in what proportions and for what objective?

These questions need to be clarified to ensure that managers
fully understand the company's risk/reward boundaries in their
search for new ideas and opportunities.

Questions Dealing with the Process of Innovation

Good innovation governance requires three additional questions to
be addressed regarding the practical aspects of innovation activities:
How to innovate more effectively? With whom to innovate? And
who is going to be responsible for what regarding innovation?

How to innovate more effectively?

Judging by the number of books, research articles, and public
seminars devoted to the practical aspects of innovation, this question is, and will remain, on the agenda of most companies, even
the most innovative ones. It has also triggered the growth of many
service providers and consultancies to guide them in their quest.
How can we boost innovation? What approaches should we adopt
to meet our innovation objectives? How can we mobilize the
organization behind this challenge? Employees expect clear direction from management to help find the answers.

These questions, which are at the heart of any innovation
governance initiative, deal with process issues, i.e. what process will

take us most time- and cost-effectively from new market needs and ideas to successful market introduction? What organization does this require? What tools should we use for implementation? What measures should we track? But they also raise a number of culture challenges that management somehow has to address despite their complexity. How do we foster a

> **Process Paralysis?**
> An executive at a power company complained: "We have all the processes for innovation we could ever need! The problem is we spend all our time trying to do what the processes call for, and almost no time really innovating!"

climate that combines creativity *and* discipline? A culture in which sensible risk is encouraged? An environment that facilitates networking and communication in all directions? A compensation system that encourages entrepreneurship and teamwork?

With whom to innovate?

The concept of open-source innovation – building on ideas and technologies from third parties – is now pervading most businesses. Many companies advocate it as part of their innovation strategy, but advocating it is not enough. The management team needs to define: Its purpose – why do we engage in open innovation? Its scope – what are we looking for and how far are we ready to go in our partnership and alliance strategy? And its implementation process – how should we proceed to create win–win opportunities? Companies that have followed the recommendations of management scholar Henry Chesbrough[8] (Professor and Executive Director at the Center for Open Innovation at the University of California, Berkeley) and embraced the open innovation challenge, like P&G[9],

> **Eli Lilly's Office of Alliance Management (OAM)**
> It has helped the company to manage and improve its partnerships and alliances. OAM recommends: Don't expect alliances to work on their own; help alliance partners to develop a common language; and keep track of what works and what doesn't.

Eli Lilly, and Philips among many others, have clearly included it in their innovation governance agenda.

Who is going to be responsible for what regarding innovation?

The *who* question is the last but by no means the least important innovation governance question. It deals with defining and allocating specific innovation management responsibilities at all levels. As part of it, management needs to choose the overall governance model or mechanism that will stimulate and orchestrate all innovation activities in the company. It will identify the owners of all key innovation processes and help in deciding whether to allocate innovation management responsibilities to a dedicated group of managers, as opposed to current business and functional managers. If dedicated innovation managers – whatever their title – are appointed, management will have to define their role, reporting level, resources, and degree of empowerment in relation to the line organization and other established staff functions.

In summary, if sustaining innovation is an important corporate objective, it is essential to address explicitly the six questions listed above – three on *content* and three on *process*. In this chapter, we have tried to provide a broad definition of all aspects of innovation governance. In the next two chapters, we shall see, concretely, what innovation governance means at the board of director level and for top management.

NOTES

[1] http://www.ecgi.org/codes/documents/hampel23.pdf (Cadbury Committee, 1992) European Corporate Governance Institute.

[2] *OECD Principles of Corporate Governance*, 2004, OECD. http://www.oecd.org/dataoecd/32/18/31557724.pdf. Retrieved 2011-07-20. Tricker, A. (2009). *Essentials for Board Directors: An A-Z Guide*. New York, Bloomberg Press.

[3] Galbraith, J.R. (1993). *Competing with Flexible Lateral Organizations*, 2nd ed. Boston, Addison Wesley Publishing Company, Figure 1.1, p. 4.

[4] Grove, A.S. (1996). *Only the Paranoid Survive*. New York, Currency Doubleday.

[5] http://www.doblin.com/thinking/

[6] http://www.gintana.com/govern/legomatrix.html

[7] Deschamps, J.-P. (2008). *Innovation Leaders: How Senior Executives Stimulate, Steer and Sustain Innovation*. Chichester, Wiley/Jossey-Bass.

[8] Chesbrough, H.W. (2003). *Open Innovation: The New Imperative for Creating and Profiting from Technology*. Boston, Harvard Business School Press.

[9] Huston, L. and Sakkab, N. (2006). Connect & Develop: Inside P&G's New Model for Innovation. *Harvard Business Review* 84(3), 58–66.

CHAPTER 2

GOVERNING INNOVATION IN PRACTICE: THE ROLE OF THE BOARD OF DIRECTORS

I said: I am going to challenge my board! Because what is a board for?

For me, I think the board basically has two tasks:

The first one is to assure that they have a good CEO and that he performs.

And the second one is to assure that the direction is the right one for the interest of the group.

Peter Brabeck-Letmathe, Chairman of Nestlé SA[1]

A first look at the board's role in governing innovation raises a paradox. On the one hand, the board must manage risk, ensure stakeholder benefits, and, in general, keep the company on an even keel into the future. On the other hand, in fulfilling that mission the board is likely to dampen the company's appetite for innovations that go beyond incremental improvements of offerings already on the market. In this chapter we will argue that the board's involvement in innovation is critically important if the company is to articulate and pursue an innovation strategy that reflects the considered judgment of the board and top management.

Although there may be room for the board to become involved in issues that touch on innovation governance, this is not spelled out in any of the board roles that we have reviewed. For example, the responsibilities of the board at Herman Miller, a Michigan-based furniture company, are:

a) Selecting, regularly evaluating the performance of, and approving the compensation of the Chief Executive Officer and other senior executives;
b) Planning for succession with respect to the position of Chief Executive Officer and monitoring management's succession planning for other senior executives;
c) Reviewing and, where appropriate, approving the company's major financial objectives, strategic and operating plans and actions;
d) Overseeing the conduct of the company's business to evaluate whether the business is being properly managed; and
e) Overseeing the processes for maintaining the integrity of the company with regard to its financial statements and other public disclosures, and compliance with law and ethics.[2]

Although there is no mention of innovation in Herman Miller's board responsibilities, the company has included a board member with impressive innovation experience. And indeed, despite the apparent absence of innovation responsibilities in the description of the role of most boards, we firmly believe that the board is critical in shaping management's approach to innovation.

CLARIFYING THE SCOPE OF THE BOARD'S ROLE IN INNOVATION

The role of the board is critical whether or not it takes an explicit role in defining an innovation strategy and approach, since – as we suggest above – management will respond to the board's *tacit* attitudes to innovation, even if they are not spelled out or addressed explicitly. Promoting innovation and ensuring that management addresses it appropriately should therefore be a key duty of the board. Otherwise, management is left to guess about innovation parameters, and the results too often cause major waste and missed opportunities. Whether the company's innovation portfolio includes the pursuit of radical innovation, what the innovation payback time frame is, what the company will invest in innovation – these are all questions that should be explicitly discussed between the board and top management. It is essential to weave innovation issues into the board's overall governance mission, while recognizing the differences between top management's executive role and the board's governance duties.

Among the many governance duties of the board, five areas should draw our attention because of their potential impact on innovation:

- strategy review;
- risk management;
- auditing;
- performance review; and
- CEO and top management nomination.

In order to address the governance duties of the board as they affect innovation, we will regroup these missions into two major areas. The first is innovation strategy, including regular audits of both leading and lagging indicators of the company's innovation performance, as well as the board's role in defining acceptable ranges of risk. The second is the board's role in performance review and replacement of top company officers. We will conclude this chapter with reflections on selecting and developing a board that has a deep interest in innovation, with the experience and expertise to act as a competent partner for management.

REVIEWING THE COMPANY'S INNOVATION STRATEGY

Participating in Strategy Discussions

Boards generally take their role as company strategy reviewers seriously. At the very least, the CEO informs them of the major strategic issues facing the company and of the options management proposes to address them. These strategic issues often come up and are discussed when board approval is required for major investment decisions. In some cases boards may be invited to attend off-site strategy retreats and participate actively in formulating strategy together with management.

Despite their general involvement in strategy – and apart from discussions on specific and vital new products or new technologies – boards often lack the opportunity to discuss innovation strategy in detail, at least in a regular or structured way. One reason for this may be that management has not always explicitly formulated innovation strategies. This is partly because "innovation" covers a wide range of corporate activities. There is no simple formula a company can follow that describes its relationship to innovation.

For some companies, innovation means having a full portfolio of innovations, from radical new markets and technologies to incremental improvements of existing products and services, to cost reductions. To be successful, these companies have to accept some long payback times and a relatively high degree of risk. Other companies insist that innovation must pay off in a short time frame. To succeed, they have to limit their innovations to areas in which the uncertainty is low, their familiarity with technology, market, production, and financial issues is high, and the time frame from initiation to launch is short.

Confusion over a company's innovation strategy may be one of the major causes of innovation waste and failure. When the board is not engaged in governing innovation, when the company's innovation strategy is not made explicit, then top management has no choice but to guess what the board wants. Although most companies want to be known as "innovative," a number of factors push boards toward a conservative position. The one that has the most impact is the stock market. Publicly traded companies are judged on the basis of investors' confidence and willingness to invest. Stock prices are evaluated quarterly or biannually. An innovation that will not pay off for several years is generally seen as a loss in that equation, and investors hate to see their investments take a hit. Companies such as Nestlé or Corning, which boast a willingness to invest "patient money," are rare.

If the board is likely to view innovation conservatively, then top management, whose performance and compensation are dictated by the board, will probably follow suit. It is all too frequent to see top management touting innovation and even funding exploratory projects that might unearth new and innovative opportunities, yet giving the clear signal that serious investment – the resources needed to get a product to market – will be limited to projects that have low risk and short-term payback.

Communicating the Company's Innovation Thrusts to the Board

In order to ensure that the company has a clear and explicit innovation strategy, which is agreed by board and management, the board should ensure that top management communicates its views and intent in four areas pertaining to innovation:

- How it rates the strategic importance of innovation for the business and where it expects major innovations to emerge.
- How that might change in the future in terms of intensity and focus, and what this means for the company.
- How it plans to meet future market demands for more innovative offerings and for more competitive new products and services.
- And, more generally, how it plans to invest in innovation, not just in R&D, to boost its innovation performance.

To help clarify what the innovation strategy will amount to in practice, the board should go further. It should expect management to communicate its innovation priorities and provide an estimate of the resources the company is planning to invest by type of innovation. The distinct innovation thrusts, which have generally been described as an innovation portfolio, should include at least the types of innovation described below:[3]

- Internal development of *incrementally new and improved* next generation products, processes, or services.
- Internal development of *radically new categories* of products, processes, or services (i.e. new to the world, not just new to the company).
- Development together with partners and/or complementors of a *radically new business model or system*.
- Development together with partners and/or complementors of *incrementally new customer solutions*.

The innovation portfolio is in fact an investment portfolio, and the board needs to know where, how much, and how management intends to invest in these four broad strategic innovation categories and to review how the company is progressing in each of these areas. With innovation investment made explicit in this manner, top management will be better able to resist the conservative drift to incremental innovation, and the board will be better able to judge the performance of the top team in relation to the board's innovation strategy. Developing this investment plan requires the board to work with management to define the risk parameters.

Being Aware of and Managing Innovation Risk

Boards have a fiduciary responsibility to shareholders to be the ultimate guardians of the company's risks. In most cases, the risks they scrutinize are financial in nature and their audit mission aims to recognize and address them. In some industries and companies, other risks are regularly reviewed and assessed by the board, e.g. environmental risk and political risk. In other industries, such as the pharmaceutical industry, product liability and class-action risks are important subjects of board review. All of these kinds of risk can be relevant to innovation: innovation affects stock prices; innovation is a critical aspect of avoiding environmental risk and achieving environmental gain; and innovation plays an important role in preventing risks due to product liability.

The key issue for the board to consider with respect to innovation, however, is how much risk the company is willing to take on. Here again we see the push toward innovation conservatism. If the board has not been explicit about its risk tolerance, management is most likely to limit risk in order to limit its exposure to board criticism and censure. In such companies, the board should therefore see its mission as stimulating management to take sensible risks to innovate. In the absence of clear mandates from the board, companies that can be truly innovative need strong governance from within the top management team. The paradigm for this today is Steve Jobs, and there are plenty of examples throughout the history of innovation, including Edwin Land at Polaroid, A.G. Lafley at P&G, and Sam Palmisano at IBM. At 3M it was William L. McKnight, who became president in 1929 and served as chairman of the board from 1949 to 1966. He encouraged the company's management to "delegate responsibility and encourage men and women to exercise their initiative," thus creating 3M's iconic "culture of innovation." But CEOs come and go and the board needs to create and communicate a clear understanding of the limits of innovation risk.

So the board needs to be aware of and oversee the risk that accompanies innovation (both internal risk and external risk), and it needs to agree on and clearly communicate the acceptable *innovation risk profile* for the company.

Internal Risk

Part of the innovation risk may be purely internal, for example when the company commits significant resources to a new and untested technology, a risky and uncertain product concept, or an unfamiliar new market. Often this kind of internal risk can be handled by the management team. Managing the innovation portfolio, if made explicit, will allow for such risk. If it is clear that a percentage of the innovation portfolio will be invested in radical new ventures, then when, for example, a radical new technology under development is found to be unworkable this will be seen as an acceptable outcome.

Another kind of internal risk deserves board oversight. This is when the activities of individuals and teams seriously – and in some cases irrevocably – alter the practices or the character of the company. It is usually up to top management to recognize the importance of involving the board in such instances, and it is up to the board to be willing to deal with such issues. Recent experiences in the banking industry indicate that neither senior bank managers nor board members were fully aware of the risks introduced by the new and complex derivative products conceived by some of the most innovative traders. In some banks, the board clearly did not exercise its governance mission in relation to innovation and new products. In this case, of course, it was not only a failure of innovation governance – the bank executives and board also failed in their responsibilities to "oversee the processes for maintaining the integrity of the company."[4]

The bank example is a matter of integrity, but frequently internal risk occurs when external forces such as disruptive technologies or market opportunities, or a combination of them, threaten to change the very nature of the company. Many years ago, Polaroid hired a consultant to help it begin to navigate the perils of the "digital age." But the company never seriously explored what it might be able to develop and market given its vast technology resources and understanding. Perhaps worse, it was not willing to devote significant resources to digital projects that would not provide revenues through the sales of film cartridges. When a company needs to radically reinvent itself, it is important that the board be a partner in helping to navigate this tricky terrain.

How does a company move from one business model to another? John Seely Brown, who now sits on the board of directors at Corning, was previously the chief scientist at Xerox and director of its Palo Alto Research Center (PARC) in the 1990s. He had this to say about understanding the importance of the business model:

> Not everything we start [at Xerox] ends up fitting our businesses later on. Many of the ideas we work on here involve a paradigm shift in order to deliver value. So sometimes we must work particularly hard to find the "architecture of the revenues" . . . Here at Xerox, there has been a growing appreciation for the struggle to create a value proposition for our research output, and for the fact that this struggle is as valuable as inventing the technology itself.[5]

Open innovation has been accepted in recent years as a "new paradigm" for innovation. Henry Chesbrough[6] opens his book, *Open Innovation*, with a chapter on Xerox PARC, which is famous for having developed many of the technologies that have radically changed our world, but for having benefited from relatively few of them. Chesbrough notes that many people blame "Xerox," "corporate management," or simply "the corporation" for the failure to harvest value from PARC's work. He, however, has a different perspective. Perhaps a better explanation, he tells us, would be that Xerox was executing a system of innovation within which the success of the innovations that PARC spun off "was largely unforeseen – and unforeseeable." At the time, Xerox's innovation system was closed, not open, and therefore there was little or no understanding of how to develop and manage the fruits of the company's research.

One of the key issues in Chesbrough's book is the business model, which is "how companies of all sizes can convert technological potential into economic value." When companies are struggling with such radical decisions, it is essential to have leadership that can help negotiate the terrain, and this includes a board with a clear and ongoing commitment to the issues of innovation. What was the role, one wonders, of the board as IBM opened its coffers, gave away what it had considered to be its treasure, and moved to a whole new business model based on service?

External Risk

The other part of the innovation risk is external and deals with competitors' development and spread of disruptive technologies that can make the company's offerings irrelevant. Recent examples of company demises abound, particularly in the digital economy. The threat may come from a new technology chasing the old one, as with digital photography. But it can also come from a radically different perspective on the market, as happened when Apple launched its iPhone to appeal to consumers, in contrast with the professional smartphone approach followed by Research in Motion (Blackberry's promoter) and Nokia. Both companies were obviously caught unprepared by Apple's emphasis on consumer markets. Managing this type of risk requires management's constant attention on weak signals of emerging trends, a willingness to consider shifts in business models, and sufficient humility to keep challenging the company's beliefs. The board does not have to see the emerging trends on its own, but its governance function requires it to be aware of the risk of disruptive innovation, to ask management to keep a lookout and report back to the board, and to be willing to fund research to uncover such signals and trends. It must continuously ask *what if?* questions while listening to management's often reassuring strategy remarks.

Auditing the Company's Innovation Effectiveness

To take on the responsibility of a governance role in relation to the company's innovation strategy, the board will have to review the company's innovation performance, for example by including innovation in the range of activities that are audited. All boards of course focus on financial audits, and they gradually have been extending the range of their supervisory auditing missions. For example, in environmentally conscious companies, the board, together with management, often becomes involved in setting environmental performance targets and in reviewing corporate scorecards against these targets at regular intervals. Similarly, aware of the impact of the human factor in overall corporate performance, boards are increasingly encouraging management to conduct employee engagement surveys and to review them regularly.

In companies for which innovation is crucial, innovation should be on the list of board auditing missions. It is indeed within the legitimate role of the board to ask top management to set a small number of critical innovation effectiveness measures which it can regularly review and discuss with management.

Innovation measures that are relevant at the board and top management levels typically include input and output indicators which can be compared with accepted industry benchmarks. In technology-intensive companies, the level of R&D expenditures – in absolute terms and as a percentage of sales – is a classic example of such innovation input indicators. A frequently measured innovation output indicator is the percentage of sales achieved through products introduced in the past several years (the amount of time depends on the natural product renewal rate of the industry). Many companies, Medtronic, Hewlett-Packard, and Logitech among them, measure and communicate about this ratio regularly, so their boards are probably tracking this indicator.

More advanced innovation trackers go beyond these accepted innovation metrics, i.e. beyond input/output indicators, to keep an eye on measures that reflect not only *what* the company is doing but *how*. This approach allows the company to monitor the leading indicators of effective innovation. For example, if the board and management have articulated a clear strategy with respect to portfolio balance, then the board should ask management to report on this aspect regularly. Furthermore, even when the approved projects reflect the desired balance, companies frequently fail to adequately resource the portfolio. The degree to which this is done could be a key leading indicator of innovation effectiveness – it is startling to discover how often management "approves" a project but fails to resource it. The board can therefore provide an important reality check by asking management to report on the metric of portfolio resourcing.

The board can also ask management to set metrics for strategic goals and keep the board informed on how well they are being met. For example, more and more companies are rising to the challenge of open innovation. To make sure that the company is making strides in achieving such a goal, top management can easily measure the number of projects that include development partners to introduce radically new business models or incrementally new customer solutions. The board and management can set targets and together they can assess the company's progress over time.

Another type of strategic goal might be achieving critical process targets for innovation. For example, the board might want to know whether the company is good at understanding customers and their needs, or whether the company has a good grip on technology resources – its own as well as those of potential or actual partners or competitors. The board could ask questions such as whether the company is using ethnographic practices, or whether it excels at mapping technology, but we have found that a better option is to ask whether they are meeting the key objectives. Although responses to such metrics are likely to be subjective, a broad range of responses will indicate whether or not the company is proceeding as expected or whether there is a gap that should be filled.

The challenge for the board and for management – and this applies to most performance indicators – is to select only a small number of relevant indicators worth board review, and to make sure these indicators are regularly changed in line with the company's progress. This should result from regular in-depth discussions within the board, together with management, as to the company's main innovation challenges, opportunities, and deficiencies.

REVIEWING AND NOMINATING THE CEO AND TOP MANAGEMENT

Auditing Management's Innovation Performance

A vital role of the board is to evaluate the performance of the CEO and the top management team as a basis for decisions on compensation packages and CEO succession. To do this, some companies have developed sophisticated formulas similar to the traditional balanced scorecard concepts used by many human resource departments. CEO scorecards usually combine financial figures and targets – generally based on company growth, profitability, and stock price, among other things – with other qualitative or quantitative measures or specific goals pertaining to the company's strategic initiatives and priorities, such as specific turnaround targets, progress in globalization efforts, capital efficiency improvements, and the like.

Companies that depend on the introduction of "make or break" new products – think of Boeing with its 787 Dreamliner – generally include the review of these large projects in the board's deliberations. In these companies, the board is most likely to make the compensation packages of the CEO and top management team contingent on the successful completion of important milestones. But for many companies innovation results are not explicitly part of the CEO's balanced scorecard. It is somehow included in other, more general performance indicators like growth or market share gains which, as we have seen, often tend to dampen innovation efforts.

This is why it is desirable, at least in innovation-oriented companies, *also* to evaluate the top management team and CEO on the few innovation performance indicators that they will have suggested to the board as the result of their audit.

Appointing an Innovation-oriented CEO

The selection and recruitment of a new CEO after the current CEO's retirement – or his/her removal – is undoubtedly one of the board's most visible and difficult responsibilities. With the gradual reduction in the length of CEO contracts, this is capturing a lot of attention from the business media.

The appointment of a new CEO always has implications for innovation. Sometimes the new CEO will have a similar approach to innovation as his/her predecessor; sometimes it will be very different. If the board has been playing a role in innovation governance by engaging in some of the activities we have already suggested, it will be more likely to take into account the company's innovation strategy and goals, as well as strengths and weaknesses, when it makes the selection.

Boards frequently appoint what management author Robert Tomasko calls a *fixer* to the CEO position, since they generally feel more comfortable with the more predictable fixers than with the innovative but sometimes more erratic *growers*.[7] This happened at Polaroid with the transition from Edwin Land, the historic innovator, to Mac Booth – a clear shift from a grower to a fixer. GE under the leadership of Jack Welch produced a number of fixers who have joined the ranks of top management in US companies in recent years.

When 3M was looking for a new CEO in 1999/2000 the board turned to a talented fixer from GE, James McNerney, a nomination that several analysts considered a casting error for an archetypal innovative company like 3M. In conversations with several 3Mers in 2005, we gained a strong impression that McNerney was bringing welcome discipline to a company that had been, and still was, an icon of innovation. One interviewee felt that his productivity as an inventor had doubled since he began using the

Six Sigma processes that McNerney had introduced. He began averaging two patents per month. "The trick," he said, "is to have the appropriately flexible structure." Geoff Nicholson, the legendary promoter of the Post-it Note, had been pleased to learn that McNerney identified two parts of the development process – the creative front end and the disciplined back end. "The disciplined back end brings focus, but if you bring that focus too soon, you can kill off the idea." Again, the key is balance.

More recently, however, the reports we received from 3Mers were more negative. The feeling was that the structure was taking over the culture of innovation, and people were relieved when McNerney was replaced. He then joined Boeing which badly needed a fixer.

Of course, growers are often needed to challenge the status quo and get the company embarked on a new growth phase. This is another key reason why it is so important to remind boards of their innovation governance responsibility. It does not mean that they should always choose growers over fixers. But it does mean that they should put their nomination in context by considering the top management team, not just the CEO. If a fixer is needed at the top, who will take the grower's role within the executive committee? And will the new CEO support his/her colleagues as they defend an innovation agenda? In later chapters we will discuss different ways of allocating the governance responsibilities for innovation within the company. The more the board is aware of how these responsibilities are framed and carried out, the higher the chances that it will be in a good position to select the right people for the right jobs as far as innovation is concerned.

SELECTING AND DEVELOPING THE BOARD FOR AN INNOVATION FOCUS

One approach to building an innovation focus in the board is to be sure to include board members with the relevant experience, expertise, and passion. As mentioned earlier, Corning's board includes John Seely Brown, who was director of Xerox PARC, and Herman Miller's board includes John R. Hoke, former creative director and now vice president of Global Footwear Design at NIKE.

Similarly, Nestlé's board includes Daniel Borel, the innovative founder and former CEO and chairman of Logitech. Boards also often include present or past presidents or CEOs. For example, Sam Palmisano remained on IBM's board even after he retired as president and CEO of the company. And so did Peter Brabeck-Letmathe, the visionary former CEO of Nestlé. Boards with members like these are better able to articulate the board's role in innovation governance and to oversee the innovation governance models deployed in the company. It is still such a new topic that even the most seasoned innovators may not be aware of the opportunities it affords.

It is also important to develop the existing board members' understanding of their role in relation to innovation. One approach is to offer workshops on innovation to board directors, as the Malaysian Directors Academy (MINDA) has begun to do for the directors of state-owned enterprises, for example. Some executive education resources include training in innovation for directors, and some companies have begun to hold directors' retreats that focus on issues in innovation.

Perhaps the most sophisticated and intensive approach we have seen is the one adopted by Corning Inc. The day before each board meeting, a 2½ hour "technology with the board" session is held in which directors are informed about upcoming technology projects and updated on projects that have already been approved. One board meeting per year is devoted exclusively to technology issues. In addition to these regular sessions, board members travel to Corning's overseas plants, and every two years they "don smocks, protective glasses, and comfortable shoes and take a tour of the

---

A Designer in Herman Miller's Board

John R. Hoke, former creative director and now vice president of Global Footwear Design at NIKE, sits on the board of Herman Miller. Herman Miller wanted to make sure that design was factored into major business decisions, so it took the unusual step of inviting a designer to join the business professors, corporate executives, and financial experts on its board. CEO Brian A. Walker commented that "a designer can help fellow board members 'learn to see' new possibilities."

@ Issue Conference,
April 29, 2008

company's sprawling Sullivan Park research facility in Corning, where most of the new ideas are hatched."[8]

Corning is a company that has reinvented itself through technology innovation throughout its history. The boards of most companies will not need the same degree of immersion in technology as Corning's board; however, Corning provides a good example of how a board can be kept up to date with the company's innovation agenda.[9]

In conclusion, it is imperative that the board make its position on innovation clear in order to provide the necessary alignment of activities and resources so that employees can direct their efforts toward fulfilling the company's innovation goals. The board's role in innovation governance must include:

- aligning with an articulated innovation strategy;
- defining risk parameters;
- requesting regular audits which show alignment with strategy and risk; and
- discussing the innovation capabilities/performance desired in top management.

In addition to these, the board would be wise to add to its members individuals who have experience and expertise in innovation and to set up opportunities – be they retreats, education sessions, part of regular board get-togethers – for the board as a whole to become involved in and knowledgeable about the company's innovation capabilities.

In this way the board can begin to play an active and useful role in innovation governance. As board members become more aware of the governance models in use at their company and others, they will also be more able to use their position to push top managers to reflect on and improve the models currently in use.

NOTES

[1] Extract from a videotaped class session with executives at IMD on the case "Nestlé SA: The Wellness Company" by Peter Killing and Bettina Büchel (IMD-3-1666, 2006).

[2] Verbatim from the Herman Miller website.

[3] Refer to Chapter 6 of *Innovation Leaders: How Senior Executives Stimulate, Steer and Sustain Innovation* by Jean-Philippe Deschamps, Wiley/Jossey-Bass (2008); refer also to *New Product Development for Dummies* by Robin Karol and Beebe Nelson, Wiley (2007), p. 213.

[4] Taken from Herman Miller's list of board responsibilities.

[5] Chesbrough, H. (2003). *Open Innovation: The New Imperative for Creating and Profiting from Technology*. Boston, HBS Press, p. 63.

[6] Ibid.

[7] Tomasko, R.M. (2006). *Bigger Isn't Always Better: The New Mindset for Real Business Growth*. New York: Amacom.

[8] Engen, J.R. (March/April 2007). How Corning's Board Stays on Top of Technology. BoardMember.com.

[9] For Corning, one outcome of the telecommunications downturn in the late 1990s was the setting up of top management governance boards and the commitment to a more diversified portfolio. The board, along with top management, was prepared to take on the nearly fatal situation and rebuild the company. We'll hear more about Corning's innovation governance model in Chapter 8.

CHAPTER 3

GOVERNING INNOVATION IN PRACTICE: THE ROLE OF THE TOP MANAGEMENT TEAM

Companies that compete through new products or services have, of necessity, a new product development system, organization, and process. These have generally been in place for a decade or more and are regularly updated as conditions change and new practices and processes are developed and adopted. As part of these updates, senior functional and business managers may change the allocation of responsibilities for the planning, design, production, and introduction of new offerings. They also invest in new tools and work approaches, and they regularly introduce new targets in terms of new product quality, cost, and lead times. In many companies, this process now works reasonably well and smoothly. Relying on the second line of command to supervise all these activities, the top management team of large companies may not be involved *directly*, except when there are significant changes, which can include both new opportunities and failures.

But despite having a good product development process in the company, CEOs often complain about the relative lack of market and financial impact of innovation efforts, at least given the investments. New products are developed, for sure, but the results are often disappointing when compared to the predictions and promises of product managers and others responsible for the introduction of innovations. New products may provide a benefit to customers and help to maintain the company's profitability, but too few are real "game changers." How many of these CEOs, reading constantly about Apple's series of market hits, ask themselves how they can emulate the success of the Silicon Valley giant? And reflecting on the fate of Nokia, that troubled innovation star – at least in the eyes of the business media – how many wonder about what suddenly happened to the mobile phone pioneer's top management team? How can one explain why these brilliant Finnish leaders, who could launch new phones with amazing frequency, somehow took their eye off the ball and missed a deep turn in the smartphone market?

Well, these questions highlight the fact that even if a company has a competent new product development process, this does not mean that it will be able to develop a range of market-winning innovations and sustain a high level of creativity and productivity over time. Neither does it guarantee that the company will be able to detect and react adequately to all opportunities and threats. As we stressed earlier, although the new product development process was designed to enable product developers to work across the company's functions and activities, the scope of innovation is both richer in results – for example, when it leads to the creation of new business models – and more complex because it involves a combination of "hard" and "soft" elements. Because of this complexity, because innovation affects the entire company, no process or set of processes can be sufficient to meet all the demands. However, the existence of satisfactory new product development processes makes it possible to implement a comprehensive innovation management system – steered by the C-suite – which is conducive to generating streams of market-leading innovations and avoiding competitive pitfalls.

Setting up a formal innovation management system requires *proactive, personal engagement* by the top team. Unfortunately, the C-suite is often simply too busy with strategic, financial, and operational issues to devote time to steering innovation on a day-to-day basis and creating that unique environment and culture. The system in place generally reflects past legacies that are seldom challenged by management. Occasionally, a new CEO or CTO will launch an "innovation revival" campaign, but it is often limited in scope and duration. Old habits tend to survive!

It is therefore healthy practice for the top management team to regularly engage in a comprehensive reassessment of the company's innovation system – how it is organized, its processes, environment, and culture – and to introduce new innovation governance guidelines. The role of the top team in this effort is critical. It goes beyond making minor structural changes and appointing new people in charge of existing departments. Governing innovation effectively involves at least six priorities:

- Setting an overall frame for innovation by clarifying a vision and mission for innovation, proposing a set of values to guide innovation activities and auditing current performance.
- Defining how the company will identify sources of value from innovation, how it will create value, and how it intends to capture value.
- Choosing organizational models for the allocation of primary and supporting governance responsibilities for innovation, and setting up dedicated process management mechanisms.
- Establishing priorities and allocating resources for innovation as part of an explicit innovation strategy and plan in support of the company's objectives.
- Identifying and overcoming current obstacles in the company's organizational system and sources of resistance in order to build a lasting innovation environment.
- Monitoring and evaluating results on an ongoing basis, and setting up a process to address conflicts of interest within the top management team in order to make innovation sustainable.

We shall now explore each of these six innovation governance areas in more detail.

SETTING AN OVERALL FRAME FOR INNOVATION

In some companies, the innovation tradition and culture seems almost like a magic potion that is part of their DNA and ensures that all

> ### At P&G, the Consumer is Boss
>
> "Procter & Gamble is known for its highly capable and motivated workforce. But in the early 2000s, our people were not oriented to any common strategic purpose. We had a corporate mission to meaningfully improve the everyday lives of the customers we served. [. . .] But we hadn't explicitly or inspirationally enrolled enough of our 100,000-plus people around the world in our mission; it was neither fully embraced by employees nor fully leveraged by the company's leadership. Our innovation efforts suffered accordingly. So we expanded our mission to include the idea that 'the consumer is boss'."
>
> *A.G. Lafley, former CEO*

activities focus on innovation – think of Apple, Google, P&G, or 3M. But even in such companies, it is useful for top management to reflect at regular intervals on how innovation can contribute to the realization of the company's overall mission and vision. This requires a willingness to align business and innovation visions, to propose and enforce a set of values that are conducive to innovation, and to conduct comprehensive innovation audits.

P&G convincingly illustrates the link its management sees between its overall vision of innovation and its culture. Its motto "the consumer is boss"[1] (see box) shows that visions and missions are not something ethereal. They can lead to very concrete actions in favor of innovation and shape the values and culture of the company. In framing innovation in this way, P&G's top management team, under the inspired leadership of A.G. Lafley, demonstrated an innate sense of innovation governance.

Aligning Business and Innovation Visions

Aligning visions means discussing and agreeing on what management wants to achieve business-wise and how innovation can help achieve it. This is vital to ensure that innovation is closely tied to the company's overall mission. The company's vision – how it wants to see its future – can generally be expressed in the form of three basic questions:

- *Who do we want to be?* What kinds of activities do we want to pursue and what do we want to stand for as a company vis-à-vis our stakeholders? (This defines the company's desired identity.)
- *What business do we want to be in?* Which segments and customers do we want to serve as a priority? (This delineates the company's desired business boundaries and focus.)
- *What do we want our offerings to mean to our customers?* How do we intend to become the preferred supplier for our customers? (This provides a set of competitive values for the company.)

Similarly, the company's innovation vision – hence the scope of management's innovation governance mission – can be expressed in the form of the three questions on the content of innovation that we proposed in Chapter 1:

> **At P&G, the Consumer is Boss** *(continued)*
>
> "The people who buy and use P&G products are valued not just for their money, but as a rich source of information and direction. If we can develop better ways of learning from them – by listening to them, observing them in their daily lives, and even living with them – then our mission is more likely to succeed. 'The consumer is boss' became far more than a slogan to us. It was a clear, simple, and inclusive cultural priority for both our employees and our external stakeholders, such as suppliers and retail partners. We also linked the concept directly to innovation. From the ideation stage through the purchase of a product, the consumer should be 'the heart of all we do' at P&G."
>
> *A. G. Lafley, former CEO*

- *Why innovate?* What concrete benefits are we trying to achieve given our current market and competitive position?
- *Where to innovate?* In what areas should we concentrate our efforts beyond our traditional product renewal activities?
- *How much to innovate?* How ambitious and open to risk should we be, and indeed can we afford to be, and for what objective?

These are all questions worth asking regularly, even if nothing special is happening in the company and its markets. This can be done, for example, as part of an annual top management off-site strategy retreat. Formally reviewing the mission and purpose of innovation and its desired focus may generate interesting new perspectives. But even if it only confirms current management views, it will at least ensure that all members of the C-suite are aligned behind common beliefs and a shared innovation vision and can therefore speak with one voice to the rest of the organization.

Expressing Innovation-enhancing Values

Google's 10 Core Values

1) We want to work with great people
2) Technology innovation is our lifeblood
3) Working at Google is fun
4) Be actively involved; you are Google
5) Don't take success for granted
6) Do the right thing; don't be evil
7) Earn customer and user loyalty and respect every day
8) Sustainable long-term growth and profitability are key to our success
9) Google cares about and supports the communities where we work and live
10) We aspire to improve and change the world.

These innovation-specific management discussions may also be useful for reaffirming a set of specific values concerning innovation. It is therefore the role of the CEO, and his/her direct reports, to regularly review and specify the values they want to promote, values that can then be broadcast through management publications, speeches, and individual performance reviews. Of course, values should not be changed too often. However, they deserve to be clarified if they are too simplistic.

For example, including "innovation" or "innovativeness" in the company's core values – as found frequently in annual reports and other company publications – does not really say much. Management needs to express in a concrete and explicit fashion what this means practically in terms of personal attitudes and interactions.

Some of these values can be expressed as short, punchy sentences that can do a lot to promote the kind of culture management aspires to create. P&G's "the consumer is boss" motto, noted earlier, indeed conveys a clear and simple message about the company's main focus.

The same can be said about Steve Jobs' early slogan at Apple – "Let's Be Pirates" – which called for a rebellion against the dominance of the WinTel PC.[2] Similarly, Andy Grove's famous book title – *Only the Paranoid Survive* – was effective in conveying to all at Intel the importance of humility and the conviction that no innovation battle is won forever.

Google provides a good example of a number of innovation-oriented values because they sustain its unique environment and culture – that is, unique in the type of people the company hires, as well as in their attitudes and ambitions. And each of these values, including its most famous one – "don't be evil" – is broken down into concrete elements.[3]

> **Apple's Values (as viewed by Gary Hamel)**
>
> Be passionate
> vs. Be rational
> Lead, don't follow
> vs. Be cautious
> Aim to surprise
> vs. Aim to satisfy
> Be unreasonable
> vs. Be practical
> Innovate incessantly
> vs. Innovate here and there
> Sweat the details
> vs. Get it mostly right
> Think like an engineer, feel like an artist
> vs. Think like an engineer, feel like an accountant.

When a company has developed a strong innovation culture and supporting values, keen external observers of that company are generally able to highlight the main elements of the culture, even though management may not have specifically broadcast them as such. This is the case with Apple's culture as viewed by management expert Gary Hamel, who adds: "I can't even be sure whether the values I've outlined [see box] are the ones that really drive Apple – but if they aren't, they should be! For me, the case of Apple is just a convenient and plausible vehicle for driving home a fundamental truth: *You can't improve a company's performance without improving its values.*"[4] This last statement is so crucial, particularly in terms of innovation performance that it should be posted in gold letters in the CEO's corner office, in the C-suite meeting room and in the boardroom.

Auditing and Improving Innovation Performance

Finally, setting the frame for innovation includes conducting a thorough innovation audit to establish the starting base before launching improvement programs. This allows management to understand how the process currently works in reality, what its deficiencies are, and what general obstacles – whether organizational or cultural – are hindering the company's innovation effectiveness.

Tetra Pak's Innovation Benchmark

"In '96, I was given the responsibility to take a hard look at how first-class companies went about the innovation process. And that took me around to companies like Dupont, 3M, Canon, Ericsson, BMW, just to mention some of them, to see what we could learn from them. I brought that back to Tetra Pak and we had several very good discussions in our group management about what we needed to change and what change in focus we would have to bring about in order to have an innovation process that works better than it does today. From that, we discussed the implications for top management in Tetra Pak. One of them was the need to get ourselves much more involved than we had been in the past, particularly with the most important projects, which we came to call 'Pace Plus' projects."

Bo Wirsén

A thorough audit generally includes some benchmarking of the company's current innovation practices against those of companies with a great innovation track record. The results of this benchmarking may be instrumental in convincing management, and the wider organization, that the company needs to change and in indicating major areas where such change is warranted. It is also a good way to silence the skeptics and proponents of the status quo. Innovation audits can be outsourced – a number of specialized consultants offer their benchmarking services. But it can also be carried out internally using an established framework,[5] ideally focusing on the whole value creation process – business design, value identification, and value realization. Maximizing value creation is indeed one of the most important management priorities in innovation governance, as we will see below.

Many companies participate in peer-to-peer benchmarking through membership in organizations such as the Product Development and Management Association (PDMA) and the International

Association for Product Development (IAPD). These organizations have helped innovators to learn from one another and in many cases have provided a venue for the adoption of new and emerging practices. They have also enabled members to create a network within which more formal benchmarking visits have taken place as workshop participants identify peers with whom they can explore specific practices.

Tetra Pak, the world's leader of packaging systems for liquid food, provides a good illustration of the power of benchmarking. The company, whose innovation governance system will be presented in Chapter 11, was founded on a radical innovation, Tetra-Brik®, an effective carton packaging system using aseptic technology for long-life milk and juices. The company was managed for many years by its charismatic owner, Ruben Rausing, and later on successively by his two sons, Hans and Gad. Each of them promoted a creative environment, particularly in R&D. But for years Tetra Pak was unable to translate its superb R&D capabilities into successful new products because it lacked adequate processes to sense the market, select the best ideas, and manage new product development projects time- and cost-effectively.

So, in 1996 management set up a small steering group of four senior managers whose mission was to recommend steps to improve the company's innovation performance. This small group was directed by the very senior vice president in charge of European operations, Bo Wirsén. As a group, they knew, from having experienced them, many of the deficiencies of their innovation process, but they lacked references about best practices. This prompted Wirsén to visit a number of companies that had impressed him.[6]

What was unique in Tetra Pak's initial audit was that such a senior member of the top management team took the initiative to conduct these benchmarking visits himself. This gave him strong personal credibility when improvement targets were decided. It also provided him with new insights into critical innovation success factors that an outsourced benchmarking exercise would not necessarily have provided. For example, through his benchmarking visits Wirsén realized that the company might benefit from creating two new functions with a strong role to play in innovation – chief technology officer and strategic marketing officer. At Tetra Pak, this initial benchmarking exercise was used to kick off an innovation improvement program. But it was not referred to later or used as a formal auditing system.

DSM, a global life sciences and materials sciences company, whose governance system will be described in Chapter 10, provides another good example of the importance of starting an innovation improvement program with a thorough audit. When top management decided to change the company's innovation governance system in 2006 and set up a corporate innovation center, it entrusted responsibility for the center to a high-level chief innovation officer (CIO), Rob van Leen, a former group vice president for food and nutrition. Starting from scratch – the company had thus far managed innovation in traditional ways, through R&D – Van Leen felt the need to build a common language and set a base through a company-wide auditing exercise. Some of DSM's groups had a good innovation track record, others less good. All had to go through a thorough benchmarking exercise structured around a number of critical processes and capabilities, an initiative that some of them resented as being too administrative. The outcome of this exercise was a mind opener to all, as Van Leen noted (see box).[7]

> **DSM's Innovation Audit**
>
> "Basically, we had to start from scratch. Nobody knew how to do it. We had to find targets but we really didn't have good definitions behind it, so that is why we started definitions, reporting and so on. Then we started to put in place a diagnostic, which was built with the help of a consultant, to compare ourselves on many innovation practices with the rest of the industry. And when we saw that we actually scored below the average in the industry, we started to put in place best practices. We got them from everywhere, sometimes from within the company because there were business groups doing very well, and sometimes we brought them in from outside."
>
> *Rob van Leen,*
> *chief innovation officer*

Interestingly, this audit was turned into a real management tool. First, Van Leen distributed the results widely, including to the company's board of management, which forced some of the skeptics to take it seriously. He also decided to redo the assessment at regular intervals to measure progress. But the most powerful use of the tool was to initiate regular review meetings around this audit between the controller of the innovation center and members of the management teams of each business group. During these meetings, progress and remaining obstacles were discussed, together with some of the business group's most meaningful innovation projects. The review meetings were then documented in a detailed and widely distributed report. These practices have created a propensity for emulation among business group managers – the better performing groups want to stay on top and the poorer ones feel the need to show progress.

DEFINING HOW TO GENERATE VALUE FROM INNOVATION

It is a truism that innovation is about turning market opportunities into value. In established management theories, this means identifying, evaluating, creating, and – arguably the most difficult step – capturing value.

Without a clear mandate from top management, most companies will naturally search for value within their current industries and markets. In this way, value is most usually generated by developing and introducing new products or services that replace or complement existing product lines. Some of these products or services will be incrementally better or cheaper; others will be more radically new. But their common denominator is that they remain, for the most part, within the company's existing industry value chain and keep converging toward the same competitive arena, the same "red ocean" as Kim and Mauborgne put it.[8] This is why the potential value created by most new products is seldom fully captured.

In fact, it is not rare to hear CEOs complain that the new products or services generated by their organization are often less profitable than the original ones on which the company built its growth. These new products or services may revitalize current market segments, but they do not lead to a sustainable competitive advantage since they are quickly imitated or superseded by competitors' entries. An important element of top management's innovation governance mission is therefore to stop this "new product merry-go-round" and initiate new ways to redefine value.

Redefining value requires broadening the scope of the search for opportunities, as we proposed in Chapter 1. This can be done by introducing a totally new basis of competition, as well as by creating new market space using previously neglected yet critical attributes – Kim and Mauborgne's "blue ocean strategy."[9] It can also result from a systematic exploitation of opportunities to redesign the industry value chain – some authors call it the "value constellation" or "value network" – to one's advantage, or in some cases to create a totally new value chain. Such a move requires a thorough understanding of industry value chain dynamics, alternative business models and competitors' blind spots.

Charlie Fine of MIT, author of the best-seller *Clockspeed,*[10] emphasizes the need to understand the dynamic relationships between suppliers, partners, and other industry value chain players to identify opportunities to take over parts of the value chain and therefore increase total profits. In his seminar Driving Strategic Innovation, conducted jointly with IMD, he encourages senior managers to identify strategic opportunities in their industry value chain through a systematic three-step approach:

Step 1: Assess your value chain dynamics, i.e. what factors will affect the dynamics of:
- Your industry's technologies (S-curves) and its innovation pattern?
- Your customers?
- Your competitors?
- Your industry structure?
- Your governmental and regulatory agencies?
- Your environment?

Step 2: Analyze your industry value chain:
- What are the key elements in your industry value chain?
- Who has power in the chain?
- Who makes the profits in the chain?

- What are the sources of power and profit in the chain (technology, brand, etc.)?
- What are the key dynamic processes influencing the power structure in the chain?
- Where is the locus of innovations in the chain?
- What is the clock speed of each element in the chain and what are the drivers?

Step 3: Design/modify your value chain strategy
- Review your insourcing/outsourcing options and decisions (make/buy choices and/or vertical integration).
- Analyze your partner selection options and decisions (e.g. choice of suppliers and partners for the chain).
- Evaluate your contractual relationship options and decisions (arm's length, joint venture, long-term contract, strategic alliance, equity participation, etc.).

Apple provides a striking example of this value creation strategy. Its financial success is in large part the result of having recognized – before any of its hardware competitors – the importance of *content* for sustainable value creation and of having cornered this value through its novel and proprietary iTunes system and its focus on smartphone applications. Apple's winning value identification strategy consisted of controlling the marketing, sales, and distribution of other companies' content by making its customers and suppliers captive, thus capturing a large part of the value of the content. This strategy is largely attributed to Steve Jobs and his top management team. They fully exercised their innovation governance role, which was to steer the company toward greener pastures – integrating hardware, software, and content – rather than leaving it to compete against the conventional pure hardware business model of its early competitors.

CHOOSING AN INNOVATION GOVERNANCE MODEL

As we stated earlier, steering, promoting, and sustaining innovation in the broadest sense of the term – not just the new product development process – is a major task that spans all company functions and organizational units. As such, it needs to be handled directly by the CEO or entrusted explicitly by the top team either to a very senior leader or to a group of managers fully empowered to exercise that responsibility. That assignment must be public, i.e. everyone in the organization should know who is in overall charge of innovation and how that overall responsibility is redistributed across the organization. Any change in the allocation of responsibilities – because changes are bound to happen over time – must also be explained and broadcast.

In our research, we have identified nine models for the primary allocation of overall responsibility for innovation. Some companies also use one or another of the same nine models to support the primary model. As we shall describe in Chapter 4, in some of these models overall responsibility for innovation is assigned to a single individual. The CEO may hold this responsibility, which is most likely to be the case if he/she is the company founder. Other individuals who may hold this role are the chief technology or research officer (CTO or CRO), a dedicated chief innovation officer (CIO) – whose actual title can be quite fancy like 'Chief Yahoo' – or a high-level innovation manager. In the financial industry the chief information officer can play this role; in other non-manufacturing sectors another CXO or a business unit manager can assume this responsibility. There are also models in which a group of leaders takes on responsibility for innovation collectively, whether they represent a subset of the top management team or constitute a high-level cross-functional steering group or a network of "champions."

There are therefore a number of models to choose from, each with its own advantages and shortcomings. It is top management's responsibility to weigh up the pros and cons of each model and how it suits the company's position and leadership resources. The choice will indeed depend on the personal preferences of the top team – do they want to remain involved personally or do they prefer to delegate responsibility to the level below? It will also reflect the type of innovation that is pursued – for example, if technology is the main driver, this would justify allocating overall responsibility to the chief technology or research officer – and of course the availability of suitable candidates for the job. Given that choice is available, top management would be well advised to refrain from sticking to the model they adopted years ago, or choosing the one most frequently found in their industry, for example the CTO model in the engineering industry.

Choosing a suitable organizational model is essential, but it is equally important to realize that conditions change. It is therefore good practice to review regularly the adequacy of the model in use given the company's changing market situation, leadership structure, and strategy.

In Chapter 4 we will explain the nature and purpose of these organizational models and in Chapters 5 and 6 we will describe these models individually and discuss how effective they seem to be, at least in the perception of companies that have adopted them.

ESTABLISHING INNOVATION PRIORITIES AND ALLOCATING RESOURCES

Steering innovation, i.e. deciding on the company's priorities concerning where, how much, and in what domain to invest in innovation, is one of the key governance missions of top management. It is generally done, at least indirectly, through project portfolio decisions. Managers understand the value of seeing the portfolio as a way of distributing resources across incremental, platform, and "radical" projects.

Going Beyond Traditional Portfolio Management Approaches

Business units typically identify their most attractive projects and management can then consolidate the various portfolios to check whether, once combined, they provide the right balance of growth, margin, and risk. Such a bottom-up approach is sometimes complemented by the addition of a few corporate projects resulting from a proactive and ambition-led, top-down innovation push. The sum of business projects included in the consolidated portfolio reflects the company's implicit innovation strategy.

The limitation of this approach is that it allocates corporate resources on the basis of the perceived attractiveness of projects as seen by business units, since business portfolios tend to weigh heavily in the company's total resource allocation. This business project attractiveness often reflects the perceived level of competitive urgency of the projects and their impact on short-term business performance in terms of sales and profitability. In other words, unless the portfolio includes proper guidelines for investment, "game-changing" projects with a long-term impact on the company are at risk of being short-changed, thus weakening the implementation of the company's vision.

To offset that risk and ensure that the strategy will meet the company's innovation priorities, and to provide investment guidelines, it is useful for top management, as a first step, to decide on how much the company should and can afford to spend on innovation in general and on innovative projects in particular. This will determine an overall "envelope" of resources for innovation, which can then be compared with other investment funding needs. This envelope should cover not only R&D – as a total amount and as a percentage of sales – and other product development expenses (the upstream investments) but also investments in manufacturing capacity and commercialization (downstream investments).

Allocating Resources between Different Innovation Thrusts

This broad "innovation envelope" should then be allocated among the different types of innovations being pursued, and this is the second step in the resource allocation process. To do so, it is necessary to characterize the main innovation thrusts being pursued. The book *Innovation Leaders*[11] proposed to do so by combining broad options derived from the questions listed in Chapter 1:

- *Why innovate?* (Innovation objective)
  Innovations can be pursued for two broad objectives: to energize and expand a current business in its existing markets or to create a totally new business. These objectives can be combined.

- *Where to innovate?* (Innovation scope or focus)
  Innovations can focus on products or services – introducing a new "black box" or stand-alone service – or, alternatively, on developing a new business model or business system.
- *How much to innovate?* (Innovation intensity level)
  Innovations can be incremental in the changes brought to current products, services, or processes, or they can be more radical, leading to completely new product and service concepts.
- *With whom to innovate?* (Innovation boundaries)
  Innovations can be developed and implemented internally, using the company's capabilities and resources, or externally through deliberate collaboration with partners.

Note that both innovation intensity and boundaries – if restricted to an either/or option (incremental or radical; internal or external) – are always subject to debate. An innovation that is radical in one company may be characterized as incremental by a competitor. The level of innovation is relative to the reference models of the beholder. Also, innovations are rarely conducted only internally – external factors like suppliers are usually involved – which means most innovation projects fall somewhere between the two extremes.

These four dimensions can be combined, as shown in Figure 3.1, into four entirely different innovation thrusts. Top management should recognize them explicitly, choose the ones that it will pursue as a priority, and use them to characterize and communicate its innovation strategy and investments, which will usually come from a combination of the chosen thrusts.

These four thrusts propose a simple typology of innovation choices:

- The internal development and launch of a *new and/or improved product, process, or service offering*, typically to grow and reinforce the current business in an incremental innovation mode.
- The internal development of a *totally new product category or service offering*, typically to grow and create a totally new business, next to the existing ones, in a radical innovation mode.

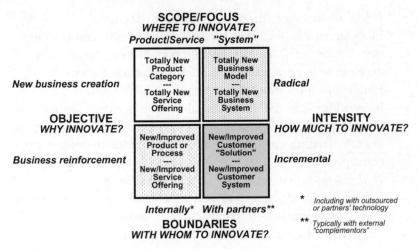

Figure 3.1: Typology of Innovation by Strategic Focus

- The development and launch, together with selected partners, of a *totally new business model or integrated system*, typically to grow and create a new business in a radical innovation mode.
- The development and launch, together with partners or complementors, of a *new and/or improved customer solution or customer system*, typically to grow and reinforce the current business in an incremental innovation mode.

This classification reflects the fact that, from a management point of view, developing a "black-box" product or service is very different – and carries a different type of risk – than introducing a new business model or business system, or even a complex product solution. Indeed, whereas the development of a new product or service is often the result of an internal process, even though it may involve the use of outsourced technology and suppliers, the development of a radically new business model or system often requires the cooperation of several external partners, outsourcing suppliers, or complementors.

As mentioned earlier, these four thrusts are not mutually exclusive – innovations can be pursued simultaneously across several of these areas. Once displayed on a two-by-two matrix (refer to

Figure 3.1), they provide a useful framework and lens for examining the complex reality of innovation thrusts.

Ideally, once the overall innovation envelope has been established, management should propose how the envelope should be split between the four quadrants:

- How much the company should spend internally on incremental projects to reinforce the current businesses.
- How much it should invest, again internally, in radical projects to create a totally new business next to the existing ones.
- How much it should commit to attempts to introduce a radical new system or business model with partners.
- How much it should devote to the creation of incrementally innovative customer solutions, once again with partners.

Management can now go back to the original project portfolio and position specific innovation projects in the four quadrants to see whether the investments that they represent add up to the predetermined envelopes (refer to Figure 3.2). If they do not – if some quadrants lack projects – then management can indicate where additional efforts are expected (see arrows on Figure 3.2) and how much they represent in terms of new resources to be committed, thus starting a search for new opportunities.

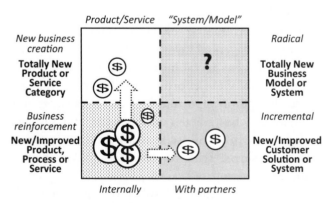

Figure 3.2: Portfolio of Innovation Projects by Type

This approach allows management to introduce an innovation dimension in the traditional project portfolio approach by: (1) indicating how the various objectives of the company's innovation strategy will be funded; (2) specifying how much management plans to spend on innovation in general, and on activities that will reinforce current businesses vs. innovative efforts to create entirely new activities; (3) providing guidelines on how much should be spent on each main type of innovation; and (4) suggesting new market domains that need to be explored as a priority for these new activities.

Three general remarks can be made on this definition of priorities and management allocation of resources.

First, in their effort to reinforce their current market position, most business management teams tend to focus on only a few areas where innovation can make a difference, i.e. new better and cheaper products, new technologies, and new production processes. It is therefore useful for the C-suite to stress the importance of other reinforcing innovations, for example in new business models, in the supply chain and/or value chain, in service, in marketing and channel distribution, and the like. These could stimulate business managers to look more broadly at innovation, as recommended in Chapter 1.

Second, deciding how much to invest by type of innovation, i.e. incremental vs. radical, determines how much risk the company is willing to take (or avoid). By addressing this issue directly – for example, by setting up specific envelopes by quadrant – management can establish a general company policy that may be helpful when the company is leaning too far to one side or the other. For example, some managers always seem to look for breakthroughs. They behave as if incremental innovations such as product derivatives are not worth their efforts, with the result that they miss major market and profit opportunities. Other managers, in contrast, stay permanently within their comfort zone and shy away from risky developments. In each case, it will help if management specifies, for each business, what it considers as the right balance between incremental and radical innovation.

Third, and finally, defining a policy on open innovation is an important element of an innovation strategy, particularly in the new social network environment and with the growing importance of crowdsourcing. It goes beyond a simple exhortation to build upon external ideas and competencies. A policy on open innovation ought to specify:

- the domains where external cooperation is desirable;
- the boundaries of cooperative deals and the types of partners to be considered off-limits;
- considerations on the protection of intellectual property; and
- indicators to measure the level of achievement of the policy.

By specifying this type of broad resource allocation – covering not only R&D but also other upstream and downstream investments – management can achieve three important benefits of good governance:

- Send a clear message regarding the company's priorities.
- Set the frame for the development of its new business activities.
- Ensure that these activities will be adequately funded.

OVERCOMING OBSTACLES AND BUILDING A FAVORABLE INNOVATION ENVIRONMENT

As Gary Hamel suggested, there is generally a strong correlation between innovation culture and innovation performance. The success of Google, for example, cannot be separated from the emphasis the company puts on its "can-do" entrepreneurial culture or from the concrete steps management takes to sustain it. Google's famous rule – modeled on 3M's "15% rule" – that allows people to pursue their own ideas for up to 20% of their time, is just one example of the company's innovation-enhancing environment. By contrast, some excellent companies with huge technological resources never seem to reach the status of top performers in their industry, largely because of an internal culture that stifles innovation.

Innovation calls for openness, experimentation and risk taking, and, above all, cooperation and constructive challenges across functions and organizational units, and all of these aspects need to be explicitly encouraged by management. In a seminal article, two Harvard Business School professors[12] summarized the lessons learned from a two-day colloquium held at their school on "Creativity, Entrepreneurship, and Organizations of the Future." The colloquium gathered over a hundred people who were "deeply concerned with the workings of creativity in organizations," including research scholars and business leaders from companies whose success depends on creativity – such as design consultancy IDEO, technology innovator E-Ink, internet giant Google, software specialist Intuit, and pharmaceutical leader Novartis among others. Even though the colloquium focused on creativity, it provided a number of lessons that apply more generally to innovation. The lessons can be summarized in a number of concrete exhortations to senior management to:

- Draw on the right minds:
  - Tap ideas from all ranks
  - Encourage and enable collaboration
  - Open the organization to diverse perspectives.
- Bring process to bear carefully:
  - Map the phases of creative work
  - Manage the commercialization hand-off
  - Provide paths through the bureaucracy
  - Create a filtering mechanism.
- Fan the flames of motivation:
  - Provide intellectual challenge
  - Allow people to pursue their passions
  - Be an appreciative audience
  - Embrace the certainty of failure
  - Provide the setting for "good work."

But creating this type of open and creative environment may not be sufficient. Management must also address several organizational and cultural obstacles that hinder innovation. We have observed them – the seven vicious innovation killers – in a wide range of companies and propose a number of antidotes to each below.

Killer # 1: Excessive Operational Pressure

The first innovation killer, present in most companies, is the excessive pressure put on managers as a result of their operational and organizational responsibilities and of a constant fire-fighting atmosphere within the business. These pressures tend to be reinforced by a management performance evaluation system that encourages short-term results. Managers may be willing to spend time on innovation, but there may simply not be enough time for these innovative undertakings in many organizations.

Management can counteract this pressure in two ways, which have proved to be effective antidotes.

First, the pressure can be alleviated if management identifies, appoints, and guides dedicated and passionate innovation coaches to motivate, challenge, and support local innovation teams. These champions are generally found among younger high-potential managers. To be effective, these coaches or champions should be highly energetic as well as socially skilled so that they are not viewed as interfering in the business or "bossing" the local managers. They should also be practical and resourceful in identifying bottlenecks, suggesting solutions, proposing best practices and tools, and generally helping business managers move forward with their innovation agenda and projects.

Second, management can create a counter-pressure in favor of innovation, for example by introducing specific innovation performance measures in every manager's balanced scorecard. This assumes, of course, that management is true to the very principle of balanced scorecards – in other words that it judges managers on all dimensions of the scorecard and not just on financial or budget performance. Once managers are penalized in their personal performance review for letting their innovation activities lag behind, even if they make their budget, it is probable that they will revive their interest in these undertakings and find a better balance of their time and efforts.

Killer # 2: Fear of Experimentation and Taking Risks

This second innovation killer usually results from unrealistic financial benchmarks or from a culture that does not tolerate failure. Financial benchmarks – for example, assigning unreasonably high hurdle rates of return on totally new and innovative projects – are an innovation killer because they may discourage people from undertaking uncertain projects. Note that full-blooded entrepreneurs will often pay lip service to these financial goals – be it in terms of net present value created or payback time – and they will provide whatever numbers management expects to see, knowing full well that such kinds of number games are irrelevant at the early stage of risky innovation projects. But circumventing the existing benchmarks can only work sometimes. After a failure or two the real true-blue entrepreneurs will soon find it more attractive to find a company that really values innovation.

Risk averse innovation cultures exist in many companies, particularly those with a strong focus on operational excellence and performance predictability. Even though management may encourage risk taking in their speeches, managers are quick to sense what the top team really means. Most companies carry a whole cemetery of failed projects and ventures, and managers are quick to find out what fate befell their promoters. This often kills early desires to take risks.

There are two powerful antidotes to the fear, which can convince managers that top management values and actively seeks risk taking.

First, management can set the example at the top by asking senior leaders to personally coach high-

> **Sponsoring Post-it Notes©**
>
> The most cited innovation of all time was developed under the auspices of 3M vice president Geoffrey Nicholson. Even though it was in most ways a "skunk works" project, a senior manager took the time and the risk of working with the team and providing "coverage." If it had failed it would have been on his watch. It succeeded beyond anyone's wildest dreams, but Nicholson's role is rarely mentioned.

risk/high-reward projects. Often, this means making themselves regularly available to the project team – for example, after normal hours – for informal reviews and problem solving.

When this is done – and this is the first benefit – the whole organization quickly learns that (1) risky projects are perceived as acceptable and management is ready to back them, even if they end up failing, and (2) a high mortality rate for such projects is considered normal and nobody should be penalized for trying and failing.

A second benefit of this approach is that within the top management team innovation discussions become more concrete as policy decisions can be tested on real projects.

If every member of the top team personally sponsors a project, the third benefit is that the decision to pull the plug on a given project is taken collectively without undue pressure on the sponsoring leader who does not risk losing face.

The second antidote is for management to adopt the philosophy of venture capitalists (VCs) regarding investments, resource allocation, coaching and return expectations, as recommended by Gary Hamel in his famous article on Silicon Valley (see box).[13] Hamel advocates creating an internal market for ideas, talent, and capital, and making projects compete for resources. Knowing that only a small proportion of projects will be successful, VCs look for the upside and not the downside of projects, and they will do their utmost to support the projects that have the highest chances of winning. In cases of failure, they move fast to start new ones.

> **Bringing Silicon Valley Inside**
>
> "Venture capitalists are risk takers, but they are not *big* risk takers. [. . .] Out of 5000 ideas, a five-partner VC firm may invest in ten which it views as a portfolio of options. Out of that ten, five will be total write-offs, three will be modest successes, one will double the initial investment, and one will return the investment 50- to 100-fold. The goal is to make sure you have a big winner, not to make sure there are no losers."
>
> *Gary Hamel*

Killer # 3: Insufficient Customer and User Orientation

Market Immersion at Hilti

Hilti, one of the world's global leaders of professional hand tools for the construction industry, sells directly and through retailers to thousands of building contractors around the world. The company has built its innovations and market success on an in-depth understanding of its customers and users. Visiting customers, not to sell to them but to observe them, is a habit that came from the very top. Hilti's former CEO, Dr Pius Baschera, was known for regularly accompanying salesmen on their customer visits . . . without telling them in advance, thus avoiding being presented only to friendly customers. In so doing, he passed a strong message to his organization, i.e. "To succeed, know thy customers deeply!"

Relying on superficial market knowledge or outdated knowledge or, worse, believing that the company "knows better" than customers – the typical arrogance of established market leaders – are also innovation dampers. Note that the reverse – taking customers' expressed wishes at face value – can also be misleading, since customers are often unable to talk about their latent or future needs – the needs that, if well addressed, can build competition-crushing, or disruptive, innovation. Who would ever have thought that we "needed" and would pay for a telephone that holds an entire address book and calendar! Insufficient customer and user orientation can also lead companies to neglect to define and target specific customer groups. Companies that launch a new product concept without clearly identifying a specific target group beforehand – at least initially – and without understanding how that customer group will benefit from it are likely to waste resources. The approach of "raising-the-flag-and-seeing-if-anyone-salutes" is a costly way to bring innovations to market. It is only valid if the company is very agile, learns fast from the initial launch, and quickly reorients and relaunches to target a specific customer group.

Once again, there are at least two types of antidotes to this lack of customer intimacy.

First, management can overcome this deficiency, not by multiplying ad nauseam the amount of traditional market research done by the company, but by making staff temporarily share the life of various customers to understand their total experience.[14] The point is not so much to search for what customers say they want – they may often trail behind the times – but to become immersed in their environment in order to understand what they do, how they feel, what frustrates and delights them, thus being able to anticipate what they might need and want in the future. Customer-oriented companies encourage a significant proportion of their staff – and not just marketing specialists – to conduct such customer immersions at regular intervals.

Second, management can also encourage staff to engage selected customers to join them in their idea searches and innovation projects. Some industries, like aerospace, do this as a matter of routine. No new aircraft could be developed and commercialized without the active involvement of lead customers, for example airlines, from the very early stages onward. But this habit, which some companies refer to as organizing "customer clinics," is not always encouraged, for fear of losing confidentiality on new products or for lack of trust in the wisdom of customers, or often because selecting customers for such tasks is not easy. Whatever their actual contribution to the company's projects, this habit of involving customers in idea searches and projects creates strong customer intimacy.

Killer # 4: Uncertainty on Innovation Priorities

Not knowing what management expects from innovation is often perceived by many in the organization as a major innovation obstacle, particularly if it is combined with a risk averse culture. It leads to ad hoc idea generation (where should we search for ideas?); difficult concept evaluations (against what objectives should we evaluate our ideas?); fuzzy screening and selection (on what basis should we favor one project over another?); and poor project justifications.

As we recommended earlier, this uncertainty can be overcome by clarifying the company's innovation strategy, which means defining and broadcasting why, where, how, and with whom to innovate.

Management can also beef up the project briefing process by requesting that projects be linked explicitly to the company's announced innovation objectives and strategy.

Killer # 5: Lack of Management Patience Regarding Results

Nestlé's Patience with Nespresso

With $3.8 billion in highly profitable sales in 2012, Nespresso is a jewel in Nestlé's product and brand portfolio. Yet few outsiders know that it took 16 years for the project to reach breakeven, as all kinds of market applications and channels were tried one after the other before achieving success. How did Nespresso manage to escape the hatchet of Nestlé's corporate financial controllers for so long? The answer is that there was strong advocacy for the project from several members of Nestlé's top management team, including Camillo Pagano, former executive vice president in charge of strategic business divisions and marketing worldwide.

Leaders who press their teams unduly for faster results – not so much for shorter lead times, which is understandable, but for quick returns on investment – can be strong innovation inhibitors. Indeed, if short payback is introduced as an important criterion for the selection of innovative project ideas, then staff will, of necessity, screen out all ideas with a long-term high-risk/high-impact profile, to focus exclusively on predictable, incremental innovations. The same leaders may also be tempted to pull the plug too soon on very attractive projects with a long incubation phase and payback outlook.

The top management team can fight this temptation in two ways.

First, it can earmark specific resources for long-term projects, alongside the company's "normal"

R&D budget, and personally become involved in selecting these high-impact projects.

Second, it can ensure that hurdle rates of return, whatever the type, are not introduced as criteria in the initial screening process for innovative project ideas. Financial payback considerations should appear only at a much later stage, when big capital investments are being considered. Instead of payback criteria, management should emphasize the project's potential to create value, i.e. the superiority of the future product or service provided to the company's customers, *as perceived by the market*, and ideally the price these customers will be ready to pay for the product or service, which will make the project attractive. This potential to create a quantum leap in value should obviously be validated through customer contacts and early feedback. If positive, this should convince management to be patient!

Killer # 6: Functional and Regional Silos

Large, complex organizations are often characterized by the coexistence of communities of specialists, each with its own identity, values, and professional norms. These communities exist at headquarters at the functional level. They are also present in decentralized operations, manufacturing plants, or regional and national commercial organizations. Unless strongly unified under the same corporate culture banner, these various groups tend to develop an "us vs. them" mentality, which can be detrimental to a cross-functional and cross-disciplinary process like innovation.

There are multiple dangers:

- Organizational isolationism, which slows the process down by making functional project handovers complex since each function wants to keep full control over its own field of expertise.
- The inability to build on one another's ideas because of the lack of opportunities to work together on the project from the start. This often happens when regional organizations feel left

> ### Working across Disciplines at Eli Lilly
>
> Eli Lilly was developing a drug intended to prevent breast cancer in women. Trials showed that, although it worked, it did not work well enough to be worth marketing. Under usual circumstances, the product would have been shelved, along with several years of the complex activities that go into drug development. Instead, several people who had worked on the project began to realize, after attending a PDMA Frontier Dialogue, that the essential hormone makeup of the drug was able to build bones. They crossed therapeutic areas, a move almost unheard of at the time, and several years later the successful osteoporosis medicine Evista hit the market.

out of the initial project specifications, which are decided upon at headquarters level "for the world."

- Domineering attitudes of some departments, which claim to have the final say in all project matters. This can be the case with marketing dominating R&D in fast-moving consumer goods, or with engineering overpowering everyone in technology-intensive companies.

- Fights over ideas and budgets may also prevent people from cooperating across organizational boundaries. This can happen when a project team requires additional resources from functional departments.

The best and most classic antidote to this danger is the systematic adoption of A to Z cross-functional and/or cross-regional innovation project teams – from idea and concept to market launch – combined with a high degree of empowerment of the project leaders in relation to the functional organization. By working together on the same intense projects, people start building bridges across functions and geographical areas, and they are more likely to adopt a "we" attitude as opposed to an "us vs. them" mindset. In addition, because they share the same performance measures – it is the team that succeeds or fails, not individuals or functions – this helps create a strong sense of solidarity within the team.

Another way to fight silos and develop a "one company spirit" is to multiply opportunities for joint innovation training programs. When people from different functions and regions spend time together discussing current management issues, visions and perceptions *do* change and collaboration becomes easier.

Killer # 7: Rigid and Over-regimented Environment

Last but not least among the most widespread innovation killers is an overregulated environment. This situation exists in many large and traditional companies. Company policy, management rules, and standard operating procedures are definitely necessary to run operations but, by limiting the freedom of would-be entrepreneurs and slowing down teams with unnecessary paperwork and controls, they can discourage people and ultimately stifle innovation.

Management can overcome this risk in two steps.

First, it can make an explicit effort to review all the management rules that were designed primarily for conducting normal operations and generally controlling non-project expenses, and free the project teams from most of these rules. Among the rules to be eliminated are all those that (1) impose standard work processes; (2) limit or organize horizontal and vertical communications; (3) restrict the project team's free access to customers, suppliers, and partners; and (4) require considerable justifications for an authorization to travel or to spend small amounts of money, for example for information or tools.

But because a certain number of rules are necessary, management should ask the project team to define the process they intend to follow and the specific rules that they are willing to accept and apply in their work. Management could then check on how well team members abide by the process and rules that they themselves have chosen.

MONITORING AND EVALUATING RESULTS

Finally, management needs to set up and monitor a range of performance indicators to track progress and identify new improvement targets as some of the initial goals are reached. At the very least, indicators ought to cover both input factors – how many resources the company pumps into innovation – and output measures – how much the company is getting out of its innovation investments. But advanced innovators will typically go beyond these two broad categories and introduce a pyramid of metrics with four types of carefully selected indicators:

- *Lagging indicators* measure process results, typically on the basis of market or financial performance. The percentage of sales that comes from products introduced in the past few years, depending on the industry life cycle, is a typical lagging indicator. So is "time to profit," which measures the time it takes for cumulated profits to pass cumulated investments.

- *Leading indicators* measure process input quality and/or quantity or factors conditioning innovation. The number of patents issued and granted is an example of a leading indicator – and not an overall innovation performance indicator as some companies believe! Another example is the percentage of R&D spent on long-term, high-risk/high-impact projects.

- *In-process indicators* measure process quality in terms of deliverables and time or cost compliance. Classic indicators in this category include the number of non-value-adding changes in projects past a certain point, or the percentage of project review gates passed according to schedule.

- *Learning indicators* which measure the improvement rate on critical performance targets for the business. Examples include the product stabilization period (from launch until quality and performance meet expectations), or more generally the "half-life" of a specific improvement (the time it takes to improve a given performance by 50%).

> **Innovation Scorecard at Solvay**
>
> "The Innovation Scorecard seeks to provide an overall picture of the Group's performance in terms of innovation. It takes account of the extent of employee participation in innovation projects and the proportion of projects carried out in collaboration with external partners, which is a key component of Solvay's sustainability strategy."
>
> *From Solvay's website*

The range of innovation performance indicators companies use

Performance indicators

Results (outputs)	1a. New sales ratio (%) – Products/services 1b. New sales ratio (%) – Technology 1c. New sales ratio (%) – Countries	
Growth pipeline	2. Expected value of new business project pipeline (MEUR)	Target and/or benchmark
Competitiveness pipeline	3. Expected value of competitiveness Improvement project pipeline (MEUR)	
Partnerships	4. % of innovation projects realized with external partners	
People involvement	5. Number of accepted innovation ideas per employee (on average) 6. Management involvement (%)	
R&D	7. Radical innovation spending (%) 8. Number of patents issued/filed	

Figure 3.3: Solvay's Innovation Scorecard
Reproduced with permission of Solvay SA. All rights reserved.

varies from very few (typically reflecting sales and profit growth from new products) to too many! It is indeed difficult to find the right balance and mix.

Solvay, the global chemicals and polymer group, provides a good illustration of a balanced innovation scorecard. It is impressive because it focuses on a manageable number of ratios, eight in total, but in the main categories of performance which reflect the company's innovation priorities: results, the growth pipeline, partnerships, ideas generated, people involvement, and R&D (refer to Figure 3.3 shown in Solvay's 2012 annual report).

The merit of Solvay's approach is that it has set specific corporate targets in three key areas that have been selected as main innovation challenges within the Group, as indicated on its website:

• Growth objective: 30% of Group income should come from new products or technologies.
• Partnerships objective: 50% of projects should be developed in partnership with external partners (customers, universities,

public authorities, start-ups, etc.) in the framework of structured agreements.

- People objective: 100% of executives should define their personal innovation objective every year and have the occasion to
evaluate it at least once with their managers. All employees
should produce at least one innovative idea every year.[15]

IN CONCLUSION: A CALL FOR ACTION

The six innovation governance areas described in this chapter
highlight a number of responsibilities that will typically not be
carried out by the second or third line of a company's hierarchy.
These employees can be expected to manage processes and projects
within a set of overall guidelines, not to come up with an overall
framework for innovation.

The six domains essential for organizing and mobilizing for
innovation are:

- setting an overall frame for innovation;
- defining value;
- choosing an innovation governance model;
- establishing innovation priorities and allocating resources;
- overcoming obstacles and building an innovation culture; and
- monitoring and evaluating results.

They condition the way innovation is carried out and sustained by the organization. They therefore belong to the prime
innovation governance duties of the top management team. It is
vital for the C-suite to address them collectively, broadcast their
outcomes and include them as a regular topic on the top management agenda.

We conclude with one caveat: the mission of innovation leaders
is to steer and support innovators. Governing innovation means
making sure that innovators have as smooth a path as possible, that
their commitment and hard work pay off as much and as often as
possible. We have seen many cases where people work hard on
projects that should have been successful, only to see their work

side-lined, defeated, or disrupted by the kinds of "killers" outlined in this chapter. This problem is often caused by the leaders who should be in charge of smoothing the path to success. They fail to follow the kinds of practices we have discussed above. Problems lie in the way the system is designed and the way the work is organized. Now that companies have discovered increasingly better ways of designing and organizing the work of innovation, it is time for top management to take full responsibility for making sure that the design and organization are optimized so that the innovators have a chance to produce the value they are capable of delivering.

NOTES

[1] Lafley, A.G. and Charan, R. (introduction) (2008). P&G's Innovation Culture: How We Built a World-class Organic Growth Engine by Investing in People. *Strategy+Business*, August 26, http://www.strategy-business.com/article/08304?pg=all

[2] Refer to Young, J.S. and Simon, W.L. (2005). *iCon Steve Jobs, The Greatest Second Act in the History of Business*. Wiley, p. 88.

[3] For the full list of these values, refer to http://www.askstudent.com/google/list-of-google-core-values/

[4] Hamel, G. (2010). Deconstructing Apple – Part 2. *Wall Street Journal*, March 8.

[5] Refer to the framework proposed by Beebe Nelson and Valerie Kijewski. http://www.nkaudits.com/

[6] Excerpt from a 2005 videotaped interview "Steering and Coaching an Innovation Project" with Nils Björkman and Bo Wirsén, members of the Group Leadership Team of Tetra Pak International by Prof. J.P. Deschamps, IMD, Lausanne, Switzerland.

[7] Excerpt from a 2009 videotaped interview "DSM: Mobilizing the Organization to Grow through Innovation" with Rob van Leen, chief innovation officer at DSM, by Prof. J.P. Deschamps, IMD, Lausanne, Switzerland.

[8] Chan Kim, W. and Mauborgne, R. (2005). *Blue Ocean Strategy – How to Create Uncontested Market Space and Make Competition Irrelevant*. Harvard Business School Press.

[9] Chan Kim, W. and Mauborgne, R. (1997). Value Innovation: The Strategic Logic of High Growth. *Harvard Business Review*, January–February 1997.

[10] Fine, C.H. (1998). *Clockspeed: Winning Industry Control in the Age of Temporary Advantage*. Perseus Books. Used with permission.

[11] Deschamps, J.-P. (2008). *Innovation Leaders: How Senior Executives Stimulate, Steer and Sustain Innovation*. San Francisco: Wiley/Jossey-Bass, Chapter 6.

[12] Amabile, T.M. and Khaire, M. (2008). Creativity and the Role of the Leader. *Harvard Business Review*, October.

[13] Hamel, G. (1999). Bringing Silicon Valley Inside. *Harvard Business Review*, September/October.

[14] Gouillart, F.J. and Sturdivant, F.D. (2009). Spend a Day in the Life of Your Customers. *Harvard Business Review*, March.

[15] Innovation Scorecard, copyright Solvay 2013, source: http://www.solvay.com/EN/Innovation/innovationscorecard.aspx

PART II

CHOOSING BETWEEN ALTERNATIVE GOVERNANCE MODELS

CHAPTER 4

WHY FOCUS ON INNOVATION GOVERNANCE MODELS?

Companies that have a commitment to ongoing innovation also have, whether explicit or implicit, a governance model by which they allocate authority and responsibility for innovation within the organization. Our research has shown that even though they may not talk about "innovation governance," most companies manage innovation according to a governance model that senior managers can describe. The mission to promote and oversee innovation might be entrusted to a particular person – who may or may not be fully dedicated to the task – or it can be taken on by a group of managers working together in the context of different types of organizational mechanisms. Our respondents' experience also shows that these models tend to evolve over time.

The evolution of governance models may reflect changes in innovation processes, for example the maturation of innovation practices and the shift from "developing products" to "innovation." The evolution may also be justified by changes in the innovation context, such as the rise of global innovation, digitization and the internet, and partnering or "open innovation." There may also be changes in staffing and structure, often linked to the appointment of a new CEO or CTO. Some of these evolutions represent management's desire for a more effective innovation process or a broader or different innovation focus. Others simply reflect a change in management philosophy or personal commitment at the top.

But one thing stands out – few companies we know seem to have adopted a systematic approach to identifying and comparing possible models before choosing one. And equally few are able to review possible models when they feel that their existing model needs improvement. In fact, often senior managers' descriptions of existing innovation governance practices are basic and incomplete. In our survey, several managers in the same company described the company's governance model differently. There is often a lack of clarity and comprehensiveness in the way governance is understood by top management. We feel therefore that it is critically important to specify and evaluate the range of possible models (1) so that companies can be more reflective and explicit in their choice of governance model, and (2) so that they can choose the ones that best fit their current conditions and aspirations and be able to keep improving them.

WHY DO COMPANIES NEED AN INNOVATION GOVERNANCE MODEL?

Innovation is a complex, company-wide venture carried out by people who assume very different roles and responsibilities within the company. Although they belong to different groups and functions, which are typically committed to different goals, their efforts must be aligned in order for innovation to be successful. They must also be aligned with top management's goals and strategies. Top management must decide who is going to be responsible at the highest level for innovation in the company and who will play a supporting role. It is this combination of primary and supporting responsibilities for innovation to achieve critical alignment that we refer to as a "governance model."

Like other complex, company-wide issues that need a proper governance system – including quality management and commitment to environmental sustainability – innovation must have a governance system that enables the adjudication of disputes, the allocation of resources, the alignment of strategies, and so on.

Corporate governance is most usually associated with the board's role – the board has a clear and articulated responsibility to oversee the actions and strategies of the company and to ensure that these align with both legal directives and the interests of stakeholders. But, as we saw in Chapter 2, although in some companies the board has an explicit interest in innovation, in most companies innovation is left to the employees, and the board is merely informed of strategy and outcomes. We hope it will become evident, in this chapter and in subsequent chapters, that the board should play an important and supportive role in innovation and innovation governance. It should, at least, be aware of the company's governance model. This does not mean that the board should meddle or try to take the place of innovation-focused employees!

WHAT ARE THE KEY ELEMENTS OF AN INNOVATION GOVERNANCE MODEL?

At least three key tasks must be dealt with when implementing an innovation governance model:

* Assigning primary responsibility.
* Defining the scope and level of responsibilities.
* Planning the support mechanisms.

Here again, we address the need to make governance explicit. As we have seen, often people do not know for sure who holds primary responsibility for innovation. Is it the CTO or the CMO? What is the role of the CEO? How empowered is the innovation steering group? The duties of those who are responsible for governance are far too complex and important to leave these questions unanswered.

Defining the scope and level of responsibilities is also a key task; and of course, as management deals honestly and explicitly with these two tasks, each will help to shed light on the other. If the two tasks are well executed, addressing the third will not be so hard. This last task requires a level of understanding of innovation best practices, and the details can be entrusted to those whose expertise is in that realm.

Assigning Primary Responsibility

The main element of an innovation governance model is assigning primary responsibility for innovation in the company. In some companies it is obvious who is responsible. For example, in Chapter 8 we will see that at Corning responsibility for front-end or radical innovation is assigned to the Corporate Technology Council (CTC), while responsibility for getting innovations to market rests with the Growth Execution Council (GEC).

In many companies, however, it is not so clear who is responsible. Our experience is that descriptions of who has primary responsibility for innovation tend to be basic and incomplete. When managers in the same company describe its governance model differently, this highlights a lack of clarity and comprehensiveness in the way governance is understood.

Duties that we include under *primary responsibilities* are often split or shared: for example, in companies like Nestlé, the head of all strategic business units may be responsible for defining *where* and *on what* the company should look for innovation, while the CTO defines the *how*. This kind of teaming can succeed when the pair works well together; if it does not, this can seriously disrupt the organization's chances of articulating and pursuing a coherent innovation strategy.

If primary responsibility for innovation governance is not assigned in the context of a holistic view of innovation, the assigned roles are likely to be at odds with each other. For example, one company adopted the mission of "growing by innovation" and appointed a director of innovation, but its annual portfolio assessment set its sights on projects that would have short-term payback. As a result, although the explicit assignment held the promise of setting and meeting innovation targets (and, in fact, under this director's leadership identified a number of promising opportunities), the tacit commitment of the company's leadership to conservative investment stymied any positive results that might have emerged from creating the director of innovation position.

Defining the Scope and Level of Responsibilities

The second element is the scope of innovation responsibility and the level of empowerment of those who fill innovation governance roles. This aspect of innovation governance also presents challenges. Most positions within a company are limited to particular functions and/or divisions. A key feature of successful innovation is that it crosses boundaries. Those who are assigned leadership roles in governing innovation must, likewise, cross boundaries. This calls for clear assignment of roles and empowerment that might upset the usual ways that business is done.

Explicit allocation of responsibilities requires corporate alignment on what is necessary for successful innovation. For example, what processes and subprocesses are essential? How will their effectiveness be judged? Who will be responsible for launching improvement initiatives? A reflection of the complexity of these questions is the degree to which leading innovation companies have gained value from the dialogues of the International Association for Product Development (IAPD) and other such peer groups. Many companies now have specific roles for *process architects*, or *process owners*, but the scope of innovation goes way beyond the design, implementation, and continuous improvement of processes. Companies need to make these questions clear and create alignment to ensure successful governance.

Planning the Support Mechanisms

The third element is the creation and implementation of supporting organizational mechanisms to manage specific aspects of innovation, or to manage innovation in specific parts of the company. By its very nature, innovation demands that innovators have the freedom to experiment, to change direction and to break with old habits and patterns. This is why some people raise their eyebrows when they hear the phrase "innovation governance." Some companies, usually those with powerful innovator CEOs (who are often also founders), can be run rather like dictatorships. At Polaroid, innovation came from the top, from Edwin Land. His chief support mechanism was to start several teams working on an idea.

The 15% Rule at 3M

At 3M, under its famous 15% rule, innovators were encouraged to work on projects that they found promising, with or without permission from top levels. This may seem more like anarchy, but it is in fact a clear mandate of governance. Andy Ouderkirk, speaking at an IAPD workshop, said that one of the most important benefits of the 15% rule was not the time you could devote to an unassigned project. It was the fact that no one questioned your spending time in other places or doing other things than those you were assigned to. In this way the varied resources of the company were able to mix and combine and find new ways of using their talents.

He could then choose the inventions and designs that best matched his idea. The rest of the company was set up to carry out the required actions to bring the idea to market.

More "democratic" companies, where innovation is bottom up or a combination of top down and bottom up, require a more subtle governance model. They need one that will enable freedom in the pursuit of novelty and change but at the same time reduce the anarchy and confusion that ensues when no one "knows the rules," when the rules conflict, and when those who make the rules are not in alignment, or sometimes even in communication, with one another.

In this context, IBM's characterization of its approach to innovation as "managed anarchy" seems to be right on target. As we will see in more detail in Chapter 7, Sam Palmisano, like many successful CEO innovation leaders, was a great spokesman for innovation, not limiting his passion to within the company but sharing it with other organizations that might help spread the word among innovation partners. He also found effective ways of conveying his message on innovation to the whole company using social media and allowing everyone to participate. Although IBM's governance model is basically top down, the company also has a carefully designed and regularly updated set of processes for innovation that specify who does what. We might conclude that, at IBM, innovation is inspired from above, spread wide through intranet connections, and kept on track by precise and well-implemented processes.

THE GOVERNANCE SYSTEM AND AN EXPLICIT CONSTITUTION

While the kinds of governance mechanisms described above work well in some companies, there is often an element of "magic" – something that is hard to explain, even hard to understand, and often dependent on particular people (e.g. Jobs at Apple). A successful innovator, in order to tip the scales toward long-term success, needs to allocate innovation responsibilities and define the nature and the boundaries of those responsibilities. Otherwise, as happens too often, decisions made by one person or group may be undermined by another, and often there is no recourse, no system of adjudication for settling disputes. One of the obvious causes of innovation failure is a lack of alignment of decision makers – people with the authority to set limits, give the go-ahead to projects, and identify the markets, technologies, or potential partners that innovators should be exploring. One decision maker gives the go-ahead; the other fails to resource the project. One decision maker points the innovators toward a particular market; the other – after considerable resources have been spent – declines to allow any innovation in that arena. And so forth.

In our research, it became evident that although our respondents were able to identify a governance model that had been implemented in their company, only rarely could they explicitly state the nature and boundaries of the allocated responsibilities. For example, a respondent might state that the CTO is in charge of innovation but not be able to specify what this means in any detail. Does the CTO determine levels of acceptable risk for innovation projects? Does he/she determine the balance of the innovation portfolio? If the company uses a phase/review process to take projects from early approval to commercialization, what is the exact task of the reviewers and what is their relationship to the CTO? These are important questions, and in many companies – though certainly not all – there are no explicit answers to them, and this lack of clarity is a major cause of waste, frustration, and failure.

Accomplishing the three difficult tasks that we have described above allows a company to move from an intuitive approach to innovation to one that is clearly communicated and clearly understood. And, perhaps equally importantly, the accomplishment of these tasks positions the company on a path to continuous improvement. Clarity about its own approach will help it to overcome the typical blind spots when it comes to seeing and appreciating what is new – be these opportunities or challenges. And such clarity can pave the way for developing what might be called an innovation governance constitution.

In Chapter 1 we suggested that a form of constitution is necessary for proper innovation governance in order to provide a frame for innovation activities that cut across organizational units, as well as to curb individual and functional interests in favor of corporate interests. The innovation governance constitution should include the three tasks outlined above, as well as:

- Specifying rules of legitimacy, which define who owns what, who does what, who is responsible for what, and what legitimizes these responsibilities.
- Identifying desired targets regarding growth through innovation and use of resources.
- Defining methods for resolving conflict, especially when innovation activities conflict with accepted line responsibilities and activities.
- Stating how the company will protect stakeholder interests, both internal (e.g. employees) and external (customers as well as other beneficiaries and/or potential victims).

Few companies have an explicit constitution. One of our purposes in this book is to elucidate the models that companies are using so that the value and the practicality of addressing these kinds of issues can be apparent.

WHAT MODELS DO COMPANIES USE?

Our research has identified nine models that companies use today (10 if one includes the option of no one being in charge). These models range from having single individuals in charge to duos or groups, and they range from top to senior to middle management. The models in place in a company are often influenced by the company's history and culture and they reflect the choices management must make when allocating responsibilities for innovation.

The first choice relates to the type and number of bearers of that responsibility. Will innovation oversight be entrusted to a single manager or leader? Will that person be fully dedicated to the task or not? Will it be given to a duo of managers or leaders or to a small group of leaders? Or will it be distributed among a larger group of managers?

The second choice deals with the management level of the appointed innovation heads and their reporting relationships. Should the jobs be filled by top managers reporting directly to the CEO or to the executive group? Should they involve less senior or even middle managers reporting to a lower level of management?

When they are combined, these two choices determine nine different models of governance, as illustrated in Figure 4.1. In practice, large companies tend to use several models to steer innovation.

Multi-business corporations may not steer innovation centrally but rather let each business group or division choose its own model. For example, Elanco, the veterinarian business within Eli Lilly, has developed its own model of innovation governance.

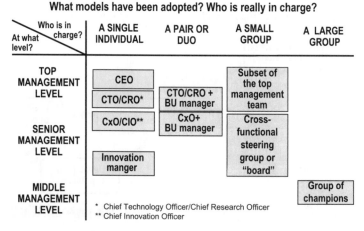

Figure 4.1: Typology of Governance Models

Although Eli Lilly's governance model is a high-level cross-functional steering group, Elanco's model places the main responsibility with the division's president and teams of innovation champions.

But even if companies have adopted a single corporate approach to innovation, they may opt for several models, for example a general model to promote and steer innovation overall, and one or several supporting models or mechanisms to leverage the first one and deal with specific missions. The overall model typically deals with the three *content* questions (why, where, and how much), while the supporting models tend to focus on the three *process* questions (how, with whom, and who). Figure 4.2 illustrates the different focus of these two types of models.

Models Dealing with the Why, Where, and How Much Questions

These important questions are the three keys to innovation strategy. In short they should be resolved by top management and the board

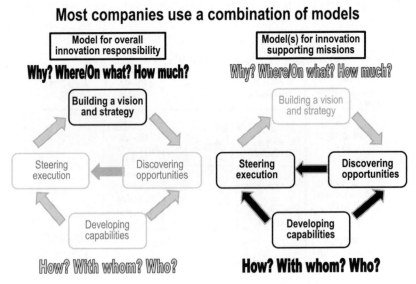

Figure 4.2:   A Different Focus for Each Type of Model

> **Resourcing Projects**
>
> Professor Nelson Repenning's research has shown that many companies use resources that were intended for early stage projects to support projects that are closer to the market but behind schedule. Of course, this results in even more projects being delayed and, all too often, in the company being in a state of permanent under-resourcing which chokes the product development pipeline and is very hard to recover from.
>
> *Professor Repenning presented his research at an IAPD workshop*

should also play a role in addressing them. If overall innovation responsibility has been entrusted to people in a lower hierarchical level than top management, then they ought to make their own assumptions regarding the answers to these questions and propose them to top management for approval (or modification).

The answers to the second and third questions (*where* and *how much*) will obviously be influenced by management's answer to the first. Just as innovation models have moved over the past couple of decades from an emphasis on developing new products to a much broader scope that includes, for example, business model innovation, so the question of where the company will look for innovation has broadened. Companies now look to markets and capabilities that would have seemed way out of their realm of interest in previous decades. The question of *where* needs to be addressed in the context of research and understanding of markets and of competencies and capabilities, and it should be seen as a moving target. Those tasked with answering this question need to be sure that the company's innovation system is up to date in this respect.

The last question, *how much*, is probably – even more than the other two – one that only top management can address. If it is not well handled, it can cause much undue waste and leads not only to great inefficiency but also to unnecessary discouragement of innovators. How much is top management prepared to spend on innovation? How will it define innovation – as limited to breakthrough new projects, or encompassing all of the ways in which the company changes its value proposition? Or something in between? The answer to *how much* needs to be considered not only in terms of percentages or funds but also in terms of *on what*, and the decision-making processes need to be aligned with top management's position on this topic.

Models Dealing with the How, With Whom, and Who Questions

The second set of questions is more in the domain of *process* and is often guided by what we call supporting mechanisms. There may be different types of supporting mechanisms for different processes, which is why most companies use a range of supporting mechanisms. For example, the supporting mechanism for idea management will often be different from that for portfolio management or project review and control. Addressing these questions builds the company's capability for innovation and steers the actual project work that is necessary to take opportunities from possibility to reality. Of course, this aspect of governance flourishes when the first three questions have been dealt with effectively and is virtually crippled when they have not been. Many companies have had "process owners" or "process architects" for many years now, whose responsibility is to keep these processes working, to upgrade them, and to identify new ones which might add to innovation effectiveness.

Companies have always relied on external partners or suppliers to add to their own capabilities. In the past, this was most frequently limited to suppliers who could provide the required elements of a product – for example, a company might contract with a supplier to make an electronic part that the company did not have the know-how to produce. This is why the *with whom* question could be delegated to functions and people close to operations. Then, the theory of supplier relationships was largely based on how to get the best deal from the supplier. But today, the question *with whom* has become an important and strategic aspect of open innovation as companies work with partners around the world to expand capabilities and market access. And this is why this question – at least in terms of policy – has moved back to the top management level.

The question of *who* – who in the company should be involved in innovation – also has an impact requiring some top management involvement, inasmuch as it can present problems and issues that can stall and disrupt innovation activities. The answer to who should be involved is, in our opinion, anyone whose talents and interests might be helpful in creating value – for the customer and for the company. Of course we do not mean that everyone should swarm to every project that is of interest – part of the job of innovation governance is to protect innovators from the frequent tendency to assign too many projects and stretch resources beyond the breaking point. However, it has become increasingly apparent that when innovation is carried out in functional silos, the company's ability to succeed is diminished. Governance of the question "Who will participate in innovation?" needs to ensure that functional boundaries do not prevent collaboration across organizational units.

In summary, however the responsibilities for governing innovation are deployed – whether there is a single model in use or responsibilities are allocated to two or more people or groups – governance must take into consideration these six questions. Innovation is a systemic enterprise and if the answer to any of these questions is missing or incomplete the whole structure will suffer.

The Nine Governance Models

- *Model 1: The top management team (or a subset of that team) as a group.* In this model – which seems to be the most widely used – members of the C-suite share the duties of governance, although most often membership is limited to those who are directly involved with innovation – e.g. business leaders plus marketing and R&D.
- *Model 2: The CEO or, in multi-business corporations, a group/division president.* When the CEO is in ultimate charge of innovation, the message that innovation is a top priority for the company is usually loud and clear. Many get that message out beyond the limits of the company. Steve Jobs, Jeff Bezos, A.G. Lafley, and Akio Toyoda, among others, have all contributed to

the fact that the whole world is more engaged in innovation – not just their companies.

- *Model 3: The high-level, cross-functional innovation steering group or board.* Members of such steering groups or boards are chosen based on functional responsibilities and frequently also on their personal interest in and commitment to innovation. Often a CTO or CRO chairs the group, but other members may span a couple of levels under the executive committee.
- *Model 4: The CTO or CRO as the ultimate innovation champion.* This model is most usually employed in companies with a strong technology and/or engineering tradition. The CTO/CRO model focuses on the content of innovation, i.e. on the promotion of technology-based initiatives, and the CTO or CRO is rarely involved in the non-technical aspects of innovation.
- *Models 5 and 6: The dedicated innovation manager or chief innovation officer.* The difference between these models and the CTO/CRO model is that responsibility for innovation is entrusted to a single, dedicated manager, not to a busy CTO/CRO with operational duties. In this model the innovation manager's focus is more on the process than the content side and he/she is usually responsible for tracking innovation success and identifying and sharing best practices.
- *Model 7: A group of innovation champions.* This model is more frequently found in a supporting model role than as a primary governance model. Typically, champions are innovation enthusiasts, sometimes referred to as "intrapreneurs." In some companies their focus is mostly on content, i.e. specific projects. In others it is more on the process side as they work to share innovation practices and experiences.
- *Models 8 and 9: The duo or the complementary two-person team.* The duo might be a CTO who shares innovation responsibility with a business unit manager, a functional manager, or a CXO. Few companies use either of these models, but they do exist.

An additional model is when *no one is in charge.* In some companies innovation is so much part of the company's DNA that everyone feels responsible and so they believe that there is no need for governance. In other cases, restructuring or reorganization may have temporarily (or in some cases more permanently) disrupted the usual governance mechanisms. And finally, in companies where innovation is not perceived as particularly important there may be no one in charge.

Choosing a Model

Identifying and comparing possible models before selecting one is always beneficial. When this important step is not taken, a company runs the risk of using an inappropriate model for its condition and state of innovation maturity. Given that no model is perfect, we recommend that a company evaluates the advantages and disadvantages of each model before selecting one or changing from one to another. We also suggest that care should be taken in deciding who should be involved in the deliberations.

When choosing an innovation governance model for the company, top management needs to review and discuss several issues. Key considerations include the company's size, its place in the industry's competitive landscape, and its organizational structure. Other important considerations are the management philosophies of the top team and the board, as well as the innovation interests and capabilities of members of the top management team. For example, if the CEO or the CTO is an obvious choice for innovation leadership, this will move the choice of governance model in that direction. If there are many strong innovation leaders in the ranks of middle management, then the company might choose Model 7: a group of innovation champions.

It is also important to address the more cultural and historical parameters – for example, how the different functions work together, how important innovation is to the company's perception of itself, and the company's core capabilities (some core capabilities lead fairly easily to innovative changes; others tend to restrict the company to a limited scope when it comes to innovation).

Another question to ask is how open the company is to change, and this is a difficult question to answer. We are all open to change, or so we think. It is only after we have failed to see the opportunities or challenges that we missed that we realize that we have been wearing blinders. In our experience, some of the more sophisticated models for understanding customers, markets, and technologies can help a company to be open to a wider world. Using practices such as voice of customer (VOC) or technology mapping usually reveals that there are, as Shakespeare said, "more things in heaven and earth than are dreamt of in your philosophy."

How Many Models Do Companies Use?

Companies – especially large ones – frequently use more than one governance model. For example, the CEO may be the person in overall charge of innovation in the company (Model 2), yet that same CEO may benefit from the advice and recommendations of a high-level innovation steering group (Model 3), while mobilizing a group of middle management champions to preach the innovation gospel across business units (Model 7). In fact, in our research we found that almost every possible combination of models was used.

Using a variety of mechanisms can make it difficult to identify who, if anyone, ultimately bears overall responsibility and coordinates the tasks of all these mechanisms. This is, of course, especially true when governance practices have emerged over time and have never been properly defined. For this reason, the question of how many models to use is best answered in the context of reviewing and selecting governance models, both primary and supporting.

Do Companies Change Models?

The scope of innovation has broadened dramatically in the past decades. From the late 1980s until the early 2000s innovators, particularly in larger companies, were puzzling how to improve their capacity to develop new products. The maturation of new product development (NPD) practices in the early 2000s, along with many other factors, totally transformed the scope of innovation – it became a global phenomenon, entered into with partners and open to changes in profit/business models. Companies whose innovation governance models still focus on the architecture and implementation of "product development processes" will benefit greatly from a shift in innovation governance that addresses and includes these radical and important changes.

Companies do indeed change their models for governing innovation. Often companies alter models when there are staffing changes, especially the appointment of a new CEO or CTO. If the company adds people with experience and expertise in innovation, the model may shift to include these new hires. Conversely, if the company loses people with such expertise, a different model may need to be applied to bring the remaining talent into a more central role.

In companies where innovation governance is weak – ill-defined or affecting only some of the company's innovation concerns, for example – models may simply drift from one to another. In these companies, models are also subject to change according to the whims of senior officers – a phenomenon that is sometimes referred to as "process of the month" and which can (1) confuse people about what their goals and responsibilities are, and (2) lead people to ignore the whims of senior management ("they'll just change their minds next month – might as well keep on doing what we're doing").

There are two motivations for change that are most likely to improve a company's innovation governance system. One is the move to a more empowered model; the other is the transition from a narrower to a broader innovation scope. In Chapters 8 and 11 we will review in more depth how Corning and Tetra Pak, respectively, empowered and broadened their model of innovation governance. At Corning, the change was triggered by the disaster of the telecom downturn, after which the company decided to create two governance models, one focusing on the radical front end of innovation and the other on projects leading to medium-term growth. Although Corning has always been a company in which innovation has played an important role, the current governance model has been greatly reinforced and made explicit, and this has had a positive effect on Corning's approach to innovation over the past few years. Similarly, Tetra Pak has considerably broadened the scope of its initial governance model – the innovation process board – by creating different high-level "councils" dealing with both process and content (i.e. strategy).

Which is Better, a Centralized Model or a Decentralized One?

Companies' response to this question varies. The major factors seem to be (1) the top team's management philosophy, and (2) the degree to which the company's business is homogeneous. Smaller companies will tend toward a centralized model, but there are also larger, diversified companies that have chosen to centralize innovation governance.

Corning is a good example of the first factor. Its top management team insists on centralized governance. Although the company has pursued many different innovations and worked with many different partners, its approach to innovation governance has remained centralized since it was founded.

We can see several reasons for this. First, innovation at Corning focuses on the use of glass. The uses have varied widely – from electric bulbs to TV monitors to photonics – and the company identifies current uses as well as what it calls "white space" potentials for this fungible substance. The location of the core of Corning's scientific resources at Sullivan Park, not far from company headquarters in the town of Corning, enables scientists working on widely different projects to cross boundaries and help one another.

Second, Corning's top management has always been centrally involved in innovation. For example, when Jamie Houghton – a scion of the Houghton family which founded Corning – returned as CEO after the telecom downturn nearly put the company out of business, his first visit was to the scientists at Sullivan Park. He did not want there to be any doubt about what he considered key to Corning's past and future success. (See Chapter 8 for more on Corning.)

The second deciding factor on whether a centralized or decentralized model is better is the degree of variability of innovation.

Homogeneous companies are likely to have a centralized govern-ance model. Like small companies, they have consistent answers to the questions of *why*, *where*, and *how much*. If, as the company explores innovation, these answers change, then it might be time to consider a more decentralized model in order to enable different parts of the company to pursue different paths.

An example of such a shift can be seen in Nestlé's approach to innovation governance. Although, in the main, the company's governance model is centralized, the rise of a number of so-called globally managed businesses like Nestlé Waters or Nespresso enabled it to create products and exploit markets that were very different and much more global than usual. Nestlé's globally managed businesses have therefore gained a considerable amount of freedom in their innovation governance, despite the fact that their R&D resources are managed centrally.

More heterogeneous companies are more likely to have a decentralized governance model. A clear example is United Tech-nologies, whose business units are businesses in their own right − Sikorsky, Otis Elevator, Pratt & Whitney, and so on − and have their own governance models. Of course the models within each of these businesses may be centralized or not.

In conclusion, a clear focus on the possible models of innova-tion governance enables a company to raise and address questions that affect its ability to use its capacity for innovation. If these questions are not addressed, the work of innovation will fall prey to "mixed signals" from management. If they are addressed, the company will have a far better chance of succeeding in its innova-tion efforts − those that use existing talents and capabilities, as well as those that must be deployed to sense and respond to change. In the next chapter we will find out which models are most widely used by companies and how different companies choose, imple-ment, and modify their models.

CHAPTER 5

INNOVATION GOVERNANCE MODELS

In sophisticated innovation-driven companies, it may not be easy to define in simple terms precisely who "owns" or "governs" innovation because of the multiplicity of owners and actors. In addition the number, nature and roles of these governance mechanisms usually evolve naturally over time, as management reinforces or keeps enlarging the scope of their responsibilities. Innovative companies do not change their governance models overnight at the whim of a new CEO or CTO. They work on their models to perfect them and enhance their effectiveness. Good innovation governance builds upon experience and calls for consistency over time and constant improvements.

Solvay's Innovation Charter

- The Group wishes to emphasize the need for dynamic and responsible innovation that can generate growth and sustainable improvements.

- The function of each member of the Group includes an innovation dimension with a significant weight. Personal evaluations, compensation and career evolution are linked, among other factors, to that criterion, which is applied at individual and team level.

- At all levels, Group management includes among
(Continued)

INNOVATIVE COMPANIES DEPLOY A RANGE OF GOVERNANCE MECHANISMS

Solvay, one of the world's top 10 chemical groups, illustrates how companies deploy a range of innovation governance models and how these evolve over time to respond to new business demands. The example of Solvay may be inspiring for companies that are embarking on the complex process of building an organizational framework and allocating a range of responsibilities for innovation.

From its roots in long-established commodity products like sodium carbonate, Solvay has evolved to become a highly respected global supplier of advanced chemicals and plastics. This transformation reflects a strong management commitment to innovation.

With innovation as its key pillar, Solvay focused naturally on R&D and technology. However, in the late 1990s, top management broadened the scope of Solvay's innovation efforts with the objective of mobilizing staff in participative, or bottom-up, initiatives. It also formalized its innovation governance activities, first by appointing an executive committee member – the head of one of its large business sectors – as *corporate innovation sponsor* with the mission to stimulate, steer, and sustain innovation. Second, management brought in an experienced innovation practitioner as dedicated *group innovation champion*, with the mission to support all corporate innovation initiatives and orchestrate this bottom-up effort.

The first outcomes of this new management emphasis on bottom-up innovation included, among others, the creation and

---

its most important missions the development and encouragement of innovation in all its forms, including participative innovation. The Group recognizes and rewards innovators. It accepts that the approach presents risks.

- Quality ideas that fit within the Group's strategic priorities receive the means to demonstrate their validity and, if it is proven, to be deployed.
- Innovation integrates a number of external stakeholders, starting with customers.

Charter released in 2003 – translated from a 2005 innovation issue of Solvay News sharing of an innovation charter (see box); the organization of a structured idea management system; and the awarding of innovation trophies in six different categories of innovation, including success in replication, or adopting in one unit the ideas or best practices developed elsewhere.

An interesting aspect of Solvay's broad-based innovation governance model is that it recognizes that bottom-up innovation, which the company refers to as participative or *kaizen* innovation, requires different management mechanisms than disruptive innovation, which most often happens in a top-down mode.

Roles for Participative (*Kaizen*) Innovation

Solvay's participative innovation objective is to tap the brains of the entire organization, down to blue collar workers in manufacturing sites, to generate innovative ideas and to mobilize everyone behind their execution. This objective is illustrated in the management values that are specified in the Solvay Innovation Charter.

Besides the group innovation champion, who supports the overall bottom-up effort, Solvay counts on the involvement of a broad variety of actors through a "central" idea management tool. A 2005 innovation-focused issue of *Solvay News* describes the role of these actors as follows:

- *Innoplace*: The intranet-based innovation platform supports the ideation system, which is in place in most entities – businesses and functions – and which covers a number of broad categories of ideas, not just technologies, products, and processes.
- *Managers*: They are supposed to encourage innovation from all. They facilitate the realization of ideas, recognize the actors and evaluate innovation performance, notably through evaluation discussions.
- *Innovation champions* (in each main business area and function) and *Innov'actors* (down to site level in France): They propose innovation initiatives to the managers and execute these initiatives with the staff concerned.
- *Facilitators*: Within the idea management system, they identify so-called experts and steer the development of ideas.

- *Experts*: They validate the ideas they receive from facilitators, and they orient the development of ideas within the appropriate innovation structures.
- *Employees*: They are all expected to submit and react to ideas. They each have a personal annual innovation objective. They keep informed and take frequent initiatives.

Roles and Mechanisms for Disruptive Innovation

> **Solvay's Innovation Centre**
>
> Solvay has given its Innovation Center, set up in April 2011, three main missions: The first is to strengthen and encourage best practices in managing innovation, improving the innovation culture so that each entity can manage its own projects more effectively.
>
> The second is to ensure R&D transversality across the various Group entities, each of which is responsible for its own resources, programs and priorities.
>
> The third is to run the four development platforms, which represent nearly 20% of the Group's investment in innovation.
>
> *Extract from Solvay's 2011 Annual Report*

Besides focusing on bottom-up innovation, the company has progressively beefed up its ability to generate and steer disruptive innovations to create new businesses. For this purpose, a number of committees and functions have emerged over the years. But since 2010, these various initiatives have been streamlined and consolidated into fewer, more empowered mechanisms. For example, in 2010, management created the position of *chief scientific and innovation officer* reporting directly to the CEO. It also centralized into an *Innovation Center* a number of activities pertaining to longer-term, disruptive innovations, e.g. an R&D Excellence function responsible for managing new shared technology platforms, as well as groups responsible for creating new ventures and businesses.

To steer these activities, management converted the New Business Board it had created in the mid-2000s, consisting of Solvay senior leaders and external personalities, into an *Innovation Board*. It is responsible for managing the portfolio of activities in a prospective development mode, orienting innovation and long-term research programs and developing softer competencies.

In summary, Solvay's top management has launched a number of initiatives and organizational mechanisms to progressively reinforce and simplify its innovation governance practices. Its three original objectives remain to: (1) build new growth platforms and enhance the company's competitiveness; (2) encourage open innovation and partnerships; and (3) engage everyone behind the innovation agenda.

It would not be exaggerating to say that Solvay's long-term objective is to make innovation everyone's business.

As in many innovative companies, Solvay's top management team, through its CEO and its corporate innovation sponsor, is the locus of the company's innovation governance system. But the company uses a number of complementary supporting models to implement its vision of an innovation-driven company and leverage its efforts. To apply our initial terminology of governance models, Solvay's supporting models include a CSO/CIO, a dedicated innovation manager, and a high-level, cross-functional steering group or board, plus a network of champions cascading down to the operational level. Not many companies have such an elaborate innovation governance system.

Solvay's bottom-up and top-down innovation mechanisms have worked well for the company. But there is no doubt that management will have to keep improving and reinforcing its current governance system. As stated in Chapter 4, innovation governance models are bound to evolve as companies grow and new challenges emerge.

THE MOST WIDELY USED INNOVATION GOVERNANCE MODELS

Chapter 4 proposed a list of innovation governance models that we had empirically encountered in the course of our innovation management consulting practice. In order to validate this list and identify the most popular of these models, we conducted a selective online survey with 113 companies, half of them global multinationals.[1] Indeed, all respondents in our survey recognized their model in the list provided to them, with only minor differences, typically in the naming of that responsibility. So these models provide a fair representation of the range of organizational solutions available for the allocation of overall innovation responsibilities in companies.

Note that, as mentioned in Chapter 4, the same models are also used as secondary or supporting innovation management mechanisms, alongside a primary model. For example, companies that have adopted one of the models in the list for their primary allocation of innovation responsibilities will often choose one or several additional models to enhance and support their primary model. That supporting model can be of the same type as the primary model, but at a lower hierarchical level. For example, if the corporate CTO is chosen as the primary source of innovation governance in a company, divisional CTOs may be assigned a similar responsibility for promoting innovation in their specific organization. But the supporting model can also be of a different nature. For example, when the top management team or the CEO is deemed to be in overall charge of innovation in the company, they may appoint a dedicated innovation manager or a network of champions to leverage their efforts.

Our survey indicates that all these models are in use today, even though some are found more frequently than others. This applies to models for both overall and supporting responsibilities, as shown in Tables 5.1 and 5.2. These tables also highlight that rankings for the frequency of use differ significantly between models for overall and for supporting responsibilities. As we will explore in more detail later, some models, like the innovation manager or the group of champions, are more frequently found in a supporting role than as a primary responsibility.

We will now consider each of these models individually and highlight why and how they are used.

THE TOP MANAGEMENT TEAM (OR A SUBSET OF IT) AS A GROUP

In this model, the top management team – or more frequently a small subset of it, often fewer than four senior leaders – exercises

Table 5.1   Primary Innovation Governance Models Ranked by Frequency of Occurrence

Who Has the *Overall* Responsibility for Innovation in Your Company?	In % of Respondents
The Top Management Team or a Subset of It	29
The CEO or Division President	16
A High-level Cross-functional Steering Group	14
CTO or CRO	10
A Dedicated Innovation Manager or CIO	9
No one specifically	6
A group of champions	5
Another CXO or Business Unit Manager	4
Other	4
A CTO/CRO with a CXO or Business Unit Manager	3

Source: IMD survey (N = 113)

overall responsibility for innovation. This seems to be the most widespread form of innovation governance. To reflect the supervisory nature of their mission, some of these innovation-oriented top management teams call their group the *innovation board*.

This model makes sense if we

> "A divisional head and member of our top management team acts as *leadership champion* and is one of the members of a cross-functional leadership team for the company."
>
> *A large utility company*

consider that innovation – a cross-functional and multidisciplinary activity – needs to be steered from the top, with members of the top team contributing their specific competence. Companies like Corning, Nestlé Waters, Lego, and SKF, among others, seem to

Table 5.2 Supporting Innovation Governance Models Ranked by Frequency of Occurrence

Who Plays the Main *Supporting* Role for Innovation in Your Company?	In % of Respondents
The Top Management Team or a Subset of It	17
A Dedicated Innovation Manager or CIO	14
The CEO or Division President	13
A group of champions	13
No one specifically	13
A High-level Cross-functional Steering Group	12
CTO or CRO	6
Other	5
Another CXO or Business Unit Manager	4
A CTO/CRO with a CXO or Business Unit Manager	3

Source: IMD survey (N = 113)

> "Our management committee sets our Growth through Global Innovation strategy and key members drive our innovation initiatives across the company."
> *A global materials company*

> "The CEO has been involved all along, with a varying subset of the senior vice presidents who report to him."
> *A global info technology company*

have adopted this model; but both the size and composition of these groups of top managers in charge of innovation vary greatly from company to company.

For example, many of the adopters of this model in our research sample have limited the membership of their dedicated innovation governance group to those senior leaders most directly linked with innovation activities, i.e. typically a mix of technical and commercial or business leaders. Chief human resources officers, chief financial officers, and other senior staff functions are generally not part of the innovation governance group.

CEOs may include themselves in this high-level steering group – at least officially – particularly in innovation-dependent companies or firms that they founded. In most large corporations, however, busy CEOs tend to delegate day-to-day responsibility for innovation to colleagues within their top management team.

> "Innovation should be carried out throughout the value chain. Therefore the top management of all functional areas should be involved in the process."
>
> *A medium-sized trading company*

An analysis of what members of this type of innovation governance group actually do shows a diverse pattern of responsibilities and activities (refer to Table 5.3).

The degree of formality with which innovation responsibilities are allocated varies greatly, and this has a strong bearing on the level of satisfaction (or dissatisfaction) with the model, as we shall see in Chapter 6. In its weakest form, innovation is included alongside all other items in the top management team's regular meetings. It is on the agenda, but has no special time allocation. In its strongest form, members of the top management team schedule regular meetings explicitly dedicated to addressing innovation issues; they set up specific innovation objectives and measures; they share among themselves oversight responsibilities for specific projects – typically the ones with a high risk/high reward profile – and they launch various initiatives to promote innovation.

Generally, given its composition of senior leaders, this governance model tends to put stronger emphasis on the content of innovation, i.e. on projects and new ventures, rather than on process. Process improvement issues tend to be delegated to various supporting mechanisms.

Companies that have chosen to allocate overall innovation governance responsibilities to the top

> "The top level team (our innovation board) is matched by a high level steering committee."
>
> *A global engineering company*

Table 5.3 What Do They Do? The Top Management Team (or a Subset of It) as a Group

Among the proponents of this model:

69% • Dedicate specific meetings or parts of meetings to reviewing innovation-enhancing programs and issues

41% • Individually champion and sponsor specific high-impact innovation projects and chair the steering group of these projects

34% • Set innovation objectives and measures for the key executives in their businesses, functions or departments

31% • Divide responsibilities among themselves for supervising certain processes within the general theme of innovation

31% • Launch and actively follow up personally a number of innovation initiatives, e.g. to improve the innovation culture or climate

25% • Have access to a dedicated innovation excellence budget to finance innovation infrastructure investments and enhancement projects

25% • Identify, empower, and coach a network of *"champions"* and *"process owners"* to extend their reach into all organizational units

25% • Actively participate in the innovation forums and events that they organize

22% • Make a point of behaving, collectively and individually, like true innovation leaders and role models

19% • Participate in innovation-oriented management development programs and/or teach in those programs

Source: IMD survey (N = 32)

management team or a subset of it use a wide variety of other supporting mechanisms to cascade their efforts down the organization.

Not surprisingly, the most frequently found supporting model is the direct involvement of divisional management teams. The second most popular approach is to appoint a dedicated innovation manager to follow through and implement the innovation initiatives adopted at top level. These innovation managers are also generally responsible for proposing improvements to the company's innovation process and tools.

THE CEO OR GROUP/DIVISION PRESIDENT (IN MULTI-BUSINESS CORPORATIONS)

The CEO as the ultimate "innovation czar" is the second most frequently mentioned model of innovation governance in our sample. It has to a great extent been promoted by a number of charismatic personalities, often direct founders of their companies. No one at Apple would have questioned who was really in charge of innovation under Steve Jobs.

Now, as we mentioned in Chapter 4, the question *must* be asked, since Jobs' successor as CEO, Tim Cook, may not have the same personality, innovation charisma, and approach. As a consequence, Apple may have to rethink and adapt its innovation governance model to the post-Jobs era. A number of senior executives were involved under Jobs – albeit probably more in a bilateral fashion than as a collective team – and they will certainly continue to be involved, but probably more as a group than as individuals reporting to the CEO. As a consequence –

> "The CTO *was* the initiator of the formation of our innovation board, now chaired by the CEO, but fueled by the CTO office."
> *A global electronics company*

and the future will tell – Apple may well move from the CEO model to the top management team model.

Besides these large innovative companies founded by charismatic CEOs acting as innovation supremos – think of Oracle, Cisco, Amazon, Google, Facebook, and the like – some older companies like IBM, Polaroid, Bose, and Hewlett-Packard were built around that model. Nevertheless, CEOs are rarely the people directly in overall charge of innovation in more traditional large

> **IBM CEO's Commitment to Innovation**
>
> "Our company is aligned around a single, focused business model – innovation – and this document explains why it gives us confidence in IBM's outlook for the years ahead."
>
> Samuel Palmisano, CEO, IBM – "Understanding our Company," an IBM Prospectus, 2004

companies. But they can be in small and medium-sized technology-based enterprises and family-owned firms. In large decentralized companies with several divisions or business groups, the heads of these organizations – the business group or division presidents – behave like CEOs of their units and, as such, can exercise ultimate responsibility for innovation in their domain, and this is why they are included in this model.

When the CEO is in overall charge of innovation, the message is usually loud and clear for the rest of the organization – innovation is a top priority – because everyone can observe what is at the heart of the CEO's interest. Will the CEO spend time in design or R&D? Will he/she show a great interest in new products – as Toyota's Akio Toyoda has done, to the point of putting himself in the role of the ultimate racetrack tester of his company's cars? Will he/she encourage the organization to open up to innovations from outside the company as A.G. Lafley did so strongly at P&G? When they take on ultimate responsibility for innovation in their companies, CEOs tend to focus on content issues – i.e. on new technologies and products – more than on process, which they typically delegate to other supporting mechanisms.

However, and surprisingly, as shown in Table 5.4, in only a small proportion of companies that use this model do CEOs get involved in concrete innovation governance tasks, like formulating an innovation strategy or setting innovation targets and measures. CEOs seem to prefer to place their emphasis on attitudes. They preach an "innovation gospel" on all occasions, internally and externally, and they promote innovation values relentlessly, becoming the evangelists of an "innovation ethic," as Peter Drucker promoted. They generally delegate most innovation management responsibilities to whatever supporting mechanisms they have set up.

Table 5.4 What Do They Focus On? The CEO or Division President

	Among the proponents of this model:
50%	• Promote innovation by walking around and visiting regularly and encouraging people in labs and units involved in innovation projects
50%	• Participate personally in the supervision of prominent innovation projects and ensure that top management team members do the same
33%	• Speak regularly in public, write about innovation and participate in innovation-enhancing events (innovation days, awards, forums)
28%	• Set company-wide targets regarding innovation performance and growth to be achieved through innovation
28%	• Set innovation objectives and measures for their key executives and evaluate them *also* on the basis of their innovation contribution
28%	• Dedicate regular meetings (or parts of meetings) of the top management team to specific innovation management topics
22%	• Appoint, deploy, and coach a network of innovation champions and monitor their results
17%	• Set an innovation strategy and clear directions and priorities regarding where, how, how much, and with whom to innovate
17%	• Set up innovation management mechanisms (e.g. incubator; innovation hub) and personally supervise the progress of these mechanisms

Source: IMD survey (N = 19)

When CEOs decide to take on overall responsibility for innovation in their company, they often rely on their top management team and/or on their divisional presidents to support their efforts. In fewer cases, they will mobilize a group of champions to leverage their initiative or choose any one of the other supporting models.

THE HIGH-LEVEL, CROSS-FUNCTIONAL INNOVATION STEERING GROUP OR BOARD

The third model – in terms of frequency of use according to our research sample – can take several forms. Generally, several leaders or managers, chosen from various functions and sometimes across different hierarchical levels, are charged with steering innovation *as a group.* This model, which may be referred to as the *innovation committee, innovation steering group* or even *innovation governance board,* differs from the first model essentially because not all its members are part of the top management team. The chair of such a group is almost always part of the executive committee – it is not infrequent to see the CTO or CRO occupy such a position – but the other members may span a couple of levels under the executive committee.

> "The innovation board governs the strategic innovation activities. The VP of innovation is chairman of the group. The group members are VPs of marketing, production & supply and heads of business units; the secretary is the director of projects."
>
> *A global biotech company*

A number of companies have chosen the high-level, cross-functional steering group or board as a model. Dutch electronics manufacturer Philips, pharmaceutical giants Eli Lilly, Roche, and Sanofi Pasteur, oil giant Royal Dutch Shell, and packaging specialist Tetra Pak are among the companies that have adopted this model.

> "Our innovation governance board includes the CEO, the COO, the innovation director, the research director, the business development director, and our business group's marketing and R&D directors."
>
> *A large agri-business company*

The norm for these steering groups or boards is to select members on the basis of their functional responsibilities, of course, but *also* on their personal interest in and commitment to innovation. It is indeed wise to avoid appointing innovation skeptics to such groups, irrespective of their functional responsibilities, and few companies have done that. Some companies make a point of

Table 5.5   The High-level, Cross-functional Steering Group or Board Composition

Among the proponents of this model:	
75%	• Include at least one member of the executive committee (possibly more) who chairs the group
50%	• Include only senior managers chosen for their specific functional roles and business contribution potential to innovation
19%	• Include senior managers in functions not always directly associated with business innovation (like HR or corporate communications)
6%	• Include a mix of senior and more junior managers, all chosen on the basis of their personal motivation and role model behavior

IMD Survey (N = 16)

letting some of their younger, most innovative or entrepreneurial managers join the group, possibly on a rotating basis, and this even if those managers remain at a more junior level hierarchically.

Tables 5.5 and 5.6 highlight some of the key characteristics of this model in terms of its composition and empowerment level.

The level of empowerment of these steering groups or boards varies significantly from company to company. The most surprising element is that only just over one-third of the steering groups or boards represented in our research have access to a dedicated innovation excellence budget, and this limits their capacity to launch costly improvement initiatives.

Some adopters of this model call it the *innovation process board* which stresses their focus on the process side. One of the key roles of such innovation process boards is to launch a broad range of innovation process improvements and to supervise dedicated process owners. The content of innovation, these companies usually argue, should remain the responsibility of the hierarchical line management, which may not be part of this mechanism.

Other companies, by referring to this body as an *innovation governance board*, for example, highlight that it is in charge of both

Table 5.6   The High-level, Cross-functional Steering Group or Board Empowerment and Mandate

Among the proponents of this model:	
75%	• Are empowered to launch and supervise specific innovation promotion and excellence projects and to guide/supervise *process owners*
56%	• Have the mandate to build a diagnostic of the company's innovation practices and processes, set performance indicators, and monitor them
44%	• Focus on *hard* and *soft* innovation development issues, including culture/mindset change and management development
38%	• Have access to a dedicated innovation excellence budget to finance innovation infrastructure investments and enhancement projects
13%	• Focus its mission mainly on innovation promotion and *hard* infrastructure development and process excellence projects

IMD Survey (N = 16)

"Many colleagues share the responsibility. Some parts of the business have established innovation managers, but this is not systematic. Generally, marketing is responsible for defining and validating consumer insights, which form the essential basis for innovation, whereas the technology organizations (R&D) are responsible for saying what is feasible and for realizing innovation."

A global electronics company

content and process. Clearly, the membership structure – in terms of level in the hierarchy and nature of responsibilities – determines whether or not these mechanisms will deal with content issues or only with process management.

On the communication side, 63% communicate regularly upward (to top management) about actions undertaken and progress achieved, whereas only 50% communicate downward about their initiatives and results.

As with the previous models, high-level, cross-functional steering groups or boards do not govern innovation alone. They depend on other organizational mechanisms to implement their policies and decisions. The most frequent supporting model is the dedicated innovation manager, who generally reports functionally to the steering group or board and hierarchically to a member of that steering group or board. Process owners are also frequently appointed to recommend, monitor, and improve specific processes.

Companies with several relatively independent business units may work with additional steering groups or boards at the divisional level, or with groups of champions. But some have no supporting mechanism and rely on the functional organization to implement the process.

THE CTO OR CRO AS THE ULTIMATE INNOVATION CHAMPION

Allocating responsibility for innovation to the CTO or CRO comes in only fourth place on our list of preferred models. Yet it is probably one of the most traditional forms of innovation governance, particularly for technology-, science-, and engineering-based companies. CTOs are normally found in engineering companies, while CROs (and/or chief scientific officers, or CSOs) turn up more frequently in science-based companies like fine chemicals or pharmaceuticals.

Whatever the title, the CTO or CRO is generally viewed as the promoter of new technology-based products. It is therefore natural for the top management team in companies that strongly equate innovation with new technologies and new products to turn to these talented individuals for all sorts of technology-based innovation initiatives. Companies like Nestlé and Rolex have chosen this governance approach, as has Crédit Suisse. In industries where information technology is predominant – like banks and insurance companies – the equivalent of the CTO is the chief information officer. It is therefore not surprising to see these leaders playing a key role in innovation governance in their companies.

The CTO or CRO model is widely relied upon for innovation in countries with a strong technology and engineering tradition and sector like the USA, Japan, Germany, Sweden, and Switzerland. In these countries, the CTO or CRO may be called senior vice president of R&D and technology, chief engineer, research president, senior vice president of engineering, and the like. But whatever they are called, they are normally full members of the top management team and their colleagues look to them for guidance with regard to innovative developments. In large companies with a management board structure – a traditional form of collegial management in countries like Germany, Switzerland, and the Netherlands – the management board member in charge of technology may not be called the CTO, but he/she will often be viewed as the official spokesperson for and promoter of innovation within the top team.

> "Innovation includes all of new product development and new business models. As such, all of senior management is involved at least at a funding decision level (that is, percentage of revenue to devote to R&D). However, most of the front end of innovation is driven through our Corporate Innovation organization, which includes technology and business development, and which is managed by our VP for Corporate Innovation, who is also our CTO."
>
> *A medical technology company*

CTOs and CROs naturally focus on the content of innovation, i.e. on the development of knowledge, technology, and new products. In some companies – particularly technology-intensive Japanese ones – they also focus on new ventures and new business creation, but these are always technology-based. They focus on process issues to the extent that they affect the company's technology and R&D effectiveness. For that purpose, they may set up an ideation and knowledge management process, but they rarely intervene in the non-technical aspects of the company, including finance, business model development, and marketing. The same is true for culture issues: CTOs and CROs may promote a mindset change in R&D – for example, to support cross-disciplinary collaboration, open source innovation, or the creation of a sense of urgency – but they generally do not feel responsible for spreading the effort to the whole organization and supervising the development of innovative processes, for example in commercial operations.

Table 5.7   What are Their Responsibilities? The Chief Technology Officer or Chief Research Officer

Among the proponents of this model:

90%	• Cover IP strategy and implementation (licensing in and out) including its strategic aspects
90%	• Do partnerships/alliances (e.g. for the establishment of new standards) designed to enhance the company's innovation performance/position
90%	• Cover technology and innovation strategy, including its business aspects (where, how, how much, and with whom to innovate)
70%	• Include corporate internal venturing activities and the management of a new business incubator
70%	• Launch innovation culture and mindset change programs, not just in R&D, and innovation-oriented management development programs
60%	• Launch external corporate venturing activities, innovation-related acquisitions, and investments in startups to enhance capabilities
50%	• Deal with the management of innovation as a process from idea to market including its commercial aspects
50%	• Set and review indicators of innovation process performance and launch actions across business units to reach process excellence
50%	• Negotiate, allocate, and manage an innovation budget extending beyond traditional R&D activities

IMD Survey (N = 11)

Because of their wide-ranging responsibilities, CTOs and CROs tend to exercise their innovation governance responsibilities with the help of supporting mechanisms. Most have their own CTO office, staffed with a few experts on

> "The CTO is accountable, but delegates the role to an innovation manager at group level."
>
> *A global consumer goods company*

content and process. In Japan, for example, CTOs often set up a small *technology planning group* to guide them in road-mapping tasks and to assess new business opportunities linked with the adoption of new technologies. In most large companies, CTOs are supported by a more or less formal network of divisional or business unit R&D managers.

THE DEDICATED INNOVATION MANAGER OR CHIEF INNOVATION OFFICER

These models are less frequently mentioned than the previous ones but deserve attention nevertheless, mostly because they stress that responsibility for innovation can be entrusted to a single *dedicated* manager, as opposed to a busy CTO or CRO with operational duties, or to a large steering group, committee, or board. This can be done by appointing a full-time *innovation manager* (or several of them in a multi-business corporation), who will act as a catalyst for innovation and as the official supporter of the line organization in its efforts to promote an innovation agenda.

Chief innovation officers are generally entrusted with overall responsibility for innovation, whereas innovation managers are more frequently found supporting another governance model. AkzoNobel, DSM, Boehringer Ingelheim, and Herman Miller are among the proponents of dedicating a member of management to innovation.

Innovation managers tend to be chosen from the ranks of highly motivated middle to upper-middle executives from a variety of functions, typically marketing or R&D. They frequently report to a member of the top management team and operate mostly by themselves, occasionally with a couple of staff assistants. They are often responsible for tracking and measuring innovation efforts and results, identifying and sharing best practices, and supporting innovation initiatives launched by the line organization. In that sense, they deal with the process side of innovation much more than the content aspects.

Within these two models, the innovation manager model is more frequently found – and in a broader variety of companies and industries – than its more empowered version, the high-level chief innovation officer (CIO) or senior vice president for innovation. Even though the two functions may look similar in terms of mission, they often differ greatly in terms of access to top management – the CIO typically reports to the CEO – and hence in terms of influence and resources. Unlike innovation managers, who rarely supervise innovation departments, CIOs often have a staff department to support them in their mission, and they are also frequently responsible for the company's innovation acceleration mechanisms, such as new business incubators or *innovation hubs*. In that sense, they will often be responsible for process *and* content.

One of the most interesting examples of the empowered CIO model, which will be described in Chapter 10, can be found at Dutch life and materials science company DSM. Not only is DSM's CIO in charge of the company's Innovation Center, with its incubator and emerging business areas, but he also directly supervises the CTO office, hence all corporate technology development activities. This structure, according to DSM's CIO, conveys a strong message to the organization, namely that innovation goes much beyond technology. At DSM, the CIO and his Innovation Center are considered *both* as the guardians and promoters of innovation excellence within the corporation *and* as the unit in charge of new business creation.

A GROUP OF INNOVATION CHAMPIONS

A number of companies in our survey noted that they have entrusted overall responsibility for innovation to a group of selected champions. In the innovation management literature, champions are often defined as self-motivated upper-middle to senior managers who are not necessarily idea initiators, but who promote the most promising ideas of others in the organization. They secure resources to execute the ideas, often on their personal initiative – more or less independently of top management mandates. They are often self-appointed enthusiasts about the projects they sponsor and are willing to commit personal time and effort in addition to their normal job. They generally operate with the blessing of top management and do not hesitate to take career risks. In that sense, they are and act as innovation accelerators.

These champions focus mainly on the content of innovation, i.e. on specific projects. However, there are a great variety of champions besides the self-appointed *intrapreneurs* as they are some-times called. For example, a few companies have appointed *idea advocates* – usually senior managers towards the end of their careers, who are well respected in the organization. They may volunteer for the role and are assigned by the CEO to make themselves available to help idea submitters prepare and defend their proposals in front of top management.

Some of the less-empowered champions may be chosen by their leaders among middle or upper-middle managers on the basis of their communicable interest in innovation and their energy and drive to stimulate and support management colleagues. They typi-cally focus on the process side of innovation, and they network internally and sometimes even with other companies to share experience and benchmarks.

In our survey, a number of companies, mostly in the USA, reported that they rely on a group of champions to promote and steer innovation. FMC technologies, Hallmark Cards, Bank of America, and Abbott Laboratories are among them. But a company that stands out for having forcefully empowered a group of cham-pions is PepsiCo, particularly under the leadership of its former CEO Roger A. Enrico, who was recognized as a charismatic busi-ness builder and marketing wizard. Enrico prided himself on not doing things "by the book," and he strongly believed that employ-ees are seldom given a chance to fully contribute and show what they can do. So, he selected a group of promising young executives to deploy as business development and innovation champions. He personally coached them and handled their management develop-ment at his own ranch.

Groups of champions are more frequently found as a supporting model rather than as a primary innovation governance model.

THE DUO (COMPLEMENTARY TWO-PERSON TEAM)

The last governance models are also the least frequently used in practice, at least based on responses to our survey. However, these models *do* exist; we have seen them in action, in a more or less formal way.

In technology-based companies, the duo may consist of a CTO sharing overall responsibility for innovation with a business unit manager or another functional manager or CXO – for example, a CMO or the company's CFO. In other companies, like banks and financial groups, the duo may bring together a CXO – for example, the chief information officer – and a commercial or business executive.

The idea behind these models is that since innovation is a truly cross-functional activity, it cannot be fully embraced by a representative of a single function – for example, the CTO. The technical and business elements of innovation are therefore entrusted to senior representatives from these functions *working together as a team.* That last phrase points to an element that is obviously critical and may be difficult to achieve in reality.

NO ONE IN CHARGE

It may be strange to include the absence of a model in our list of innovation governance models. But it does reflect a reality. In some companies, there just is no one officially in charge of innovation. In our experience, there may be several reasons for this.

The first reason – by far the most positive and the first one given in our survey responses – is that innovation is so much part of the company's DNA that everyone feels responsible and acts to support it.

This is based on a management

> "In our company, product management is in charge for product innovation, architects for IT innovation, and everybody else for their field of expertise."
>
> *A large financial company*

belief that innovation is everyone's task and that the company can therefore count on each function to play its usual role in the process . . . hence no need for an official mechanism for allocating innovation responsibilities! This type of reasoning may be common in a range of very innovative new companies, for example in the internet area. Some will argue that a bottom-up organization like

Google fits in this category because ideas are supposed to come from everywhere in the organization, and everyone is empowered to experiment with them. However, this is debatable given the visionary leadership at play within Google's top management team. Google's founders were clearly in charge of innovation, at least at the beginning.

The second reason for the absence of a governance model may be due to temporary circumstances, such as a restructuring drive or the reorganization of a company. Some companies change their governance models so often – typically at each change of CEO or CTO – that managers may feel that no one is permanently in charge of innovation.

The third reason – which no one in our survey cited, although it exists in real life – is that innovation may not be perceived as really critical by management, and therefore it is deemed unnecessary to allocate specific responsibilities for it. We have come across a few companies in this category. They were typically active in domains requiring strong management emphasis on operational excellence, for example in the shipping industry.

And there is also a fourth reason: There are indeed management teams who are blissfully unaware that innovation will not happen on its own and that it requires some sort of governance.

COMBINATIONS OF PRIMARY AND SUPPORTING MODELS

As we have seen, all of the models listed above can be used both for the primary allocation of management responsibilities for innovation and for supporting innovation. For example, in one company the CEO could be the person in overall charge of innovation; in another he/she could be supporting whoever is entrusted with overall responsibility.

Interestingly, our survey results indicate that almost all combinations of primary and supporting models exist. For example, if the primary model is the top management team or a subset of it, some companies stated that the CEO is a supporter of the top team, while others relied on a cross-functional steering group for

Almost all possible combinations seem to coexist

Overall Innovation Models (ranked in declining order of frequency)	Innovation Supporting Models (ranked in declining order of frequency)
Top Management Team or subset	Top Management Team or subset
CEO or Division President	Dedicated Innovation Manager or CIO
Hi-level X-functional steering group	CEO or Division President
CTO or CRO	A group of champions
Dedicated Innovation Manager or CIO	No one specifically
No one specifically	High-level X-functional steering group
A group of champions	CTO or CRO
Another CXO or SBU Manager	Another CXO or SBU Manager
CTO/CRO with CXO or SBU Manager	CTO/CRO with CXO or SBU Manager

Figure 5.1:   Combinations of Governance Models

this. Yet others considered it to be the role of the CTO to act as supporter, and so forth. Figure 5.1 illustrates these multiple combinations.

ADDITIONAL INNOVATION-SUPPORTING MECHANISMS

Most companies do not restrict themselves to one primary governance model and only one supporting model. Like Solvay, many use a number of additional sources of help to support their innovation governance efforts. For example, besides relying on corporate innovation-oriented functions, such as R&D, design, new business development, incubators, and the like, most companies in our survey sample mentioned using at least one and often several of the following mechanisms:

- Thirty-two percent have appointed one or several *innovation managers* reporting to senior management. These innovation managers, who come as the third element of their innovation governance system, are generally middle to upper-middle managers embedded in the corporation's various organizational units. Their mission is similar to that of higher-level innovation managers – to help local managers launch innovation initiatives and support innovation projects, albeit in the units to which they are attached.

- Thirty-two percent rely on selected business managers appointed as *innovation sponsors*. The use of *project sponsors* is widespread in new product development as it allows management to ensure that projects meet an essential business need and proceed smoothly. But the same business managers can easily broaden their role and sponsor all kinds of innovation-enhancing initiatives.

- Twenty-nine percent have set up a dedicated *innovation department* with its own staff resources. Such departments are found primarily when the company has entrusted innovation responsibilities to the CTO/CRO or to a high-level chief innovation officer. These innovation departments typically focus on process excellence, best-practice sharing, and innovation performance tracking. Some of them – sometimes called *innovation acceleration teams*, as in Nestlé – serve as internal consultants on innovation.

- Twenty-four percent call on external resources – typically *management consultants* – to help on critical innovation tasks. On the process side, consultants are often asked to provide assistance with technology road-mapping, voice of customer research, benchmarking to help establish a diagnostic of innovation obstacles, or to propose or improve a phase review product development process. Some companies use them more broadly, for example to restructure innovation-oriented departments like R&D. On the content side, consultants' help may be used to optimize a product portfolio or launch market feasibilities for totally new concepts.

- Sixteen percent have deployed a network of officially designated *innovation coaches*. These innovation coaches are usually different from the *innovation sponsors* mentioned above. Whereas sponsors support teams and initiatives at the management level without necessarily becoming personally involved, innovation coaches tend to be much more hands-on. They are high-level champions who are accessible to everyone who has an idea, and they will work with idea submitters to refine their original ideas and ensure they are receivable by management. In many companies, these innovation coaches – or innovation advocates as they are sometimes called – are managers in the last years of their career with an interest in innovation, strong personal credibility, and a broad personal network which they can bring to bear on specific innovation projects.

In summary, as we stated at the beginning of this chapter, most companies have deployed a broad range of organizational mechanisms to govern and manage innovation. In the next chapter, we will indicate how the companies we polled evaluate their level of satisfaction or dissatisfaction with their chosen governance model. We will also highlight some of the factors that affect the effectiveness of each of these models.

NOTE

[1]This survey was conducted with 113 companies mostly in Europe and the USA. The respondents came from the following industries: healthcare (18); engineering (16); electronics (17); fast-moving consumer goods (13); trade and services (11); other consumer goods (8); financial services (6); chemicals (6); telecom operators (4); software (4); utilities/energy (3); materials (3); other industrial products and anonymous (4).

CHAPTER 6

WHICH MODELS SEEM TO WORK AND WHY?

The previous chapter listed a number of organizational models that companies typically choose for allocating responsibility for innovation, thus exercising their innovation governance mission. The question management is bound to raise is whether and under what conditions these models will work in practice. This chapter will try to answer this question and discuss how companies perceive the effectiveness – or inadequacy – of their innovation governance endeavors. To do so, we will characterize management's level of satisfaction or dissatisfaction with the various organizational models that their company has adopted. The data in this chapter come from the results of our online survey, complemented by our past work and contacts with a broad range of companies in Europe and the USA.

DOES INNOVATION GOVERNANCE WORK SATISFACTORILY?

Not surprisingly given the broad variety of companies that responded to our survey, the general level of satisfaction with innovation governance varies greatly:

- Thirteen percent of respondents declared that they are very satisfied with their company's innovation governance system. They generally feel that all aspects of innovation – both hard and soft – have been taken care of and the results are positive.
- Forty-four percent expressed their relative satisfaction with the way their company steers innovation at the top, although they recognized that some aspects of innovation still remain unaddressed or unclear.
- Thirty-eight percent stated that they are rather dissatisfied with their innovation governance system. They recognized a need for better coordination in the way functions work together and for a clearer allocation of responsibilities.
- Five percent confessed that they are very dissatisfied with the way their company handles innovation. They see a need to start with a clean sheet and establish a new overall innovation governance system that really works.

Given that the governance of innovation has not yet been carefully studied and researched, we find these numbers show a more positive assessment than we might have expected. Over half the companies in our sample expressed some satisfaction, and the 44% that expressed only "relative satisfaction" should be in a position to improve their practices and clear up those areas that "remain unaddressed or unclear." We suspect, however, that these assessments may have been affected by the opportunity the questionnaire gave participants to reflect on their governance practices. When people are asked about their innovation governance practices in, as it were, a vacuum, they generally look blank and are not sure what you are asking about.

In fact, in our consulting practice we have often heard that management devotes too little time to addressing the issues that fall within the boundaries of innovation governance effectiveness. Even practices such as managing the innovation portfolio, which is widely seen as part of governance, are often done in a haphazard manner. Many companies change their innovation governance system regularly, often after the arrival of a new CEO or CTO. When a new leader takes over, it is natural for him/her to address perceived inefficiencies by shifting responsibilities, and since the practices of innovation governance are still so poorly understood, companies frequently try to improve things by bringing in new leaders with different experience and ideas. It is our objective in this chapter to present the different levels of satisfaction with the different models so that companies can explicitly assess their own models and develop plans for changing or improving their practices.

ARE SOME MODELS MORE EFFECTIVE THAN OTHERS?

Given that many managers are rather – or in some cases very – dissatisfied with the way their company exercises its innovation governance mission, it is interesting to ask whether their frustration is linked to the particular governance model the company has chosen. In other words, do some organizational models work better than others? The answer to this question conveys a mixed signal.

On the one hand, yes indeed, the degree of satisfaction of respondents in our survey varies quite substantially according to the governance model they have chosen, as Figure 6.1 shows. This depiction shows that some models *do* seem to work better than others. The two models that receive the highest satisfaction marks are those in which overall responsibility for innovation is entrusted either to a high-level, cross-functional steering group or board, or to the CTO or CRO.

Do governance models influence satisfaction levels?

Rather dissatisfied and very dissatisfied	Who has the prime overall responsibility for innovation?	Relatively satisfied and very satisfied
42%	Top management team (or subset of it)	**58%**
44%	CEO or division president	**56%**
35%	High-level cross-functional steering group	**65%**
30%	CTO or CRO	**70%**
65%	Dedicated innovation manager or CIO	**35%**
60%	A group of champions	**40%**
100%	No one specifically	**0%**
43%	Another CxO or SBU Manager	**57%**

Figure 6.1: Overall Levels of Satisfaction/Dissatisfaction with Chosen Governance Models

On the other hand, none of the models scores a perfect 100% on satisfaction. Even the more popular models have a significant proportion of users who are relatively or very dissatisfied. And, hardly surprisingly, companies that have not appointed anyone to oversee innovation are unanimously dissatisfied with their (lack of) innovation governance.

These mixed results, even for the most popular models, require some comments and raise a number of questions.

Why Aren't the Most "Empowered" Models Always the Most Effective?

As indicated in the previous chapter, overall responsibility for innovation is most frequently allocated *either* to the top management team (or a subset of it) *or* to the CEO – or, in diversified and decentralized corporations, to a division president acting as CEO of a business unit. There is obviously no more powerful way to indicate the importance of steering innovation in a company than to apply models that mobilize the top level of the hierarchy. For this reason, we would expect these to be the most effective governance models. However, this is not always the case.

Fifty-eight Percent are Satisfied When the Top Management Team is in Charge

"We are relatively satisfied with our governance system but have opportunities to improve on the front end, to better understand customer needs and filter projects. We also have opportunities on the back end with commercialization."

An engineering company

For sure, innovation governance seems to work well in a number of companies that have chosen the top management team as their governance model, for example at Corning, Nestlé Waters, and Lego Systems, among others. In these companies, which have achieved a relatively high level of satisfaction with their innovation governance results, the involvement of top management is most probably intense and this mobilizes the rest of the organization.

However, being satisfied with the innovation governance system that is in place does not mean that improvements are not needed. This is true, of course, of all complex processes, including innovation and quality processes. One reason is the sheer complexity of these processes. Another reason is that *continuous improvement* is particularly critical when the processes themselves mature, with better practices continually being developed and the range of the processes expanding. For example, several companies among those that have established a well-functioning innovation governance model recognize that their emphasis so far has mostly been on *hard* issues, like processes, tools and projects. Several of them are now putting more emphasis on *softer* cultural elements, such as team dynamics, program and project leadership, and functional skills and competencies.

As the numbers in Figure 6.1 indicate, the level of satisfaction with the top management team model is seen as problematic for a significant proportion – over 40% – of companies that have adopted them. There are probably as many reasons for this as there are companies. Among the main causes of dissatisfaction, several problems are explicitly mentioned:

• Lack of formality in implementation of the innovation process, and even if the process is formalized, it is not followed strictly.
• Insufficient customer orientation in the process, leading to missed opportunities to create real value in the market.
• Difficulty in emerging from the old vertically integrated model and migrating toward a more networked approach.
• Functionally oriented organization, leading to a lack of coordination and understanding between functions.
• Lack of consistency in the project prioritization process across divisions and business units.

These problems show that the allocation of innovation governance responsibilities to the top team requires these senior managers to be willing to break down silos and to work as a cohesive team across functional and business turfs, which may not be easy to achieve. It also demands a combination of individual and collective commitment, particularly when the company is facing turbulent conditions. To be effective, innovation needs leaders with a high degree of consistency in their priorities, messages and actions, which external pressures can easily endanger. When lower level managers rely on the top management team to promote innovation, they rapidly notice the slightest change in priorities or level of attention at the top, whether these are triggered by external or internal crises, and they naturally adapt their own priorities to these changes.

The Degree of Satisfaction is Slightly Lower (56%) When the CEO is in Charge

"Our CEO always had new innovative ideas that he managed to have implemented as the executive team turned them into reality. So, innovation was really a one-man show, which was never ideal. But now that person has left, so innovation and the urge *to do* something new and different have gone too!"

A financial industry company

CEOs who see themselves as the ultimate innovation champion in their company – there are relatively few in this category – should, by definition, be highly motivated to share their enthusiasm with the rest of their organization. For this model to work well, CEOs also need to maintain their commitment even in periods of crisis. We have seen this succeed in companies such as IBM, particularly with Sam Palmisano, as well as P&G under Laffley.

But too often the reality is slightly different and the CEOs' commitment may not cascade down to all business units and functions. They need *amplifiers* and *relayers* to turn their vision into concrete implementation initiatives. In addition, CEOs come and go, and when this happens, will the new CEO be as motivated about innovation as his/her predecessor? And even if he/she accepts the mission as a matter of fact among many other duties, at the beginning he/she may be too thinly stretched to fully exercise this governance mission, despite the original good intentions.

This is why it is so important, when the CEO takes on overall responsibility for innovation governance, to appoint a dedicated manager, a group of managers, or another organizational mechanism in a direct supporting function. The combination of responsibilities that seems to work best, according to our survey, next to the CEO in full charge, includes either a subset of the top management team or a group of identified innovation champions straddling the organization.

When Does Relying on the CTO or CRO Make Sense?

Many technology-, science-, and engineering-based companies have naturally entrusted overall management of their innovation efforts to the head of their technical function, whatever his/her title.

As shown in Figure 6.1, the results of this model beat all other models, reflecting the fact that it concentrates a lot of power in the hands of a single, specialized leader, and one who is most likely to have the knowledge and resources to decide on and supervise all projects – at least the technical ones. This, of course, puts a lot of pressure on the CTO or CRO, which may help explain why the model does not work satisfactorily in all companies. Success is highly dependent on the credibility and leadership talents of the specific high-level individual.

The applicability of this model is optimal in technology-intensive industries where innovation and markets are driven by technology, and where technology choices and deployment issues are complex and critical. The main condition for the success of this model is linked to the breadth of capabilities of CTOs or CROs. In all cases, they must have a strong business orientation because ultimately all innovation efforts turn into business creation challenges. This is why they are often supported by competent staff departments capable of exploring the market potential of new technologies and linking technology and product roadmaps. This also means

> "Markets and the voice of customers should be involved much more in the process of product innovation.
>
> Innovation should also go beyond the product and be introduced in other areas of the company (service, distribution, etc.)."
>
> *A consumer durable company*

that they must develop a strong sensitivity to innovation commercialization and adoption issues to avoid the risk of sterile "technology-push" initiatives. And this, of course, implies that they need to maintain excellent relationships with their colleagues in business management.

The main limitation of this model is its primary and sometimes exclusive focus on technology deployment issues. CTOs and CROs usually have limited involvement in upstream and downstream marketing activities. In addition, their focus tends to be mainly on content, which means that their interest and involvement in non-technical processes and on softer organizational culture improvements is often limited.

What Makes High-level Cross-functional Steering Groups or Boards Effective?

> "This model has given a good insight into the innovation process for all involved parties and we have measures (KPIs) to secure that we can follow any progress in our innovation capabilities."
>
> *A biotech company*

Another innovation governance model almost ties with the CTO/CRO model in terms of its perceived effectiveness, i.e. the creation of an official innovation steering group or board (also called innovation board, innovation process board, or innovation governance board).

Such a mechanism includes members representing some of the company's innovation-relevant functions and businesses. In describing this model in Chapter 5, we emphasized that it is different from the top management team or a subset of it inasmuch as it enlists managers from lower levels of the organization, even though the chairperson of the steering group or board is often a member of the top management team. We call it a "high-level" steering group or board more for its high-level mission and visibility than to reflect the hierarchical position of its members.

Whereas the subset of the top management team may be comprised of no more than three or four members, this cross-functional steering group or board may number six to 12 members, depending on the company. They will generally be selected not only on the basis of their functional or business expertise but also because of their intrinsic motivation for innovation and their personal drive. The composition of this mechanism and the motivation of its members provide an initial explanation of why this model is perceived as more effective than most other models.

The main advantages of this approach, compared with other innovation governance models, are threefold:

1. It allows comprehensive representation of the relevant parts of the company in the decision body for innovation. This diversity of technical, functional, and business expertise, and hence of perspectives, is likely to enrich the conversations and lead to more effective decisions. In addition, the size of the board makes it easier to allocate specific responsibilities to individuals, for example for supervising processes or coaching project teams.
2. It offers a high degree of flexibility, allowing management to modify the board's composition to reflect changes in environmental conditions or company strategy. It is also relatively easy to instill new spirit in the group when needed by taking out less productive members and bringing in innovation enthusiasts. Experience shows that some companies have also used this mechanism to test the leadership qualities of younger, high-potential managers.
3. It is possible, because of the board's size and composition, to entrust it with a broad range of missions and not just the selection, launch, and supervision of projects. Even when this board focuses only on process (rather than content), its mandate frequently covers two major tasks:
   - To stimulate/supervise innovation process development efforts, for example by:
     - appointing, supporting and reviewing the work of process owners and coaches;
     - allocating and monitoring the use of innovation process development budgets;
     - setting up and monitoring innovation benchmarks and performance indicators; and
     - setting up and supervising an *innovation online* platform.
   - To take action to sustain innovation performance, for example by:

- identifying/building innovation-critical competencies;
- identifying and developing high-potential innovation leaders;
- promoting an innovation mindset and improving the culture; and
- building a communication platform to mobilize the organization.

However, this model also has some limits that companies need to fully appreciate before choosing it! The most important ones, in our experience, are twofold.

First, the scope of the model's mandate may be unclear and make for inadequate representation of critical parts of the company. The main question to be clarified concerns its focus. Is the innovation steering group or board empowered to discuss and advise (or even decide) on content issues – specific innovation projects and ventures – or is it only allowed to deal with innovation process issues? The staffing of this mechanism is clearly dependent on the answer to this question. Ambiguity in this case is dangerous, since it will quickly disqualify the steering group or board in the eyes of non-members, who are generally from line management.

> "The protection of innovation budgets continues to be difficult, especially in challenging economic times. It still often seems easier to purchase a company than to make a major budget commitment to internal ('organic') innovation, especially when the innovation activity would have a rather long time horizon. (Managers dislike the P&L impact of investments in projects with a long payback.)"
>
> *A medical service company*

The second limitation of this model is that it may lack sustained empowerment and resources, particularly when the company is exposed to severe market, financial, or operational pressures. This lack of empowerment may reflect its membership – are members of the steering group or board sufficiently credible in the eyes of the top management team? Are the members likely to be personally affected by the consequences of some of the investment decisions on risky projects? But it may also indicate a weak long-term commitment to this type of innovation governance, or to innovation as a whole. In our experience, this may happen in companies where the top management team sets up this kind of mechanism to relieve itself of its own responsibilities and rapidly stops supporting it.

Why is Having an Innovation Manager or CIO Less Appreciated?

The appointment of a dedicated manager to carry the innovation flag across the company or one of its divisions is sometimes chosen as a solution because of its apparent advantages, i.e. by concentrating accountability for innovation in the hands of a single, dedicated individual, it avoids overloading other senior managers with additional responsibilities.

Our experience shows that the effectiveness of this governance model – particularly if it is used as a primary model – is highly dependent on the intrinsic experience, qualities, and drive of the manager in question and of his/her reporting level. A lack of recognition of these two factors may explain why this model scores so poorly as a way of allocating primary responsibilities for innovation in the ratings in Figure 6.1. The difficulty of the job, if it is carried out by a middle manager reporting two or three levels below the CEO, is apparent when interviewing those who inherited it. For some of them – and we have had several in our innovation management sessions – it is an impossible task given the magnitude of their responsibilities, their low empowerment level, and their lack of resources. However, innovation managers can be quite effective when appointed in support of another, more empowered model.

The situation is completely different when top management chooses one of its members to assume this dedicated responsibility and appoints a CIO, as DSM, the Dutch life and materials sciences company, did earlier in this decade. Figure 6.2 highlights the differences between a middle-level innovation manager and a high-level CIO of the type found at DSM with a broad range of responsibilities, notably in new business development.

Although it is not specifically mentioned in our survey, the chances are that the more satisfactory models in this category are

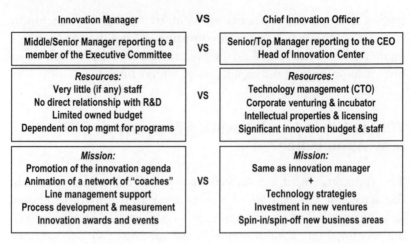

Innovation Manager	VS	Chief Innovation Officer
Middle/Senior Manager reporting to a member of the Executive Committee	VS	Senior/Top Manager reporting to the CEO Head of Innovation Center
Resources: Very little (if any) staff No direct relationship with R&D Limited owned budget Dependent on top mgmt for programs	VS	*Resources:* Technology management (CTO) Corporate venturing & incubator Intellectual properties & licensing Significant innovation budget & staff
Mission: Promotion of the innovation agenda Animation of a network of "coaches" Line management support Process development & measurement Innovation awards and events	VS	*Mission:* Same as innovation manager + Technology strategies Investment in new ventures Spin-in/spin-off new business areas

Figure 6.2: Innovation Manager and CIO: Two Different Worlds

the most empowered ones, i.e. the high-level CIO model is more likely to ensure effective innovation governance than the lower-level innovation manager model.

In both cases, success is dependent on at least three conditions:

- The company must have developed a strong process management culture to ensure that everyone understands that innovation is a cross-disciplinary and cross-functional process that needs to be managed as such.
- The leaders in question must have built strong personal credibility and possess social skills to be able to influence a wide range of managers who will not fall under their direct hierarchical responsibility.
- They need to be strongly supported by the CEO and the top management team, in word and deed, particularly when there are turf conflicts with operational or functional managers.

Is it Realistic to Rely on a Network of Champions to Govern Innovation?

A number of companies noted that they rely on a network of champions as their primary innovation governance model. This probably implies that these companies define innovation governance rather narrowly, with the main focus being on process issues. Identifying, empowering, and mobilizing a network of champions can be an effective way to stimulate innovation, for sure. But it will not be a proper way to address more strategic content issues, which always call for the direct involvement of top management.

Not surprisingly, a majority of companies perceive this model to be unsatisfactory. For many of them, this may be due to the limitations in scope inherent in the model. Given that champions are middle managers, there are only a limited number of things they can do on their own to stimulate and steer innovation. This model is more effective when it is supporting another model rather than being the primary model of allocation of innovation respon- sibilities. In our sample, networks of champions are used as a sup- porting model in three main instances – when the primary responsibility has been entrusted to either the CEO or the top management team; or to a high-level cross-functional steering group or board; and/or to a dedicated innovation manager.

But irrespective of its scope limitations, a network of champi- ons is a complex organizational mechanism. It is not easily created and keeping it productive over time remains a challenge: first because its effectiveness is highly dependent on the quality of the motivation and drive of the individual champions being selected; and second because, as with all networks, it will slowly see its energy level fade away unless it is strongly supported and rein- forced by management. It will need direct access to its high-level sponsor, adequate support in terms of resources and training, and the guarantee that some of its most important recommendations will be implemented.

SO WHY ARE MANY GOVERNANCE MODELS DEEMED UNSATISFACTORY?

This chapter started with a relatively disappointing evaluation of the perceived effectiveness of innovation governance models – 43% of survey respondents are rather or very dissatisfied with the system their company has put in place. In our experience, this poor apprecia- tion primarily reflects insufficient or inconsistent commitment and

> "While close to 70% of CEOs say innovation is a top priority, the gap between talking about innovation and delivering innovation is wide. If innovation is to become a critical capability, executives must demonstrate that innovation is crucial to corporate success, through their engagement, communication, investments and actions."
>
> *Paul Hobcraft and*
> *Jeffrey Phillips*

personal engagement by the CEO and his/her top management team regarding innovation. This observation may contradict the fact that the vast majority of senior managers see the importance of innovation growing in their company; that innovation is a stated objective in most annual reports; and that a pile of money is invested in innovation each year, typically in R&D.

This contradiction is understandable if we consider the constraints under which most management teams operate. In an insightful article drawn from their practice, two experienced innovation practitioners and coaches[1] list a number of possible reasons that senior executives may not fulfill their role and the likely causes:

"Senior executives fail when they:

- are unaware their vision needs to be framed into a compelling message;
- don't understand the importance of their role in communicating and motivating;
- miss articulating the value, importance and benefits to both the company and the individual;
- don't resolve the "hearts and minds" in engagement that innovation requires;
- are unable to set out an overall framework for innovation and define its value creation;
- delegate the role to others who don't have the power to execute and compromise too readily;
- are constrained in their role due to time pressures and/or competing initiatives;
- fail to shape, inspire or clarify the necessary linkages and synergies across the company."

[. . .]

"There are a number of reasons why senior executives can often have difficulty filling an innovation leadership role, including:

- Fixated on short term financial goals to the detriment of longer term opportunities;
- Difficulty balancing the complexities of "important" versus "urgent" tasks;
- Pressures of conflicting demands and other growing business issues that take priority;
- Convincing others to convert their vision and translating this into operational reality;
- Unfamiliar with the variety of innovation tools and frameworks;
- Unaware of the level of resistance and inertia that creates the roadblocks;
- Have an unclear or incomplete mental model about innovation and what it fully needs;
- Concerned about upsetting the status quo."

Besides a lack of top management commitment, a number of criticisms can be leveled at all these innovation governance models, at least in the way they have been implemented. We have personally observed the following problems:

- *Problem #1.* Whatever the model chosen, management has not defined the scope of its innovation governance activities broadly enough. Some companies focus mainly on content (basically projects), others on process – they rarely focus on both! Also, many companies have a narrower than optimal view of innovation. Most companies have developed a strong bias for developing product or process innovations. Those that look equally seriously at other forms of innovations – i.e. business model, service, and/or marketing innovations – are rare.
- *Problem #2.* In some companies – managers complain – innovation strategies are rather fuzzily defined or at least are poorly communicated, implying that these strategies and communicating about them are not included in the list of primary innovation governance topics.
- *Problem #3.* Almost universally, some domains remain poorly covered, even though they are critical for sustaining innovation. Questions associated with the development of values and a culture that are conducive to innovation – which often requires a change management program – are often left aside. The same

is true for programs linked to the development of management and leadership competences. The problem is not so much that management considers these issues secondary, but that these *soft* aspects are difficult to address in a meaningful way.

- *Problem #4.* Innovation policies and mandates may conflict, in some cases because they have not been made explicit, in others because mandates are not aligned and lead to decisions that are in conflict. This is most likely to occur when different parts of the innovation agenda are involved. One group may have the mandate to explore more radical kinds of innovation, while another may be working toward a conservative innovation portfolio.

- *Problem #5.* Finally, and this also happens quite frequently, responsibilities and empowerment levels often remain unclear or keep changing due to:
  - a lack of management consistency and commitment over time;
  - short-term pressures diluting management's attention and long-term efforts; and
  - a misalignment between rewards and incentives and innovation objectives.

Many companies would do well to consider this brief overview of governance models and their mediocre current level of effectiveness as a wake-up call. With any luck it will spur management teams on to react and finally put innovation governance at the top of their agenda.

Our next chapters will describe how six innovative companies – IBM, Corning, Nestlé, DSM, Tetra Pak, and Michelin – have organized to govern innovation, each with a different model that seems to work.

NOTE

[1] Hobcraft, P. and Phillips, J. (2012). The Critical Role that Senior Leaders Must Fill for Innovation Success. http://www.innovationexcellence.com/blog/2012/09/10/the-critical-role-that-senior-leaders-must-fill-for-innovation-success/. Used with permission.

PART III

LEARNING FROM THE FIELD

CHAPTER 7

LEADING FROM THE TOP

Example 1 – IBM's Innovation Governance Model: A Succession of CEOs Oversees "Continuous Transformation"

In the previous two sections, we have looked at the innovation roles of the board and the top management team, respectively, as well as describing 10 different innovation governance models. Now it is time to look at some real company examples to see how they have applied these models. As we saw in Chapter 5, according to our survey of 113 companies the two most commonly used innovation governance models – accounting for almost half of all responses – were the top management team, or a subset, and the CEO. We explore them in more detail by looking at Corning in Chapter 8 and IBM in this chapter.

At IBM, it is the CEO who is in ultimate charge of innovation – and has been for most of the company's history. The CEO as the *innovation czar* is often found in companies where a charismatic founder plays the role, and in this IBM is no exception. Thomas J. Watson Sr. ruled IBM for almost four decades until just a few weeks before his death in the early 1950s, when his son Thomas J. Watson Jr. took over as CEO. The company saw several more decades of success, becoming one of the most prosperous companies in the world and attracting the attention of the government for its near-monopoly of the computer industry. Although it defeated the government's antitrust suit, it did not deal with what we might describe as internal cultural issues of arrogance and self-satisfaction and came close to losing everything in the years from 1985 to 1993 under CEO John Akers.

The tenure of outsider Lou Gerstner brought IBM back from the brink, and its current model of governing innovation – influenced no doubt by the legacy of the Watsons followed by a succession of successful CEOs – was crafted and adopted by IBMer Sam Palmisano when he took over the reins from Gerstner. By the end of its centenary year in 2011, IBM was a worldwide corporation with revenues of $106.9 billion, total assets of $116.4 billion, and 433,362 employees.

Like many companies in which innovation is governed by the CEO, the importance of innovation is very clear. The CEO controls the *content* of innovation, but not the *processes*. IBM's collaborative culture, reinforced by internal as well as customer-focused social networking practices, provides an environment in which it is possible for employees to work together effectively without always needing explicit rules.

The Gartner Group has referred to IBM's innovation governance model as *managed anarchy*, and we have seen IBMers nod their heads in agreement. This expression is an apt description of CEO-level governance at IBM, but it does not imply a lack of discipline.[1] At IBM, governance is supported by key executives in businesses, functions, and departments who make a point of behaving, collectively and individually, as true innovation leaders and role models. In addition, over the years IBM has implemented a solid set of innovation processes that guide tasks and decisions all the way from front-end exploration to commercialization and product line management.

BIG BLUE[2]

IBM started life in 1911 as the Computing-Tabulating-Recording Company (C-T-R), which manufactured and sold commercial scales, tabulators, and punch card machines. Watson Sr. joined C-T-R in 1914 as general manager. By 1924 the company had expanded its markets worldwide and built manufacturing facilities in Europe, and in that year the name was changed to International

Business Machines Corporation. At some point in the last century, the company became known simply as IBM. The company was also known by the nickname Big Blue, some say in reference to its logo or to the blue covers of its mainframe computers, others to the dark blue suits that its employees used to wear.

Success Leads to Complacency

According to Steve Hamm, co-author of a book about IBM and now in the company's communications department, "in the late 1980s, IBM had become complacent about its position in the computer industry and rapidly lost business."[3]

Many readers will remember Big Blue in the 1970s and 1980s as a conservative company with an impressive market position and a dress code that stipulated what its employees should wear to work. Its success in the computer industry was legendary. Its sales force focused on the C-suite and sold mainframe solutions that served whole companies. IBM was committed to "selling iron" as Polaroid had been committed to "burning film." In that environment, even though it successfully launched its PC in 1981, the "mainframe bureaucracy asserted itself" and the IBM personal computer failed to achieve its market potential.

Among IBM's customers it was typical for employees to feel that they were safe with IBM. In other words, if what they bought did not work they would not be blamed if it was an IBM product; choosing a product from another manufacturer – even if it was cheaper and perhaps better – would not be worth the risk in case the product failed. The IBM sales force could count on repeat sales from existing customers.

Having led and profited from the many changes in what would come to be called the IT market, IBM found itself in "back-to-back revolutions" that "transformed the way customers viewed, used and bought technology."[4] These revolutions, of course, were the simultaneous rise of the PC and of client servers, which changed radically where IBM needed to do business: IBM's sales force had previously focused on marketing corporate applications across the whole business; now it had to shift its model to dealing with people on a more individual or departmental level.

Internally, there was a breakdown in the collaborative decision making that had been successful for years, as senior executives began to compete against one another, using a practice known internally as "nonconcurrence." This had started as a way of avoiding "groupthink" but had become a way for individuals and groups to ignore decisions and do what they pleased.[5]

In 1969 the government had sued the company because of antitrust issues. For 13 years after that, according to IBM process architect Paul Aspinwall, "We were always asking, 'Are we doing something the courts will get us for?' "[6] As a result, IBM went through a period in which it was never acceptable to make a mistake. Hamm quotes a former executive vice president: "The culture was: Be careful what you're doing. Be careful what you're saying. Be careful what you're writing. People may be watching. Fortunately we got past that!"[7]

The antitrust suit was eventually dropped in 1982 – "on the same day that a judge ordered the breakup of AT&T" following its antitrust suit.

By the early 1990s, as a result of complacency and increased competition from more nimble competitors, the company was almost on its knees. In 1991 it recorded its first loss, of $2.8 billion, which was more than doubled the following year – the biggest ever corporate loss. In an attempt to cut costs, the CEO, John Akers, had instigated layoffs – unheard of in the company's history – and divided the company into 13 autonomous units. Analysts fully expected the company to be split up. IBM's vast R&D spend of $55 billion over the previous 10 years had not borne fruit.

> "I worked for IBM for many years and left during the great 'downsizing' of the mid-90s. It was difficult for all the employees, but radical surgery was needed to save the patient.
>
> Lou Gerstner began the painful cuts that continued under Sam Palmisano to allow IBM to survive and begin to grow again. Then Palmisano completely restructured the company to eliminate dead end products and take advantage of emerging global opportunities.
>
> I'm proud to be a retired IBMer and glad I held on to my stock."
>
> *From Harvard Business Review blog, "Sam Palmisano's Transformation of IBM" by Joseph L. Bower. January 20, 2012, www.hbr.org*

IBM Hires an Outsider CEO

Against this backdrop, Akers resigned in 1993 and Louis V. Gerstner Jr. was brought in from outside to fix the problem. His solution included addressing IBM's then dysfunctional culture, as well as shifting to open-source software and creating a focus on services. In addition to his consumer orientation and his expertise in strategy, Gerstner, the first leader who had not come up from the IBM ranks, was a classic *fixer* (see Chapter 2). He cut costs, for example by reducing the company's real estate footprint, and focused on the existing product line. Perhaps most importantly, he avoided splitting the company, recognizing that its ability to provide integrated solutions was "one of IBM's enduring strengths."

In 2000, IBMer Samuel J. Palmisano was named president and COO, and two years later became CEO. His big challenge would be to pursue the transformation effort and to deliver on the potential that his predecessor had uncovered. By the time Gerstner stepped down, IBM Global Services, which he had created in 1996, was worth $30 billion dollars.

Palmisano said of Gerstner: "Without him, I don't think we would have survived. We needed someone with that tough mind and analytic skill."[8]

> "Tom Watson Jr. drove a huge transition to the modern computing era . . . the Watsons believed that every decade or so you had to reinvent the company and drive to the future. That was their bias."
>
> *Sam Palmisano. From Forbes online, "IBM Turns 100 – An Interview with CEO Sam Palmisano" by Rich Karlgaard. June 15, 2011, www.forbes.com*

IBM'S MODEL OF INNOVATION THROUGH "CONTINUOUS TRANSFORMATION"

Since its founding, the company has survived periods of near disaster, surfing the winds of change in its core field of business information and shifting its technologies, its offerings and its profit models to meet emergent opportunities and challenges. Unlike companies such as Polaroid, which spectacularly failed to deal with the onset of digital technology, IBM has managed to weather the storms of seemingly overwhelming changes in both markets and technologies.

IBM's History of Innovation

As an example of IBM's model of continuous transformation, Rometty spoke of IBM's history of "remixing" its R&D resources: "Two decades ago, 70 percent of our researchers were working in materials science, hardware and related technology. Today, 60 percent are in fields that support our key growth initiatives." These researchers include 400 mathematicians as well as specialists in a number of key fields such as biology, natural language processing, and climate forecasting.

2012 IBM Annual Report. Source: http:// www.ibm.com/ annualreport/2012/bin/ assets/2012_ibm_annual.pdf

Watson Sr. ruled IBM for almost four decades until just a few weeks before his death in the early 1950s, when Thomas J. Watson Jr. took over as CEO. The decade of the 1950s saw a number of technological transformations, including the introduction of FORTRAN, a new random access storage system (RAMAC), and a computer based on the vacuum tube (IBM 701) which greatly expanded the computer's usability in business applications. Watson Jr. served as CEO until 1971 and on IBM's board until 1984.

Foreshadowing, and indeed participating in, the vast changes that IBM would experience, Watson Jr. stated: "I believe that if an organization is to meet the challenges of a changing world, it must be prepared to change everything about itself except those [core] beliefs as it moves through corporate life."[9] The System/360, introduced during Watson Jr.'s tenure, was a real game-changer in the computer industry. Palmisano called it the boldest bet in IBM's history.

When Gerstner started at IBM, faced with an unwieldy, oversized and underfunded organization, it might have seemed like an easy solution to split the company up and sell parts of it off. However, he resisted the temptation to do so – in what Steve Hamm describes as "the signature decision of his tenure."[10] Gerstner

helped prepare IBM to achieve a leadership position in the emerging world of the internet and network computing. He was also
responsible for two extremely counter-intuitive decisions that have
paved the way for IBM's success in the 21st century: the move to
open standards and the move to providing services.

Dennis Elenburg, a technical representative at IBM, says the
following in his review of Gerstner's book, *Who Says Elephants
Can't Dance?*:[11]

> Gerstner points out that some integrator, fundamentally acting in a
> service role, controls every major industry. This was the basis for
> building IBM Global Services. Another shrewd Gerstner insight is
> that every major industry is built around open standards. It was this
> realization that led IBM Software to enable and build on open
> standards in a network-centric world, and Gerstner provides a com-
> pelling argument for abandoning proprietary development and
> embracing software standards (e.g., J2EE and Web Services). In fact,
> Gerstner argues that the most valuable technology companies are
> OEM suppliers who leverage their technology wherever possible;
> therefore, IBM must actively license its technology in order to be
> successful.[12]

Innovation at IBM Touches its Core

While many other companies remain glued to a product-oriented
approach, IBM has been able to transform its core identity with
respect to business models and market offerings and has provided
different kinds of products and services for many different customers and markets.

By 2012, the company's major operations were organized in
five business segments representing markets and offerings, only one
of which existed in the previous century: Global Technology Services and Global Business Services (which the company collectively
calls Global Services); Software; Systems and Technology; and
Global Financing. Four worldwide organizations play a key role in
serving clients: sales and distribution; research, development and
intellectual property; enterprise transformation; and integrated
supply chain.

The company's commitment to innovation – aided by the
insight and instinct of many of its CEOs – has enabled IBM to

pursue innovation in directions that were unfamiliar, foreign, and sometimes seemingly downright dangerous. Ginni Rometty, CEO since 2012, espouses a model of *continuous transformation*: "IBM is an innovation company. Both in what we do and in how we do it, we pursue continuous transformation – always remixing to higher value in our portfolios and skills, in the capabilities we deliver to our clients and in our own operations and management practices."[13] At an IBM Investor Briefing in February 2013, she reiterated that the company had chosen the route of change instead of the route of commoditization and described the three "strategic beliefs" that would "guide IBM into the decade ahead": (1) relentlessly move/remix to higher value; (2) include emerging new areas of computing; and (3) look for new markets/new clients.

Rometty was echoing her predecessor, Sam Palmisano, who announced in 2004: "As I described to you last year, we've made our choice: IBM is an innovation company." He then reflected on the job ahead, for him and for his successors: "Of course, declaring something like that is easy. It has taken a great deal of discipline to execute."[14]

Let Go to Grow

> "Leadership no longer means command and control. It no longer means 'my values' but rather shared values. It means collaboration, empowerment, and the ability to enable decision making in the business – any business – to occur closer to the customer. Although the leader's vision can be delivered vertically, it will drive growth only if it is implemented horizontally, across the organization."
> *Sanford and Taylor, p. 131*

IBM's pursuit of new identities in the 21st century was carefully crafted, thought through, and researched. Palmisano was not hoping simply to survive the radical changes that were occurring all around. He created a leadership position to accomplish the desired transformation, and to do it in a way that would enable ongoing transformation.

Senior vice president Linda Sanford was the first head of IBM's Enterprise Transformation. In her book *Let Go to Grow: Escaping the Commodity Trap*, co-authored with

Dave Taylor, Sanford outlines the approach that IBM and other companies need to take to succeed in the global digitized age.[15] On the very first page, the authors articulate an important part of IBM's strategy – to take existing and potential partners, including competitors, along with it: "You need to open up your business by building and participating in value *webs*, where value is built by a number of companies coordinating their individual capabilities."

Sanford and Taylor emphasize the importance of collaboration. This has clear implications for how IBM will understand governance. No longer, they insist, does it work for leaders to declare the direction and say, "Follow me." Instead, "leadership is about listening, about letting go of control and creating a shared sense of collaboration for the greater good of the firm."[16]

Shared values and collaboration do not, however, mean that "anything goes." It does not mean that IBM employees are all free to pursue whatever ideas they may have. On the contrary, this increase in collaborative innovation demands rigor in governance. The companies that Sanford and Taylor deem to have "set the pace for profitable growth show the primacy of coordination." In the companies whose cases are explored in their book, "workers are never left in doubt about top management's priorities and their own responsibilities to support them."[17]

Advocating for Innovation in the Ecosystem

Palmisano's belief that innovation is critical for the continued success of his own company led him to participate in, and in several instances to form, groups like the Council on Competitiveness through which he could explore approaches to innovation with others, develop new ideas, and also spread his beliefs about innovation more widely. His participation in such groups gave even more credibility to the way he used his position as CEO as a bully pulpit for innovation.

In a speech to the Council on Competitiveness Annual Meeting in Washington, D.C., in October 2003, Palmisano declared that "simply put, innovation: spawns new industries, fuels economic growth, creates countless high-value, high-paying jobs, and raises the standard of living for people around the globe. Now more than ever, innovation is occurring within a global – not just a national – ecosystem, with multiple points of intersection among business, government and academia."

GOVERNANCE AS "MANAGED ANARCHY"

For governance to work as *managed anarchy*, the entity being managed must meet certain criteria. It must have embedded in it strong and focused productivity, shared values, and robust decision-making practices – in other words, the organization must be able for the most part to operate successfully on its own, without the oversight of top management. When everyone knows what to do and does what is needed, there is less need for hands-on management.

Creating a Culture in which Anarchy Can be Managed

Palmisano expressed the need for management that works with the diversity of IBM's global business:

> Think of our organizational matrix. Remember, we operate in 170 countries. To keep it simple, let's say we have 60 or 70 major product lines. We have more than a dozen customer segments. If you mapped out the entire 3D matrix, you'd get more than 100,000 cells. You'll drive people crazy trying to centrally manage every one of those intersections.
>
> So if there's no way to optimize IBM through organizational structure or by management dictate, you have to empower people while ensuring that they're making the right calls the right way. You've got to create a management system that empowers people and provides a basis for decision making that is consistent with who we are at IBM.[18]

To provide such a basis, Palmisano – like the Watsons and Gerstner before him and Rometty after – saw a key to this puzzle as the conscious creation of the culture of the corporation. Watson Sr. believed in information and in thinking. From this core belief – both "fervent and unformed," Steve Hamm tells us –

Watson "doggedly aimed to build an organization that self-consciously embodied his mantra, 'Think'."[19]

The conscious and careful creation of corporate culture, which Hamm suggests was a radical notion in Watson's day, persists as IBM's CEOs today seek to shape the corporation so that its employees will make "the right calls the right way."

Palmisano transformed IBM "into a single globally-integrated enterprise that focused on serving enterprises in 170 countries." He got rid of the 11 member Corporate Executive Committee (CEC), replacing it with teams whose members were responsible for leadership of parts of IBM's "faster-moving widely dispersed organization."[20]

> "The potential for innovation is only magnified by the emerging knowledge-based global economy. Today, the basis of innovation is less focused on things, and more on ideas, collaboration and expertise. And in our restless, 24-hour networked world, innovative ideas can move around the world with the click of a mouse."
>
> *Sam Palmisano, former CEO. From Sophie Bechu presentation "IBM eServer." Source: http://www-304.ibm .com/jct03001c/procurement/ proweb.nsf/objectdocswebview/ file1+-+bechu+symposium +presentation/$file/1 +-+bechu+symposium +presentation_9_06_2006.pdf*

Social Networking at the Core

Early in his tenure, feeling that the core values that had driven IBM for decades had become stale, Palmisano staged a "ValuesJam." IBMers were invited to participate in a 72-hour online brainstorming session to rethink the company's values.

According to Hamm, "the jam got off to a rough start. Critics deluged the forum with negative comments."[21] Some senior executives wanted to shut the session down. But they persisted and "over time the tone changed and became constructive." The values that emerged – dedication to every client's success; innovation that matters, for our company and for the world; and trust and personal responsibility in all relationships – bear a certain resemblance to the Watsons' basic beliefs of respect for the individual, customer service, and excellence. The exercise has been credited with building

> **IBM Software Group's Social Business Adoption Program**
>
> Code-named "BlueIQ," this internal program promoted IBMers' adoption of social software such as IBM Connections, as well as pilot tools developed in IBM's Technology Adoption Program and research labs. It has now evolved into an enterprise-wide program.
>
> BlueIQ's methodology for social software adoption combined task-focused training, individualized "consulting" to jumpstart teams and communities, motivational activities, and enablement tools with volunteer early adopters.
>
> *From IBM website.*
> *Source: https://www-304*
> *.ibm.com/connections/wikis/*
> *home?lang=en-gb#!/*
> *wiki/BlueIQ*

senior management commitment to innovation and to re-creating a sense of purpose for IBM.

It is not possible to understand IBM's innovation governance as *managed anarchy* without reflecting on the extent to which IBM is what the Gartner Group, in a book by Bradley and McDonald, calls a "social organization." Such organizations "don't simply succeed here and there in using social technology. Instead, they embed mass collaboration in who they are and how they work. It's part of the way they do business; it's how they think."[22]

IBM is an information management company, so perhaps it is no surprise that while many mature companies are struggling to make sense of the value of opportunities provided by the internet, social networking, and so on, IBM harnessed them early and not only provides them to customers but also uses them internally.

Social Networking Leads to Bottom-up Innovation

A number of collaborative tools and initiatives allow and encourage every employee to engage in innovation. ThinkPlace enables IBM employees to share, discuss, and refine innovative ideas. Jams, including IdeaJam, enable brainstorming focusing on critical business, technology, or social issues among globally distributed groups. BlogCentral facilitates internal conversations.

On the Technology Adoption Program (TAP) participants can post, critique, and improve concepts that have moved beyond the "idea stage." WPTS (Worldwide Patent Tracking System) enables employees to submit inventions for patent consideration. In 2012 IBM received a record number of patents – almost 6500 – putting it at the top of the US patent list for the 20th consecutive year with a grand total of nearly 67,000 patents. The patents apply to inventions in the domains of analytics, big data, cyber-security, cloud, mobile, social networking, and software defined environments, as well as industry solutions for retail, banking, healthcare, and transportation.

IBM's programs also reach beyond the company. FOAK (First of a Kind) was established in 1995 under Gerstner. It provided a platform for collaborative relationships between leading clients that wanted to become early adopters of cutting-edge technologies and IBM scientists wishing to conduct research in the marketplace. Under Palmisano, IBM also became a leader in several *ecosystem groups*, which are not limited to IBM participation. They include employees, customers, business partners, independent software vendors, universities, venture capitalists, community leaders, and others. Participation in these groups helps IBM to stay in touch with what is happening in innovation and also to advocate for innovative practices. One such group, the National Innovation Initiative, advocates an agenda to make the United States the most fertile and attractive environment for innovation.

> "Perhaps more than anything else, IBM has always been a culture that encourages, supports and celebrates innovation. Great minds inside this company are again focusing their brainpower on how technology, and the data that drives it, can solve the most perplexing challenges both in the enterprise and in society."
>
> *Jeanette Horan, vice president and CIO, speaking at HMG's CIO Summit of America, February 2013, where she was a recipient of HMG's Annual Transformational CIO Leadership Award*

EMBEDDING DISCIPLINE WITHIN ANARCHY

At IBM innovation falls into four distinct categories: markets and offerings; business/enterprise models; operations; and sustaining enablers. Clarifying this is important to governance in two ways: (1) it helps IBMers know where to target their efforts; and (2) it widens the field of innovation so that more and different efforts can be undertaken.

IBM has a traditional product development process that is used within the businesses. The development process – IPD, or integrated product development model – was first implemented several decades ago and is updated whenever IBM finds an internal improvement or whenever it discovers improvements that have been implemented by peer companies. The group of projects that are under way at any one time is overseen by a portfolio management team within the relevant business. Riskier, more radical projects – ones that typically address new markets, new business models, and/or new disruptive technologies – are placed in the Emerging Business Opportunities framework where they are judged against six criteria: strategic alignment, cross-IBM leverage, new source of customer value, $1 billion+ revenue potential, market leadership, and sustained profit potential. If they meet these criteria they are moved into development, where their progress is subject to the framework of the IPD.

Like other companies with effective innovation governance models, IBM has carefully articulated and implemented processes for bringing products and services to market. In addition, it has an effective discipline for managing and resourcing the development pipeline and portfolio. In other words, there is a structure to ensure that decisions that are made concerning innovation and new opportunities can be acted on.

In response to a Forbes interviewer's question about how IBM balanced short-term and long-term financial goals, Palmisano's answer was, "We don't run IBM in quarterly cycles even though there's tremendous pressure to do that, to give quarterly guidance within a penny. You certainly have to make your numbers. But I just feel it is wrong for the long term to run a company like that. That's why, in 2002, we came up with our 2010 roadmap. That way, IBM could communicate to its investors about the long term . . . it [also] tells our people, here are the growth plays and here is your role in it."[23] To tie such a long-term investment outlook with the role of innovators within the company can help to align two forces that are at odds in many companies and is an important aspect of innovation governance.

In IBM's ongoing transformation journey, it has exited the commodity businesses, strengthened its position in services and open systems, and acquired over 60 companies that can forward its innovation agenda. Innovation governance at IBM is built on a corporate culture and history that elevates innovation to a high place and oversees the implementation of practices that will help to engage every employee as well as IBM's ecosystem. This part of the job is usually identified as the "soft part" and takes place at the front end of innovation. At the same time, the governance system makes sure that the later stages are effectively and efficiently carried out, so that the commitment to discovering new opportunities can be translated into valid market entries.

> "We opened up our labs, said to the world, 'Here are our crown jewels, have at them'. The [Ideas]Jam – and programs like it – are greatly accelerating our ability to innovate in meaningful ways for business and society."
>
> *Sam Palmisano, former CEO. From IBM press release. Source: http:// www-03.ibm.com/press/us/ en/pressrelease/20605.wss*

LEARNING FROM IBM

IBM provides us with an example of high-level and long-standing commitment to innovation. Throughout much of its history IBM has practiced what it preaches – that innovation, not just invention, is key to the company's very existence, and that innovation will not be held back by the company's existing structures, practices, and models. The company takes a hands-off approach to innovation. It does not want to micro-manage, Paul Aspinwall told us. Watson made it clear that there was nothing wrong with wild ducks that flew out of formation. Gerstner managed only his direct reports; he counted on them to manage the people who reported to them. Following this formula, IBM's board works only with the CEO.

IBM has always had tremendous respect for the ability and intelligence of its employees. Even now, when rapid staff turnover has become more the cultural norm in most companies, IBM has a record of employee longevity. This connects with recognizing the importance of an innovation culture that encourages employees to participate in identifying and developing new opportunities.

There are at least three important messages that we can take from the story of innovation governance at IBM. These are:

- IBM's commitment to and focus on a culture that promotes innovation;
- the CEO's involvement in building methods and opportunities for employees to participate; and
- a belief in the inevitability of change and the role of corporate values in addressing change.

A Culture that Promotes Innovation

From the very first days of the company's existence, most of IBM's CEOs have appreciated the importance of a culture of innovation. A focus on culture may have been a radical notion in the Watsons' day, as Hamm suggests, but the hands-on approach to building culture by the top levels of the company is unusual even today. Too often we hear that "culture" is the province of the HR department, or that it can be trusted to sporadic events or projects, often organized by outside consultants.

IBM's "near-death experience" in the last century can be seen in part as the result of leadership turning its attention away from a culture of innovation. The highly conservative nature of IBM's workforce, down to the adoption of dress codes, is at the opposite end of the spectrum from the company that Palmisano describes: "You have to be willing to change your core, and you have to be ahead of the shift."[24] Through their commitment to and belief in the importance of an empowered workforce, many IBM CEOs created an environment that sustains and supports a culture of innovation.

Building Methods and Opportunities for Employees to Participate

We have returned again and again to the social networking programs and practices that connect IBM's employees throughout the world. They are at the core of IBM's approach to innovation. That they are also at the core of IBM's products and services surely made the transformation to a "social organization" imperative. We should remember, however, that it was not until the arrival of Gerstner that the company was able to connect the dots and in so doing to find the path to real transformation.

To build a "social organization" is to build an organization where innovation is "emergent." As Bradley and McDonald put it: "Emergence is what allows collaborative communities to come up with new ways of working or new solutions to seemingly intractable problems; it is the source of innovation."[25] This means that leadership will not be able to call all the shots. It means that anarchy must be managed, not eliminated or ruled. In such a company, leaders must be willing to follow as the ducks fly out of formation.

At the same time, as we have stressed, leaders must encourage structures of discipline. They cannot simply stand back as groups throughout the organization come up with and pursue innovative ideas. Part of what governance means, and a significant part of what IBM's leaders have encouraged, are structures such as the integrated product development model, which give decision makers a basis for making choices about where the company's resources will be directed.

The Inevitability of Change

Watson Jr.'s statement that "if an organization is to meet the challenges of a changing world, it must be prepared to change everything about itself" has proved to be remarkably apt. Almost a hundred years later, IBM is still changing. In her first year as CEO, Ginni Rometty, began implementing a five-year strategy to use new markets like cloud computing and

"When you ask me about strategy, ask me instead what I believe. [Beliefs] are enduring, and they will mature over time."
Ginni Rometty, 2012
IBM Annual Report.
Source: http://www.ibm
.com/annualreport/2012/
bin/assets/2012_ibm
_annual.pdf

business analytics software to achieve revenue growth of $20 billion by 2015. Asked what she had learned from Palmisano, she responded: "IBM must keep evolving. What he always says is, 'Nothing is inevitable.' She went on to explain, 'Whatever business you're in – it doesn't matter – it's going to commoditize over time. It's going to devalue. You've got to keep moving it to a higher value'."[26]

NOTES

[1] See, for example, *2012 IBM Annual Report*, in which CEO Virginia Rometty points to "the discipline of our management systems" as a key contributor to IBM's overall success. From IBM website. Source: http://www.ibm.com/annualreport/2012/bin/assets/2012_ibm_annual.pdf.

[2] Much material in this section is from an IMD case study by John Weeks and Jean-Louis Barsoux, "Rebooting IBM," Case no. IMD-4-0318, 2010; and from Maney, K., Hamm, S. and O'Brien, J.M. (2011). *Making the World Work Better: The Ideas that Shaped a Century and a Company*, IBM Press (hereafter *MWWB*), as well as several consultants who worked with IBM during this period.

[3] This quote and others in this section from *MWWB*, pp. 158ff.

[4] From IBM website. Source: http://www-03.ibm.com/ibm/history/history/decade_1990.html.

[5] See Weeks and Barsoux, *Rebooting IBM*, Copyright 2010, Case no. IMD-4-0318.

[6] Interview with Paul Aspinwall, 2013. Used with permission.

[7] Steve Hamm and Jeffrey, M. O'Brien, *MWWB*, IBM Press, 2011.

[8] *MWWB*, p. 209.

[9] *MWWB*, p. 148.

[10] Ibid, p. 208.

[11] Gerstner, L.V. (2002). *Who Says Elephants Can't Dance?* Harper Business.

[12] IBM website. Source: http://www.ibm.com/developerworks/rational/library/2071.html.

[13] 2012 IBM Annual Report. Source: http://www.ibm.com/annualreport/2012/bin/assets/2012_ibm_annual.pdf.

[14] 2004 IBM Annual Report. Source: ftp://public.dhe.ibm.com/annualreport/2004/2004_ibm_annual.pdf.

[15] Sanford, L.S. and Taylor, D. (2006). *Let Go to Grow: Escaping the Commodity Trap*. Pearson Education.

[16] Ibid, p. 134.

[17] Ibid, p. 157.

[18] *MWWB*, p. 166.

[19] Ibid, p. 138.

[20] From Harvard Business Review blog, "Sam Palmisano's Transformation of IBM" by Joseph L. Bower. January 20, 2012, www.hbr.org.

[21] *MWWB*, p. 161.

[22] Bradley, A.J. and McDonald, M.P. (2011). *The Social Organization: How to Use Social Media to Tap the Collective Genius of Your Customers and Employees*, Harvard Business Review Press, p. 7.

[23] Karlgaard. R. (2011). IBM Turns 100: An Interview with CEO Sam Palmisano, June 15.

[24] *MWWB*, p. 141.

[25] Bradley and McDonald, p. 15.

[26] "IBM's Ginni Rometty looks ahead," *Fortune*, Jessi Hempel, 9/20/12.

CHAPTER 8

LEADING FROM THE TOP

Example 2 – Corning's Innovation Governance Model: Two Executive Councils Execute Hands-on Governance[1]

Corning's model of innovation governance is an example of what we call *the top management team or subset as a group*. Two executive councils are in charge of Corning's innovation worldwide: the Corporate Technology Council (CTC), which focuses on more radical innovations, and the Growth Execution Council (GEC), which is responsible for the success of medium- to short-term innovation. Members of the CTC include, among others, the CTO, the three senior vice presidents of research, development, and engineering, and the vice president of legal affairs; both the CTC and the GEC are co-chaired by the CTO and the innovation officer, and the CEO regularly attends meetings. These councils were important in Corning's recovery from the telecommunications downturn of 2002, in which a huge drop in demand for optical fiber drove Corning's stock price down from $110 per share to $1.10 and threatened the company's very existence.

The company was founded by Amory Houghton Sr. in 1851 in Corning, New York, where its headquarters and its principal Science and Technology Center[2] – called Sullivan Park after one of the early pioneers of research at Corning – are still based. Since then it has evolved from a small company, whose first major product was the glass envelope for Edison's light bulb, to a multinational corporation, with record sales of just over \$8 billion in 2012. At year-end it had approximately 28,700 full-time employees worldwide, of whom about 11,700 were in the United States. Corning is a leader in specialty glass and ceramics, and we shall see that it has discovered a multitude of ways of using this core competence to develop many different kinds of products in many different industries. Today its largest business is liquid crystal displays (LCD) for which it makes the glass substrates.

Corning has been a successful innovator – to put it mildly – throughout its history. Its leaders have been committed to innovation and to creating a culture for innovation success. In recent decades, leading companies have researched and discovered more explicitly what is necessary for innovation to be sustainable and effective, and Corning has been a leader in this advance. It has won the Product Development and Management Association (PDMA) "Outstanding Innovator" award, among other awards, and engages with peer companies to explore the most effective innovation practices. Today, senior executives use an explicit governance model to provide a structure that allows them to dig deep into the technologies and the markets that are the focus of new opportunities and innovation projects.

In this chapter, we will review the history of how Corning built its innovation competency, with particular emphasis on the first decade of the century – roughly from 2001 to 2009. This time frame saw the implementation of Corning's model for governing innovation, and although the pace of innovation as well as its scope has increased greatly in the past few

"[. . .] Corning Glass was one of the first companies in the US to invest in the idea of research and development. We really were one of the leaders in bringing research and manufacturing together. [. . .] We would ask, 'what can we do to be different from everybody else?' and that's what led us to concentrate on the whole idea of innovation as a process and the whole idea of fundamental research and development in glass as critical to the future success of the company."

James R. Houghton, former CEO and chairman. From "Interview with James R. Houghton" by Heidi Legg. May 29, 2013, www.theeditorial.com

years, the necessary adaptations to meet new challenges rest on the innovation governance structure and the innovation processes that we describe below.

CORNING'S EVOLUTION: A GLASS FACTORY BECOMES A WORLD LEADER IN INNOVATION[3]

Corning started life as a glass factory. Since then, it has discovered and created ways of using its core substance that have made it a leader in many different industries. Corning's commitment to innovation spans its more than 160-year history. CEO Wendell Weeks rarely misses a chance to remind management groups that the company's goal is another 160 years of innovation and independence. Corning's leaders have always demanded that the company *grow through innovation* and that its innovations should not only be attractive to Corning but should also have a lasting impact on society.

THE AGES OF CORNING: A HISTORY OF SUPPLE GOVERNANCE

Corning currently participates in five market segments: display technologies, telecom, environmental technologies, life sciences, and specialty materials. In addition to these market segments, the company includes one that it describes as *new business development*. This segment holds new business ventures that may or may not make it to the market but ensures that it is working on the next viable opportunities.

Many companies have trouble canceling projects, even when the chances of success are not clear. Corning has learned to be more comfortable with generating many potentially viable opportunities but only commercializing those that show the most promise of success. This ability is a clear sign of effective governance – too many companies continue to ride the projects that have been approved, throwing good money after bad even as market or technology prospects look dim or the fit with company strategy is misaligned.

> "We know that we know glass and that we probably know glass better than anybody in the world and we're going to protect that capability as a company and we're going to look for opportunities to exploit those capabilities. Most of the businesses revolve around this theme and so we are able to move people across those different technology teams at Sullivan Park."
>
> *An HR director. Source: Rebecca M. Henderson and Cate Reavis, Corning Incorporated: The Growth and Strategy Council, copyright 2008; revised April 15, 2009, Sloan School of Management*

Corning's major innovation successes over its history include the glass envelope for Edison's light bulb, Pyrex glass, silicones and ceramics, catalytic converters, and a high-throughput screening platform for drug discovery, as well as optical fiber and glass materials used in TVs. Most recently, it has developed Gorilla® Glass – initially as a cover glass for the iPhone to prevent it from getting scratched, but now extended to all display devices and enjoying explosive growth.

At an IAPD workshop in 2001, Jacques LeMoine, director of Corning's Science and Technology International Laboratories until his retirement later that year, described Corning as *toujours young*.[4] "Corning's business strategy at the most basic level," he said, "is to focus on attractive global markets where Corning's leadership in fiber optics, materials, and process technology will allow us to achieve and sustain competitive advantage and superior growth over time."

Frequently in its history, when Corning's core technology competency gives rise to a product, the product is then supported by a specific manufacturing process. For example, the light bulb envelope developed by Corning was a critical factor in bringing Edison's discovery to market in 1879, but without the "ribbon machine" that the company later invented, it would not have been possible to manufacture light bulbs cheaply enough to make them commercially viable. These machines are still in use today.

The scope of innovation at Corning has spread over the years to include more and more products that draw not just on one of Corning's competencies but on a combination of them. The process is one that Bruce Kirk, director of corporate innovation effectiveness, describes as "iterating and learning," and the outcome is often the discovery of new uses for older inventions and technologies. For example, signal lamp technology paved the way for cookware. Equally, the company's core competency in glass often provides a base from which it is able to recognize opportunities that can be fulfilled only by accessing other technologies. This has led to joint ventures, acquisitions, and partnerships, as well as licensing and contract manufacturing, which allow it to enter areas that would otherwise have been out of reach. These have taken the company into a variety of different industries, including building products (with PPG Industries), fiber glass (with Owens-Illinois), silicones (with Dow Chemical), display technologies (with Asahi Glass, Samtel, and Samsung), telecom (with Siemens), cooktops (with St. Gobain), and ceramic substrates (with NGK). Corning protects its intellectual property carefully, but it also does not hesitate to sell or spin off technologies and businesses that no longer provide competitive advantage. Unlike many companies that hold on to outmoded business models, Corning appears to be as willing to invent business models as it is to formulate materials and processes.

> Corning's core competency in the fundamental material of glass may be critical to its longevity. LeMoine describes glass as a "frozen liquid." It is extremely versatile. It can change shape and color; it can be transparent or opaque; it can take on many variations of durability and strength. Glass is formed by melting crystalline materials at very high temperatures and locking them into a random or disordered state before they can form perfect crystals. The result is a substance which, according to the Corning website, "can do most anything."
>
> *From Corning website. Source: http://media .corning.com/flash/ opticalfiber/2012/corning _optical_fiber/glass.htm*

DEFINING THE CORE

An IAPD Workshop in 2002 addressed the significance of core competencies in innovation. Jurriaan Gerretsen, then innovation process manager at Corning, provided a dynamic model of the interplay between Corning's businesses and its core competencies,

> **Corning's Core Competencies 2002**
> - Inorganic materials (glass, ceramics)
> - Melting and forming processes
> - Measurement of process parameters and materials properties
> - Manufacturing research
>
> *Gerretsen, IAPD 2002*

each business drawing deeply on the competencies and associated applications, overlapping with one another, and positioned to provide space for the new applications and businesses that will emerge as older ones fade away.[5]

Although of course the picture has expanded in the decade or so since Gerretsen's talk, his description of Corning's competencies gives us a clue as to how the company holds its assets and might help explain its ability to generate and regenerate technologies and businesses. He maps Corning's *core competencies* (see box) as four overlapping circles. Around the competencies at the center, or core, of the model Gerretsen rings more overlapping circles that represent some of the areas of application – networks, halides, surfaces, catalysis, and so on. These varied competencies and applications make it possible for Corning to develop capabilities in many areas; at the time of Gerretsen's talk, Corning participated in five industries and nine major businesses.

The four competencies at the core are not likely to change much. They are so intertwined with Corning as to represent its identity at a very deep level. However, the application areas – along with the capabilities, businesses, and products to which they give rise – can and do change in response to shifting technology and market forces. "Growing and shedding" of these application areas, according to Gerretsen, "is a continuous process." And this is facilitated by the fact that Corning has defined its core at such an elemental level.

FROM SUCCESS TO CRISIS: THE DOT-COM DOWNTURN

In the later decades of the 20th century Corning's technology focus turned to fiber optics. The company invested in the segment for 20 years before it finally turned profitable in the 1980s and took off. By 2000, Corning was deriving 70% of its revenues from telecommunications and investing the same proportion of its research budget in the sector. It was the most significant player in the fiber optic market, with a 40% share.

The decision to pursue fiber optics meant that Corning had to build capabilities that it did not yet possess. The necessary expertise was acquired, and temporary offices were built at key locations including Sullivan Park and Fontainebleau Research Center (FRC), Corning's site in France, to make space for new employees and new labs. Then came the telecom crash. Within two years, the merger in 2000 between AOL – the darling of dot-com investors – and Time Warner, the world's largest media company, had gone sour and many companies like Corning felt the effects. They no longer had the infrastructure to monetize their investments. By 2002, the company's revenues had halved, its share price had tumbled and it was on the verge of bankruptcy.

James Houghton, founder Amory's great great grandson, was brought back to fill the role of CEO for a second time. The first place he went when he was reappointed was to Corning's Science and Technology Center at Sullivan Park. He wanted to make sure that the scientists and engineers who worked there realized their importance to Corning's future. And, true to its commitment to innovation, even during the worst parts of the downturn Corning never lowered its overall R&D investment below 10% of revenue. LeMoine affirmed, shortly after the downturn, that in order to continue to lead through innovation Corning needed a solid foundation in science and technology: "Even through the downturn, although there has to be realism in research, in understanding what the company can afford in order to protect the future of the company, still there is a focus on science and technology, on innovation."[6]

BUILDING A STRUCTURE FOR EFFECTIVE GOVERNANCE

The term *innovation governance* has been more widely used only recently, but the practice of governing innovation is not new.

Throughout Corning's history we can see the impact of a steady hand on the tiller. The culture and the explicit commitment of leadership to innovation, the strategy to employ some of the best scientific talent available, and the willingness to seek partnerships with others well before the "buzz" of open innovation – all these were elements of how Corning governed innovation. They defined some of the key questions of innovation, as outlined in Chapter 3:

- *Why* – because Corning is defined by its consistent focus on innovation, and because its core enables innovation.
- *Where* – in any field in which its competencies might create something of value to Corning and to society as a whole.
- *How much* – whatever was needed to accomplish its innovation goals, even if the payback time was long.

Corning's leaders not only articulated these lofty ideals; they have acted on them over the company's long history. And Corning's employees are aware of the importance of innovation and are ready and willing to play a role.

The shock of the telecom downturn, however, influenced Corning to make its governance policies clearer and more explicit and to make sure that the discussion and decision making included voices across the top level of the company. As a result, Corning has adopted the model that we call *the top management team or subset as a group*. As we have already mentioned, the Corporate Technology Council (CTC) and the Growth Execution Council (GEC) are responsible for governing innovation at Corning. These councils, led by C-suite executives, oversee and support the projects that will continue to enable Corning to out-innovate competitors and to position itself as a valuable ally in any number of industries.

GOVERNING CORNING'S MEDIUM-TERM GROWTH: THE GEC

The GEC oversees Corning's medium-term growth projects. Generally, its innovations pass through a five-stage process that includes gathering information/building knowledge; determining feasibility; testing practicality; proving profitability; and managing the life cycle. The last stage was previously referred to as *commercialization*, but was changed to reflect the need to continue to manage innovations once they have been developed and launched and to prevent fast followers from seizing the advantage. This flexibility is a vital part of Corning's approach to innovation.

Born out of the Boom

The GEC meets regularly to work with medium-term project teams. It helps them solve difficult questions and issues that arise as they move through the stages toward launch. The question of whether a project will pass a gate is usually determined by the project sponsor on the GEC working with the project team.

The GEC, originally called the Growth and Strategy Council (GSC), was started in the days of the global telecom boom, when Corning was investing heavily in optical fiber. By the late 1990s, the industry was flourishing and the company was doing extremely well. In 2001, then COO Peter Volanakis initiated a dialogue for the businesses that were not involved in the hugely successful optical fiber business. Its purpose, according to Henderson and Reavis, was mainly to help the less successful businesses continue to thrive and grow.[7]

Joe Miller left DuPont, where he had been senior vice president of R&D since 1994, and began his career at Corning as CTO in 2001, shortly before the downturn. It did not seem to be an auspicious beginning, but in a meeting with CEO Jamie Houghton he was told that even though he might have to scale back, he could not give away Corning's core. He presided over Corning's success in the first decade of the new century as executive vice president and CTO until his retirement in April 2012.

Wendell Weeks, who is now Corning's CEO, was a lead player in the optical fiber business, serving as vice president and general manager from 1996 to 2001, and then as president. As Corning's website puts it, "he led [the business] through both dynamic market growth and the subsequent challenges of market declines." In 2002

"These councils reflect the breadth of a project by bringing in scientists, marketers, and business leaders [. . .] We spend four or five hours a month in the sessions, bringing all the stakeholders together and driving to a decision. You hear the technical facts about what's working and what's not working. Management will sometimes decide on the spot whether to continue a project and what we should spend. This eliminates older, more formal, more stratified practices. We put it all together at the same time so that no one has to leave the room saying to their direct reports, 'They said A, but what I really want you to do is B.' We agree on the plan in that room."

Interview with David Morse, CTO, adapted and reprinted with permission from "The Gorilla of Agile Business" by William J. Holstein from the strategy+business website (http://www.strategy-business.com/article/00192?gko=589bd), published by Booz & Company Inc. Copyright © 2013. All rights reserved.

Weeks was promoted to Corning's president and COO: "In this role, he helped lead the company's restructuring and return to profitability following the telecom industry crash. Weeks was the chief architect of Corning's Corporate Strategy Framework, which provides a foundation for mitigating the company's inherent volatility and managing through good times and bad."[8]

Immediately after he became president and COO, Weeks shifted the focus of Volanakis' group to address investment in research and innovation at the corporate level in order to protect Corning's level of involvement in R&D. The group was renamed the Growth Execution Council (GEC) and repurposed. Its role was to make sure that Corning avoided the likelihood that the downturn would seriously damage its commitment to innovation, and the council succeeded in this. Even in this situation, top management's commitment to innovation did not falter. Corning's core competencies, in particular, were kept intact, and investment in R&D was maintained at roughly 10% of revenue.

Leading from the Top – Always

Since its inception, the GEC – and its earlier incarnation the GSC – have benefited from active top management support. When

Jamie Houghton returned as CEO, he was on the council, along with the COO (Weeks), the CTO (Joe Miller), and several of their direct reports. Now CTO David Morse and innovation officer Marty Curran, whom the board elected to the newly created position in 2012, co-chair the group. Curran is a Corning veteran, having been general manager of the optical fiber unit.

The CEO regularly attends GEC meetings and visits the people in the labs at Sullivan Park almost monthly to understand how the various technologies are advancing. A key part of Corning's culture is top management's belief and engagement in its technologies. The council's focus is to support ongoing innovation projects as well as to have an overall view of investment in innovation.

GOVERNING LONG-TERM GROWTH: THE CTC

Corning's radical innovation projects spend more time in the first two stages of the innovation process, under the guidance of the Corporate Technology Council (CTC), which was set up in 2003 to focus on long-term growth. Although it is important in this early stage to make sure that resources are directed to the most promising opportunities, the focus of the CTC is more to support and help than to winnow and decide. Group members are experienced in and knowledgeable about the early stages of innovation. They can help teams to identify the robustness and unique qualities of potential future technologies, and support them in differentiating offerings and building market opportunities.

They often encourage players to look more broadly. For example, they might provide a sense of the IP space for a particular opportunity and encourage teams to explore further on issues where needed. When initiatives are approved for further exploration and work, CTC members continue to provide advice and encouragement, and they often participate in overseeing significant investments until near the end of the second stage, i.e. determining feasibility.

Many of the projects that the CTC is concerned with have emerged from Corning's Strategic Growth Organization (SGO), which includes Project Magellan, the company's front-end exploratory program. The SGO was established in 2002 like a separate business division within R&D to help identify and incubate radical innovations that might develop into new businesses. It was staffed by people with technical experience in NPD and/or market development expertise. Today, it is known as Emerging Markets and Technologies, possibly a more apt description of its current role.

GOING OUTSIDE-IN TO FIND WHAT'S NEXT

> "Some of the best parts of Magellan workshops are the dialogue and debate among our external experts, who come from such widely different fields and often have different points of view."
>
> *Deb Mills, director of early stage marketing, IAPD 2007*

Project Magellan's task is to research attractive markets and promising technologies, especially those that can fill new, as yet unidentified, needs. The focus has recently been broadened to include what Corning calls *adjacencies* – i.e. new markets, purposes, and uses for existing technologies. According to Deb Mills, director of early stage marketing and leader of Magellan, their approach is largely "outside in – teams of marketing and technology professionals systematically look for important systems problems that require a technical or materials solution."[9]

Mills describes their process as "far from linear." It includes "creative collision" between outside thought leaders and internal Corning technologists, scientists, strategists, and business people. Project Magellan workshops, which focus on a market/technology megatrend, bring outside and inside experts together. The outside experts provide specific market or technology knowledge, or informed points of view on social or technology trends. Magellan project teams use white papers to screen potential themes, and spend four to six months assessing those that they deem the most promising. The content and form of the white papers is prescribed in order to make it easier to compare different possibilities, and teams use *tools and frameworks* to allow them to put the information in a common format.

Hands-on Governance and Top Management Oversight for Multi-functional Teams

Although Corning regards both the CTC and the GEC as governance bodies, these two councils play a role in innovation that is often more hands-on than governance functions in other companies. Cross-functionality is the norm at Corning – teams that develop products include at a minimum one person from marketing and one from technology. The Magellan teams include strategic marketing and early stage technology members who pair up to help develop the projects. The CTC's role is to support Magellan's ability to develop these market opportunities and new technologies so that they can provide an avenue for future innovation. These opportunities often require Corning to take a new business focus, which is a key reason that early oversight and support must be provided at the corporate level.

The CTC, which was started by then CTO Joe Miller, is now – like the GEC – co-chaired by CTO Dave Morse and the innovation officer Marty Curran. Other members of the team include the senior vice presidents of research, development, and engineering – all three the CTO's direct reports. The vice president of legal affairs and the group responsible for mergers and acquisitions also sit on the CTC, alongside the two heads of Project Magellan – Deb Mills and Daniel Ricoult.

> "In 161 years, Corning has been through recessions, depressions, world wars, industry meltdowns, and numerous evolutions driven by changing markets. Corning is no stranger to tough times, and the leadership team has worked hard to ensure that the company is stronger than any challenge we face."
>
> *Wendell Weeks, CEO. 2012 Corning Annual Report. Source: http://www.corning. com/assets/0/15/19/59/ 133/3BDCF1B8-CF5E-429B-8BE3-E2F4C 5197000.pdf*

CORNING'S INNOVATION RECIPE[10]

On April 25, 2002, Houghton gave his first address to shareholders since his return as the company's chairman and CEO. In his talk,

Houghton sounded two chords: Corning's technology leadership and his commitment to the company. "We must remember that technology and innovation are at the heart of this company's future, a future we will never allow to be jeopardized."[11]

Corning's experience after the telecom bust motivated it to reenergize its commitment to radical growth through innovation. In reflecting on past cycles of innovation, leadership spelled out the DNA of, or the recipe for, the company's culture of innovation. This recipe includes deep understanding of a specific technology combined with the identification of customers' difficult systems problems. Corning's objective, in using this recipe, is to increase the number of large new businesses it initiates each decade.

In his role as director of corporate innovation effectiveness, Bruce Kirk is responsible for developing and deploying the current innovation process, as well as defining next generation processes. Employee education and training and global benchmarking are also part of his remit. At the IAPD Roundtable on Innovation Governance in 2009, he enumerated the following critical success factors that he and his team had extracted after considering Corning's R&D history:

- Belief in the power of technology
- Sustained leadership commitment
- Real understanding of what Corning was capable of
- Connected to customers and big problems
- Took big but well understood risks
- A steady stream of successes.

A diagram of core competencies reminiscent of the one Gerretsen used back in 2002 depicts the growth and emergence of what Corning can do and has done with its core substance, glass. These reflections, held at the highest levels of the company, yield Corning's *innovation recipe*, and the recipe drives strategic actions.[12]

PATIENT MONEY: INVESTING FOR THE FUTURE

Corning is a publicly traded company, but its way of doing business sometimes looks more like a privately held one. Its willingness to shift from one "age" to another and the exploration of the "white spaces" between established technologies have sometimes made its pattern of growth quite "bumpy." It has often preferred to take chances on long-term growth opportunities instead of ensuring stock performance in the short term. Nonetheless, its stock performance over the long haul continues to be excellent.

According to Henderson and Reavis, "Innovation at Corning has always meant being willing to make significant, sustained investments knowing that the payback would likely be well into the future. Internally this is known as 'patient money'." [13]

Patient money has played a role through Corning's history – the long-term view of the investment in optical fiber is a good example. Significantly, patient money does not imply that Corning will be willing to continue to invest in projects that are not likely to be successful in the market; it does, however, give innovators confidence that their work will be supported even if the payoff time seems long. It may take anything from seven to 15 years, or even more, to get innovations to market on a large scale.

Patient money also means that Corning will invest in projects when money is tight. "In 2001, the company approved the appropriations request for a $250 million new factory for the diesel [particulate filter] business at a time when the telecom business was crashing and the emission regulations for 2007 were not yet in place." [14]

THE ROLE OF INFORMATION IN GOVERNING INNOVATION

Corning divides its time horizons into *today*, *tomorrow*, and *beyond*. *Today* focuses on expanding existing businesses; *tomorrow* anticipates business needs; *beyond* engages the research community in trying to expand core competencies for breakout businesses. Each is funded independently in order to maintain development of the longer-term areas and resist the temptation to divert funds from *tomorrow* and *beyond* to *today*.

"But it's also critical for senior leadership to understand what the people in the lab are doing. Launching a product shouldn't be like having a gauntlet to run, but rather having a series of people holding water for the person running the marathon, getting behind them, coaching them, and participating with them. Personally, I've always believed that the function of technology management is to enable those people. We work for them. We should make sure that the smartest minds we have can succeed. This includes knowing what they are doing, giving them resources, and exposing them to the needs of relevant industries."

Interview with David Morse, CTO, adapted and reprinted with permission from "The Gorilla of Agile Business" by William J. Holstein from the strategy+business website (http://www.strategy-business. com/article/00192?gko= 589bd), published by Booz & Company Inc. Copyright ©

The company has a set of well-developed processes for gathering and sharing information. It uses business/technology roadmaps and what it calls *event mapping* to allow it to show *today, tomorrow,* and *beyond* visually – and at a glance. Emerging Markets and Technologies continuously maps the landscape, both internally and externally. Event maps bring in technical trend analysis and anticipation of new waves of innovation and opportunity domains in a time horizon that provides for planning and response. Product and technology roadmaps allow planners to link opportunity with capacity and create specific plans for resource allocation to close the gap between opportunity and reality. The existence of a clear understanding of its science and material assets allows Corning to plan how to move into future opportunities. In his presentation on technology road mapping at the 47th IAPD Workshop in 2007, Kirk emphasized that the key to effective portfolios is their link with ongoing business practices.[15]

CONSTANTLY EVOLVING INNOVATION PRACTICES

Corning has never been content to rest on its laurels where innovation processes are concerned. It first implemented an explicit innovation process in 1987, based on Robert Cooper's then new stage-gate™ process. The process was customized for the company after analyzing around a hundred of its most successful projects to identify their key success factors, which enabled them to draw up guidelines for its model. Once again, Corning's top management commitment to innovation was evident. For roll-out, the management committee was trained first, followed by division general managers and their employees, and then the project teams themselves. This meant that everyone was quickly up to speed on the whole innovation process.

The company now employs an ongoing practice of *continuous improvement*. For example, innovation effectiveness facilitators constantly interact with the innovation teams to understand what improvements to their system might deliver more value. Some of the facilitators are experts in understanding specialty areas such as value propositions, manufacturing process development, and commercialization, and they are called in to help when needed by the other facilitators. The innovation processes make it possible to combine multiple competencies in the service of discovery and learning, and – as we have seen above – multi-functionality is a key part of how innovators at Corning work together.

LOOKING TO THE FUTURE

To stay young – or *toujours young*, to borrow LeMoine's earlier description – Corning must remain alert to the dynamics that play around its core. It has achieved this by constantly monitoring its competencies against market opportunity, by developing new scientific and technological capabilities, by widely investigating markets in which its competencies might provide value, and by identifying key partners that might extend its ability to enter any of these areas. As we have seen, the core is not depicted as separate areas that meet different criteria, as is often the case in other companies. Instead, by presenting the core as a set of overlapping circles, innovators and decision makers are encouraged to speculate on how these different circles might interact to create new uses and open new areas of exploration.

HOW WILL THE GOVERNANCE OF INNOVATION STAY FRESH?

As we have seen, the governance of innovation was not invented overnight at Corning. It has been integrated into the practices and culture of the company since the beginning, becoming more explicit – i.e. overseen by named councils – only quite recently. The design of the governance practices included dialogue among the people involved, work with a consulting firm, and a series of templates, all of which encouraged participants to think deeply about the steps they were taking and to focus on the most important issues. The top management team has not been reluctant to make changes where it sees problems and the operation of the councils has already been altered in some ways.

Corning's leaders' level of hands-on engagement with project teams is impressive. It will be interesting to see how these practices might evolve in the coming years, but one thing seems sure: Corning's leaders will remain committed to innovation and will use their experience and expertise to ensure, to the best of their ability, that those who are responsible for carrying out the actual work of innovation get the best support possible.

One thing that will not change is the inevitability of change itself. According to Charlie Craig, senior vice president of administration and operations; science and technology, Corning's innovation governance is adapting again to changing markets and technologies – "faster paced markets, shorter product development life cycles, and intense technology competition." In response to the CEO's exhortation in late 2012 to pursue agile innovation, Corning must now take into account the need for "dramatic strategic changes to accelerate innovation," which are necessary to achieve near-term growth in consumer electronics, as well as the "significant change in approach" that the soaring growth in Corning's Gorilla® Glass is demanding. To date it has been embedded on 1 billion devices worldwide.

Corning's long history of innovation success provides it with the culture, the practices, and the ongoing commitment to make it work yet again, and the innovation governance structure and processes implemented in the early part of the century are providing a foundation for the necessary adaptations today.

NOTES

[1] In this chapter we draw on presentations by Corning employees at a number of International Association for Product Development (IAPD) Workshops and information from the Corning website (www.corning.com). Reproduced with permission from Corning Incorporated.

[2] Corning seems to use the terms R&D (research and development), R, D & E (research, development and engineering), and S&T (science and technology) interchangeably.

[3] This chapter also references a case prepared by Rebecca M. Henderson and Cate Reavis, *Corning Incorporated: The Growth and Strategy Council*, copyright 2008; revised April 15, 2009, Sloan School of Management (hereafter H&R).

[4] Jacques LeMoine, Sustained Innovation: How Companies Foster Innovative Cultures, IAPD Workshop #34, March 2001, Peachtree, Georgia.

[5] The 37th meeting of the IAPD, Seabrook Island, South Carolina. The title of Gerretesen's talk was "Core Competencies at Corning – Realizing Strategic Intent – Positioning for the Future." Gerretsen joined the company in 1997 as manager of surface and interface technology at Corning's Research Center in Fontainebleau, France (FRC).

[6] Jacques LeMoine, interview.

[7] H&R, p. 14.

[8] From Corning website. Source: http://www.corning.com/investor_relations/corporate_governance/our_leadership/Wendell_Weeks.aspx.

[9] Deb Mills, Early Stage Opportunity Identification and Development: Using Early Stage Teams to Link Market and Technology Together, IAPD Workshop #47, January 2007, Coral Gables, FL.

[10] The text in this section draws on a 2009 interview with Bruce Kirk in "The Innovators: Conversations on the Cutting Edge," http://www.innovate1st-str.com/newsletter/february2009/BruceKirk.pdf, as well as Kirk's presentation at the IAPD Executive Roundtable on Innovation Governance, September 2009, the Harley Davidson Museum, Milwaukee, WI.

[11] Press release, 2002, Corning Incorporated Annual Shareholder Meeting. Source: http://investor.shareholder.com/corning/secfiling.cfm?filingID=24741-02-22.

[12] Bruce Kirk, Innovation Governance and Continuous Improvement – Creating an Environment for Effective Innovation, IAPD Roundtable on Innovation Governance, 2009.

[13] H&R, p. 13.

[14] Ibid.

[15] Bruce Kirk, Road Mapping to Link Business Strategy, Market Opportunity, and Product Evolution, IAPD Workshop #47, Linking Product/Market & Technology Strategies, June 2007, Niagara on the Lake, Ontario, Canada.

CHAPTER 9

APPOINTING INDIVIDUAL INNOVATION CHAMPIONS

Example 1 – Nestlé's Innovation Governance Model: CTO in Partnership with Business Heads

A quarter of the companies who participated in our survey have entrusted overall responsibility for innovation to a single individual, a high level innovation champion. This person can be either the most senior representative of the technical functions – we call it the CTO/CRO governance model – or a dedicated senior innovation manager or chief innovation officer – which we refer to as the CIO governance model.

In describing these two models in Chapter 5, we emphasized the main structural difference between them, i.e. the fact that CTOs/CROs maintain important corporate functional responsibilities at top management level alongside their innovation governance duties, whereas CIOs tend to be 100% dedicated to their innovation governance mission. This difference can in fact be marginal, since many if not most CTOs consider innovation to be their core mission, and some CIOs may oversee the technical functions in their organization. In theory, CIOs may also define their mission and innovation more broadly than the more traditional CTOs or CROs, who tend to focus mainly on technological and product or process innovations. But again, some CTOs, particularly when they sit at top management level, as at Nestlé, think beyond technology and see themselves as and behave like new business sponsors.

To illustrate these two champion-driven models, we shall describe the governance approach chosen by two innovative companies – the world's largest food group, Swiss giant Nestlé, and Dutch life sciences and materials sciences company, DSM. Nestlé has chosen to give the ultimate responsibility for governing innovation to its CTO. DSM has appointed a fully dedicated CIO with the mission to stimulate the development of new businesses. Even though there are differences in the scope of these leaders' responsibilities, both are perceived as the *leaders in charge* for all aspects of innovation in their company. But of course, all of them operate in close partnership with their business colleagues.

THE WORLD'S LEADING NUTRITION, HEALTH, AND WELLNESS COMPANY

Nestlé, one of Europe's oldest food companies, is also the world's largest with sales in 2012 of CHF92.2 billion (over US$98 billion). Given its size, the company's organic growth rate of close to 6% in 2012 is commendable, particularly in an industry that seldom expands more than 2 to 3% per year. And with a 15% trading operating profit on sales, it ranks among the most profitable of its peers.

With more than 80 global and regional brands, Nestlé is present – and often the market leader – in a broad number of product categories. Its product portfolio reads like a list of supermarket processed food departments: baby food, bottled water, cereals, chocolate and confectionery, coffee, culinary specialties, chilled and frozen food, dairy, drinks, ice cream, pet care, sports nutrition, weight management, and so on. In addition, the company has strong positions in food service and healthcare nutrition.

Not surprisingly for a global company of such a size, for most of its businesses Nestlé combines a highly decentralized market organization with a relatively centralized approach to strategic innovation, operations, and R&D. Each geographical market head enjoys a great deal of autonomy in product portfolio and local market operations under the supervision of his/her zone director. Nestlé is split into three broad geographic zones: Europe; the Americas and Caribbean; and Asia, Oceania, Africa, and the Middle East. But product strategies are handled by a number of centrally located strategic business unit (SBU) leaders, who report to an executive vice president in charge of all SBUs as well as the strategic aspects of marketing and sales. Similarly, all operations are managed centrally under the supervision of an executive vice president for operations and "Globe" (Nestlé's resource planning system). All R&D and innovation activities are supervised by an executive vice president, who is also CTO and head of innovation, technology, research and development.

In addition to its geographically based businesses, Nestlé operates a number of globally managed businesses like Nestlé Waters, Nestlé Nutrition, Nespresso, Nestlé Professional (its business for catering customers), and Nestlé Health Science. These organizations enjoy a greater level of autonomy in their operations and resources than other Nestlé businesses. Some of them are represented in the executive board by their respective head or CEO. Nespresso, while technically run like a globally managed business, is reporting to the head of strategic business units, marketing and sales, a member of the executive board. The company has also established a number of joint ventures, in both food and beverages, like Cereal Partners Worldwide (with General Mills), Beverage Partners Worldwide (with Coca-Cola), and Dairy Partners of America (with Fonterra), as well as in pharmaceuticals (with L'Oréal).

Nestlé is one of the most innovative companies in the rather traditional and slow-moving food industry, as illustrated by the enormous success of its Nespresso coffee system and the inroads it is making into the emerging market of science-based, personalized nutritional solutions. In fact, it was to leverage its powerful R&D capabilities and meet new societal demands that Nestlé redefined itself as a "nutrition, health, and wellness company." *Innovation and renovation* – as radical and incremental innovations are known within the company – are at the heart of Nestlé's technological and market activities. The company has one of the industry's broadest networks of R&D and technology development facilities, with more than 30 centers worldwide, and it introduces hundreds of new products per year under its many global brands. So, as might be expected, Nestlé's top management pays a lot of attention to the governance of innovation, a key corporate priority.

One of Nestlé's most popular and successful recent innovations, the Nespresso premium coffee system, illustrates several aspects of the company's innovation governance philosophy, which is characterized by a combination of long-term vision, patient money, strong management championing, consumer quality focus, adaptive persistence, and creative marketing.

GOVERNING INNOVATION AT NESTLÉ: THE NESPRESSO BREAKTHROUGH EXAMPLE[1]

Starting as an R&D-led Project with a Long Incubation Phase

In 2012 Nespresso was a fast-growing global business, with sales exceeding $3.8 billion, 8300 employees and a high margin level. It also enjoyed a premium profile image and a wide degree of brand recognition. Yet, most people do not know that it took 16 years – from 1980 to 1996 – for the project to break even. During this time, Nestlé's top management kept supporting and funding the project, despite many internal critics and marketing uncertainties.

Nestlé had bought the high-pressure coffee extraction technology that led to the Nespresso system from Geneva's Battelle Institute in 1974, but no one worked on it for several years. Then, the coffee R&D center in Orbe, Switzerland, decided to design a new espresso system using this proprietary technology. The idea was to add value to a commodity like coffee and create a unique taste experience by packing coffee in hermetically sealed aluminum capsules and extracting the flavor in specially designed high-pressure steam machines. Spurred on by their strong belief in the concept, a number of champions in R&D worked for several years to solve all the main technical problems. They ultimately developed a full system – comprising a patented machine and proprietary capsules – with a premium taste and, importantly in an espresso, an appealing *crema*, the visually distinctive creamy foam on the coffee's surface. The Swiss manufacturer Turmix produced the first machines for Nestlé, which maintained complete control over machine design and the intellectual property of the system.

Nestlé's food service division saw an opportunity for the new system in the Swiss restaurant market. But a market test performed in 1982 proved disappointing. The system was too slow and could not accommodate several cups at the same time, a typical restaurant requirement. Besides, the cost per cup was too expensive, at least compared with large institutional Italian espresso machines. So, the idea was abandoned in favor of the *office coffee* sector. A distributor of appliances present in the Swiss office coffee market was approached to distribute the Nespresso system (machines and capsules) in the institutional market.

Championing the Project at Top Level and Protecting It

Nestlé's top management had followed the project with a combination of skepticism on the part of some members and interest on the part of others – like Camillo Pagano, executive vice president in charge of several worldwide strategic product divisions and business units.

Conscious of the unique nature of the Nespresso system within the group, in June 1986 management decided to create a separate company and appointed one of its members at its head to market the new system. At first the company was called Nestlé Coffee Specialties (NCS) before the Nespresso name was adopted. This move, it was felt, would allow the new business to be independent of the powerful

> "I saw this contraption in Orbe that somebody said was going to be fantastic. I discovered that the R&D team had developed this system without even really talking to the marketing side. There is no doubt that technical development can bring innovation. But internally, there was a lot of skepticism about the possibility to commercialize Nespresso. The business was physically moved out of Nestlé so that it could establish credibility and so that it didn't have to fight against all the company's rules."
>
> *Camillo Pagano, former executive board member*

coffee business unit and its competing Nescafé brand. It would also allow Nespresso to develop its unique identity. From that moment, the business stayed under top management scrutiny.

The system was tested in several markets for office coffee machines in Switzerland, Italy, and Japan, but with disappointing results. This, combined with quality problems with the machine, led some members of the top management team to suggest dropping the project. But a number of champions in the same team defended the system. Camillo Pagano was among the most enthusiastic Nespresso advocates, arguing convincingly that the quality of a cup of Nespresso was beyond all comparisons – and as a true Italian, he obviously knew a lot about espresso. He was strongly backed by several other members of the top management team, including Peter Brabeck-Letmathe, who was senior vice president in charge of a large worldwide division and who became Nestlé's CEO in June 1997. Another leading advocate was Rupert Gasser, executive vice president in charge of technology, production, environment, and R&D. All three strongly believed in the concept while recognizing that the office market might not be the right one. So in 1988, management hired an "outsider," i.e. an entrepreneur with a strong commercial and marketing track record, to help market Nespresso.

Backing an Entrepreneur with Marketing Flair

The new Nespresso team was convinced that Nespresso could have strong potential in the household market provided it targeted affluent consumers with discerning taste. The growing market for expensive espresso machines and the trend for gourmet and specialty coffee chains indicated that espresso coffee was becoming an appealing drink with the social elite. They therefore proposed a change in strategy and obtained management's green light to target the Swiss premium household market. Despite grim market research data, which the Nespresso team embellished somewhat, Nestlé's management backed the new team and its strategy.

Since the outlook for selling Nespresso in supermarkets appeared uncertain and unattractive, the Nespresso team conceived a direct marketing approach by creating a Nespresso Club, with customers ordering via the phone or web. This direct channel approach is what ultimately made Nespresso extremely successful. The external entrepreneur became the CEO of Nespresso and additional machine manufacturers were licensed, sales boomed, and the company extended operations progressively in all European markets. Breakeven was achieved in 1996 and Nespresso became the fastest-growing business unit in the Nestlé organization. By 1998, it had paid back its entire investment and the company was starting to develop a version of the system for professional applications, for example in offices.

Nestlé's top management members followed the progress of Nespresso with interest. They challenged the CEO regularly but abstained from interfering in operations. They all accepted that the new company needed a maximum amount of freedom to continue experimenting with the new channel strategy and brand building efforts. To some extent, Nestlé's top management accepted the fact that Nespresso would not be run in the traditional Nestlé way.

> "There were not many people in the company who believed in Nespresso – there was a concern that it would distract us from our core business in instant coffee – but our new manager was totally convinced of the opportunity. Nespresso was purposely run at arm's length and not built into Nestlé's main coffee structure. Our CEO challenged him a lot. He found the challenge motivating, he liked it!"
>
> *Rupert Gasser, former executive board member*

> "Nespresso's manager was very demanding of management's time. Like all entrepreneurs, he was insecure. You need to hold an entrepreneur's hand once in a while and give reassurance. Entrepreneurs are particularly keen on this because they are very alone. For me, the responsibility of being a manager is really to deal with the ideas of people. You need to spend a great deal of time with your people, communicating with them."
>
> *Camillo Pagano, former executive board member*

Pagano and Gasser kept in close contact with Nespresso's management team, which they coached regularly. Up to his retirement at the end of 1991, Pagano held what he called "monthly confessionals" with his protégé. These were coaching sessions during which Pagano tried to contain the ebullient dynamism of his entrepreneur while attempting to alleviate some of his relationship problems up and down the organization. The personality of the entrepreneur-manager was indeed quite controversial, both inside and outside Nespresso. He accepted structure when it served his purpose and "helped people to do a good job." He rejected it when "it stopped people from doing crazy things!" But he fought constantly to keep the Nespresso concept alive, sometimes doing things on the edges of Nestlé's organization. Keeping him at the helm of Nespresso for much longer would be an issue now that the company was on a fast growth track.

Changing Management to Build a Professional Organization

Nestlé's top management team was convinced that the time had come to change management at Nespresso. Late in 1997, the company had reached a critical stage in its evolution and needed to build a structure and industrial scale operations that its current entrepreneur-manager could not easily lead. So, after the entrepreneur left, he was replaced by an experienced Nestlé leader, Henk Kwakman, with the mission to spearhead this transformation and build the brand's prestige. By that time, all the skeptics within Nestlé's top management had been converted to Nespresso's business model. Brabeck, who was then Nestlé's new CEO, rapidly saw the corporate benefits of leveraging Nespresso's premium image. He also liked the direct distribution model, which allowed Nespresso to become independent of the trade and hence to generate healthy margins that could be reinvested in brand building. He set an ambitious target for the new management team: Take the business from CHF150 million, where it stood in 1997, to CHF1 billion within the next 10 years. That target was largely exceeded thanks in part to additional major innovations in other key business dimensions (distribution, client management, machine design, leveraging of digital technology, etc.) that Kwakman and his successors introduced. They contributed significantly to transforming the business in successive phases.

Drawing Management Lessons

The Nespresso story may have irrevocably changed the way managers at Nestlé look at innovation. First, it demonstrated the market power and consumer appeal of branded beverage systems, consisting of a purpose-designed, proprietary machine and exclusive consumables in the form of patented capsules and pods. Second, it made management realize that sustainable competitive advantages often result from multiple or combined innovations. Food manufacturers have traditionally considered that innovation is purely a matter of new products, in terms of concept, dietary profile, organoleptic qualities, and packaging convenience, combined with smart marketing positioning. Certainly, Nespresso's success can clearly be ascribed to unique product and taste attributes and clever consumer targeting, but it is also due to the innovative business model and novel channel strategy. The concept of mutually reinforcing innovations has been extended by the various Nespresso CEOs who have run the business since Kwakman. In the past decade, besides growing fast, Nespresso has embarked on a series of additional innovations across the value chain, namely in:

- sustainable coffee farming policies;
- coffee quality and choice, with the selection of ever more specialties;
- new machine designs and machine features, including for the institutional market;
- home delivery and client services;
- distribution channels and service, with the opening of over 300 Nespresso boutiques;
- brand communications, with the hiring of George Clooney as main spokesperson;
- information technology tools and processes for e-business and call center management.

Thanks to this continuous flow of innovations, management hopes to maintain Nespresso's capsule volume and margins against the combined attacks of generic producers following the expiration of the system's patent protection.

Reflecting on the managerial aspects of this new innovation philosophy, Brabeck commented:

> You can't impose change from the top. You can only create an environment that stimulates change. Many managers in large institutions have been trained to keep things running as they have been. They have learned to comply with an enormous number of detailed procedures and systems. They were taught by experience that they are better off following the expected tracks of routine rather than venturing out into the new and unexpected.
>
> We need to create a climate where there is a certain freedom to fail and where those people who are promoted have made decisions and carried them out, even if they were not always 100% successful. We don't want to advance the careers of those who have never made a mistake because they've never done anything except apply the rules. We have to identify, foster and mentor people who have proven that they are willing to stick their neck out, who made a mistake, learned from the mistake, and are willing to continue taking risks.[2]

LEVERAGING NESPRESSO: THE CREATION OF AN INCUBATOR FOR BEVERAGE SYSTEMS

The success of Nespresso convinced Nestlé's management of the commercial benefits of proprietary beverage systems. Once consumers have bought a particular branded machine, they will of course continue buying the corresponding beverage capsules or pods. The creation in 2010 of Nestlé's System Technology Center (STC) was a move to leverage Nespresso's system development capabilities and introduce new beverage systems. Management recognized that it was important to continue conceiving innovative new beverage systems while letting Nespresso focus mainly on developing its own systems. Indeed, while extending the company's markets geographically, Nespresso's management focused on growing the business worldwide, introducing new machine designs and coffee varieties and opening boutiques in prime locations.

The STC was set up in Orbe, alongside other R&D entities such as Nestlé's product and technology center (PTC) for beverages. A number of Nespresso's research innovation engineers were transferred to the STC, which brought together all system research and most of Nespresso's innovation competences. Alfred Yoakim, a Nespresso veteran who had been with the company since the beginning in 1986, was appointed as head of this new system incubator. Originally, Yoakim was in charge of Nespresso's service organization and establishing the company's customer data management system, after which he became the head of Nespresso's research innovation team.

> "Nespresso was successful because Nestlé's management let the team go to the end of their ideas and they fully championed the project. To continue on this track and launch new systems, we need to identify champions in SBUs who have both power and personal credibility."
>
> *Alfred Yoakim, head of the STC*

With the 2012 expiration date of the company's main system patent approaching, the Nespresso research innovation team started working on a new concept for a multi-beverage system, which was proposed to the Nespresso management team. They turned it down, perceiving it as being incompatible with Nespresso's exclusive, luxury image. But Kwakman, who had since joined Nestlé's large beverage SBU (Nescafé), supported the concept and the research innovation team developed it further over several years. The product appealed to the Nestlé coffee beverage community which was originally quite worried by the threat of Nespresso cannibalizing its lucrative instant coffee business. Once the new concept was finalized, Nestlé decided to launch it in Europe, through the trade, as a multiple coffee variety system under the name Nescafé Dolce Gusto. The new system was very successful and created a new volume segment of the coffee market.

Full of ideas on how to exploit the Nespresso model and introduce new system concepts, Yoakim's research innovation team developed a super-premium tea system that also conflicted with Nespresso's priorities. But once again, Kwakman championed the

> "I believe that we need to develop many different concepts in order to have one that ultimately makes it and wins in the market."
>
> *Alfred Yoakim, head of the STC*

new concept which has since been introduced as Special T. In the same way, working with the nutrition SBU, another Nestlé R&D entity came up with BabyNes, a revolutionary infant formula system based on the Dolce Gusto technology, which has also been introduced in the market.

Today, the STC develops and prototypes a wide range of totally new system concepts each year, for both the consumer and professional markets. Its objective is to stimulate the imagination of the most advanced market companies, for example Japan, and the SBUs concerned in the hope that one such system will be picked up and marketed, as happened with BabyNes. All the while, it continues its innovation and renovation work for its existing system businesses. As one of the centers belonging to Nestlé's broad R&D and innovation organization, the STC is becoming an important innovation source for the company.

Nestlé is keen to maintain a highly innovative yet business-oriented culture within the STC. It encourages the team of innovators, designers, and engineers to remain in touch with the market by doing consumer tests and watching consumer panels react to new concept prototypes.

NESTLÉ'S STRONG TOP MANAGEMENT INVOLVEMENT IN INNOVATION

Nestlé has always benefited from CEOs with a keen interest in innovation. Its previous CEO and current board chairman, Peter Brabeck, was indeed perceived by many at Nestlé and beyond as a visionary and the main innovation driver within the top management team. Brabeck backed important innovations like Nespresso and led the company into the new field of nutrition. He was seconded in his task by Gasser, a strong and experienced head of technology, manufacturing and R&D, who sponsored and coached many innovative projects. Even though Gasser was involved in most large innovation projects as a result of his functional responsibilities, he did not have *innovation* officially in his title like his successor Werner Bauer, executive vice president innovation, technology, research and development.

Since becoming Nestlé's board chairman, Brabeck has kept his strong focus on innovation and, together with current CEO Paul Bulcke, convinced his board to enter into the new area of science-based personalized nutritional solutions. Conscious that Nestlé needed to be able to scientifically justify its claims about the nutritional benefits of these future products, he was instrumental in establishing the Nestlé Institute of Health Sciences – a fundamental research organization – at the Federal Polytechnic Institute of Lausanne, and he chairs its board of directors.

> "Is Peter remaining active in innovation now that he has become board chairman? More than ever! But Nestlé's board of directors doesn't keep involved directly in innovation issues. It reacts by emphasizing the strategic directions of research and it gives them impetus."
>
> *Werner Bauer, executive vice president innovation, technology, and R&D*

Promoting Innovation-oriented Values

Paul Bulcke, Brabeck's successor as Nestlé's CEO, shares the same interest in innovation but with a different management style. He promotes a *global inspiration–local execution* philosophy. One of his primary management objectives is to align energies within his huge global organization – 339,000 employees in more than 150 countries – on a one-page roadmap that puts innovation in a broad strategic perspective. This roadmap details, in Bulcke's own words:

- **What we want to be and do as a company** (Nestlé's mission):
  To be the leader in nutrition, health and wellness, and the industry reference for financial performance, trusted by all stakeholders.
- **How we are going to measure our success** (the Nestlé model):

Through four dynamic drivers: top line (organic growth); bottom line (trading operating profit margin in constant currency); underlying earnings per share in constant currency; and capital efficiency.

- **What we are going to leverage** (Nestlé's competitive advantages):
  Unmatched product and brand portfolio; unmatched research and development capability; unmatched geographic presence; people, culture, values, and attitude.
- **Where we want to focus** (Nestlé's growth drivers):
  A nutrition, health and wellness agenda; emerging markets and popularly positioned products; out-of-home consumption; "premiumization" (value creation).
- **How we are going to do it effectively and efficiently** (Nestlé's operational pillars):
  Consumer engagement (consumers in the middle); bringing products to where consumers are (wherever, whenever, however); operational efficiency; and today's most important pillar: innovation and renovation.[3]

Bulcke spares no effort in ensuring that his roadmap is understood and accepted by the new generation of leaders. He uses the company's management development center near its Vevey headquarters for this purpose. The center trains 2500 future company leaders each year, and Bulcke goes there many times per year to talk to them, emphasize his roadmap, and share his personal philosophy on what he calls "meaningful innovation." In all sessions, he exhorts staff to adopt a long-term approach and to be open minded in order to cope with a rapidly changing world.

> "I like to give examples of extraordinary employee commitment, like what our people did in challenging circumstances such as in Egypt, Syria and in other countries around the world. I also speak about how I embrace big ideas and fight against ego-driven innovation. It doesn't matter who *owns* an innovation. What matters is who makes it happen!"
>
> *Paul Bulcke, CEO*

Continued success in innovation, according to Bulcke, will come from a mindset change. People at Nestlé, he claims, have to understand how they can create value for consumers across the value chain and how they can take waste out of their processes to free up time to enhance that value. To promote this mindset change, he established the Nestlé Continuous Excellence (NCE) program, which is a set of continuous improvement initiatives. So far, the program has reached 220,000 people and helped identify best practices everywhere. It has been credited with unlocking creativity in all functions.

Supporting Innovation Concretely

Bulcke contributes to the company's innovation efforts at three levels: (1) at the board of directors level, (2) at the executive board level, and (3) at the operational level with SBUs, globally managed businesses, geographic zones, and individual markets.

With the support of Brabeck, Bulcke likes to keep innovation on the agenda at board meetings. For example, he has devoted a session to new ideas and new platforms such as the Nestlé Institute of Health Sciences. Once a year the board travels to a foreign country that is important for Nestlé, and he takes directors into the local R&D center to discuss innovation issues.

Innovation is also a regular agenda item for Nestlé's executive board. At each monthly meeting, Bulcke introduces a review of the top 10 or 20 most important corporate innovation projects and launches. And one executive board meeting a year is entirely dedicated to innovation issues, for example a focus on the STC, Nestlé's development unit for beverage systems.

At the operational level, Bulcke plays an active innovation support role in the course of his one-to-one contacts with the head of SBUs, Patrice Bula; the heads of Nestlé's globally managed businesses; and the CTO and innovation chief, Werner Bauer. With them, he emphasizes the importance of taking a broad view on technology platforms (for example, on extrusion technology), on consumer benefit platforms (for example, on obesity or aging), and on geographical needs.

> "Paul drives innovation by his consistent way of making things happen! He keeps asking people about their progress: 'How are you doing with project abc; when will project xyz be rolled out?'"
>
> *Werner Bauer, CTO*

Bulcke also supports the company's innovation agenda during his numerous market visits. He makes a point of reminding all the market heads of the importance of showing a *five-generation product pipeline*, hence being long-term oriented (an aspect that has become a key innovation performance indicator at Nestlé).

In addition, every six months he gathers the heads of Nestlé's 10 to 15 key markets – typically accounting for around 80% of the company's sales – and discusses new ways to face the world with them. And every two years, in the presence of all market heads, he stresses the values he promotes: "Have an open mind; encourage creativity; be part of the solution; promote entrepreneurship!" He also encourages geographic zone and market managers to organize innovation days.

Finally, as CEO, Bulcke has set a number of innovation-oriented priorities for the corporation:

- Evolving Nestlé's product emphasis from mass-produced products to personalized products, systems, and services.
- Making choices, which means being able to cancel projects, since he feels that Nestlé has not always been good at saying no in the past.
- Seeing the opportunity, i.e. challenging people to come up with solutions to consumers' problems.
- Valuing what consumers value, which is linked to the Nestlé Continuous Excellence program.
- Connecting with the wider society by creating shared value, for example through nutrition.
- Developing people and talent (hence his regular participation in Nestlé's management development programs).
- Embracing digital, by creating a *digital acceleration team* with young managers from the markets who pioneer new ideas and leverage social networks.

Sponsoring Radical Innovation at the Top Management Level

Since the creation of Nespresso and Nestlé Nutrition, the company's top management has become deeply involved in developing radical innovations and disruptive technologies. These innovations are often sponsored by lead markets. Nestlé claims to be a consumer benefit-oriented company, and this means that everyone in the organization, including R&D, places the consumer at the heart of the innovation process. However, being *consumer oriented* does not mean being *consumer driven*. In fact, Bulcke very much follows the same approach as his predecessor, Brabeck, who personally pushed for the creation of Nestlé Pure Life, the company's global bottled water brand.

Bulcke encourages the creation of new technology-based and market-oriented ventures, and he makes sure that these projects are personally coached by members of the executive board, himself included. He pushes everyone in the organization to steer consumers into new areas, and provided R&D is linked to the business, it is viewed as the main instrument for creating new value for consumers. The setting up of Nestlé Health Science, which builds on science-based personalized nutrition solutions for chronic diseases at the interface of nutrition and pharmaceuticals, is a good example of science- and technology-based new business creation.

The three new beverage system ventures initiated by Yoakim and the STC and launched starting in 2006 – Nescafé Dolce Gusto, Special T, and BabyNes – illustrate the personal involvement of top management. All three were developed by a special venturing team before being turned into self-standing units. Given their complexity and need for resources, they were – and some continue to be – personally coached by members of the top management team.

> "For me, governing innovation entails a willingness to accept mavericks who make the company progress, and a top management team which is engaged, supports innovators and shows patience."
>
> *Patrice Bula, executive vice president SBUs, marketing, and sales*

As mentioned earlier, Nescafé was interested in Dolce Gusto, but since it could not devote enough time and resources to developing it, it was quickly put under the overall responsibility of the CTO, who personally supervised the development team. The executive board first considered it as an experimental project. But its favorable outlook – it is one of Nestlé's fastest-growing businesses – justified

> "An incubator like STC cannot keep incubating for the sake of it, developing new concepts relentlessly. Its new concepts need to find champions in the business willing to test and launch them, hence the importance of top management's involvement in this process."
>
> *Alfred Yoakim, head of the STC*

creating a special unit within the beverage SBU. Internal observers consider that, without the strong involvement of the executive board – it was one of the 10 key projects regularly reviewed by them – Dolce Gusto would not have made it to the market.

The BabyNes infant formula system has followed the same pattern. Despite the interest expressed by Nestlé Nutrition and given the resource requirements and different business model, this project was entrusted to the CTO who coached it personally, as he did Dolce Gusto. The project is now reaching its roll-out phase and the project leader will become the head of the new BabyNes business within Nestlé Nutrition.

Since its inception in 2008, Special T is supervised by the beverages SBU and reports to the head of SBUs. It is now being rolled out as a full internet-based business.

LINKING R&D TO INNOVATION: THE KEY ROLE OF THE CTO

> "Innovation governance? We don't call it that, but we are doing it at the highest level! How? Through our R&D strategy conference which is aligned with the global business strategy, handled at the executive board level. We have an innovation model; we have an innovation territory; and we have well-defined governance responsibilities."
>
> *Werner Bauer, CTO*

When asked who is in overall charge of innovation in the company, Nestlé managers all point to Bauer, the company's CTO. A senior scientist and university professor in Germany with considerable business experience, Bauer is a member of Nestlé's 13-member executive board. His predecessor, Gasser, was in charge of technology and R&D but also of manufacturing operations, as was Bauer at the start of his tenure. But the job was subsequently split in two to ensure that both sides – the CTO side and the operational side – were managed by dedicated leaders, so Bauer now focuses on technology, R&D, and innovation.

The CTO is officially responsible for overall innovation governance within Nestlé. He is also perceived as an element of continuity in innovation within the company, reflecting the fact that he has occupied his position for a number of years, whereas SBU heads frequently change. He supervises all the company's R&D activities, including the Nestlé Institute of Health Sciences – a fundamental research lab; a central research lab – the Nestlé Research Center (NRC); 32 Product and Technology Centers (PTCs), which conduct product development around the world; and a couple of Centers of Excellence.

To guide the development and deployment of technical resources necessary for the future, Nestlé has established a symmetrical or parallel process between the mechanisms for business governance and those linked to R&D and innovation. On the business side, the global business strategy is discussed and agreed annually at the executive board level; then a market strategy is formulated at the zone and market cluster level and, finally, at the individual market level. All business strategies include an innovation element.

> "The head of SBUs is my counterpart in the strategy process taking place through our R&D conferences. He decides on the *what* of innovation! The *how* is the CTO's job! But we sometimes help the businesses decide on the *what* by indicating to them what is scientifically or technically feasible."
>
> *Werner Bauer, CTO*

On the technology side, an annual R&D strategy conference mirrors and supports the global business strategy. Discussions on technology are then carried out at zone level – typically on portfolio issues – then at market cluster and individual market level for specific projects. Nestlé's globally managed businesses, like Nestlé Waters and Nespresso, do not work through the zone system. They typically enjoy relative freedom in their innovation strategy and route to market, but they depend on the overall Nestlé R&D organization for their technological and R&D resources.

Nestlé's Innovation/Renovation Governance Model

In a $98 billion food and beverage company, even one in which technology plays a critical role, a top level CTO cannot govern innovation by himself. He has to work in close partnership with his business colleagues, namely the head of all the company's SBUs, Patrice Bula, and the heads of the globally managed businesses and joint ventures. They operate as the company's most senior innovation leaders and are part of the company's executive board.

Bula is a key driver of innovation at Nestlé, in full partnership with the CTO and the R&D community. The SBUs that he oversees, including Nespresso, account for about 73% of the company's global sales. SBUs are responsible for globally managed brands, all product categories, and the strategic and marketing staff they employ. They also drive the renovation/innovation process in their categories. In Nestlé terminology, *renovation* deals with incremental product development in existing categories, while *innovation* describes more radical attempts to create new categories, either within the business boundaries or through the creation of new ventures like Nespresso, Dolce Gusto, Special T, and BabyNes.

The heads of the globally managed businesses – Nestlé Nutrition; Nestlé Health Science; Nestlé Waters; Nestlé Professional – play the same role as the head of SBUs for their businesses. They drive all renovation/innovation activities within their businesses with the support of R&D.

> "Most SBU heads are former market heads. They are therefore very much market-oriented, hands-on and very professional. Under them, they have a team of younger marketing specialists who will typically spend some time in a SBU before returning to a market. SBU heads are generally very engaged in innovation. It wouldn't work if they weren't!"
>
> *Patrice Bula, executive vice president SBUs, marketing, and sales*

> "It is the job of our globally managed businesses to allocate responsibilities for innovation the way they want, but their resources are globally managed and report to the CTO. It gives them much faster access to Nestlé's global resources."
>
> *Werner Bauer, CTO*

The bulk of Nestlé's new product development projects proceed through the combined efforts of three complementary parties: SBUs, PTCs, and zone and market management. The Nestlé Research Center is a fourth element that comes into play when totally new technology or new ingredients need to be developed for the new product.

> "R&D, SBUs and markets are the magic triangle at Nestlé. Our common objective with the CTO is to have them fully aligned."
>
> *Patrice Bula, executive vice president SBUs, marketing, and sales*

Being responsible for the product strategy in their category – and innovation is a chapter of every business strategy – SBUs work with the various zone and market managers concerned to define their new product concepts and their specifications.

Two types of annual conferences allow all the market players to share strategic information on innovation and establish the framework within which renovation/innovation activities will take place. These are the global business strategy conferences (GBS) and the market business strategy conferences (MBS).

In the past, Nestlé's market organizations were unevenly involved in specifying the nature and characteristics of new products. This is changing and most are now increasingly active in identifying new product opportunities and helping define product specifications. In fact, the largest market companies have appointed senior business executives by category, and these managers work with the SBU staff, PTCs, and even the NRC on innovation/renovation projects. Some of the larger ones, such as Germany, France, Spain, the USA, and China, have even set up their own innovation board with key local market leaders and high-level corporate members representing the SBUs, R&D, and technical operations involved in innovation projects.

But the key forums in which renovation/innovation projects are discussed and financing decisions are made are the annual R&D conferences mentioned earlier. These one-day events are organized at the level of the SBU or globally managed business. For very large or diverse SBUs, they are held at the level of a large product category. These conferences bring together:

- the CTO and his key staff, including the head of the NRC;
- the executive vice president SBUs, marketing and sales and his staff, or the heads of the globally managed businesses concerned;
- representatives from the operational side, including manufacturing;
- key members of the management team of the SBU or globally managed business concerned;
- representatives from key markets, like Japan, France, China, and the USA.

Discussions during these conferences relate to Nestlé's so-called five-generation pipeline.

Managing a Five-generation Pipeline

Nestlé uses the idea of a five-generation pipeline to map its renovation and innovation activities. Under this concept, SBUs and globally managed businesses are asked to propose, in a bottom–up mode, their plans for incremental renovation activities. These plans typically cover the first three years of the cycle. At the same time, they are encouraged to come up with visionary ideas to create new categories – real innovations in Nestlé's terminology – in years four and five. The role of R&D and the NRC is both to support and to challenge the proposed pipeline and, ultimately, to accept funding projects to test the new concepts proposed for years four and five.

The process followed is a very classical one. It addresses three questions:

- What is needed for the consumer? (Responses come from SBUs, the markets and R&D.)
- What is technically possible? (Responses come from R&D and technical operations.)
- What is economically achievable? (Responses come from SBUs, markets, R&D, and technical operations.)

Geographic zones and individual markets – the ultimate profit and loss centers of the company – have operational responsibility for their territory, including in innovation. This means that they

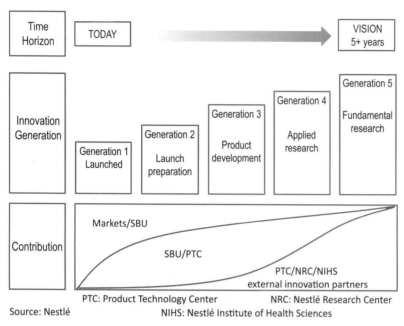

Figure 9.1: Innovation/Renovation: Building a Robust Pipeline

launch the products defined by the SBUs and developed by the PTCs, and they commit to volumes and profits.

The structure of the five-generation pipeline and the various players is shown in Figure 9.1.

Nestlé has also established at least two processes that are applied globally for the entire company, for both renovation and innovation projects. The first is the Nestlé Product Development and Introduction (NPDI) process. It specifies the various tasks, responsibilities, and decision gates to be followed from product concept to launch. The second is the internally famous "60/40+ rule" process, which ensures that all new products meet rigorous standards for nutrition and consumer preference. Products are blind-tested with consumer panels, and at least 60% of the people must prefer the Nestlé product over the competitors'. Next to the sensory preference (60/40), each product under development is expected to deliver at least nutritional adequacy according to the "Nestlé Nutritional Profiling System" and "NF criteria" (Nutritional Foundation – determining the maximum content of public health-relevant ingredients such as sugar and salt, in line with international reference values). New products are developed to achieve NF and, where possible and meaningful, to achieve a "nutritional competitive advantage" – i.e. a nutritional superiority vis-à-vis competitors' products. Products having this characteristic in addition to a sensory 60/40 advantage, are given a 60/40+ rating.

Encouraging Innovation Partnerships

Given its unique technology resources, Nestlé has long been tempted to rely on its own forces for all of its technology and product development initiatives, and indeed many of its most successful innovations have been developed internally. But the rapid expansion of new scientific and technological developments in all areas – ingredients, processing, packaging, and the like – and the company's ambitious move into totally new fields like nutrition showed management the limitations of this traditional self-sufficiency. In the early 2000s, Brabeck in his role as CEO challenged this internally focused attitude and, like many companies, Nestlé began following the *open innovation trend*, which it refers to as *innovation partnerships*.

> "Upstream partners represent early, mid and mature stages of innovation. Typically, these partners come from universities, start-up companies and inventors. They also include large industrial partners (i.e. ingredient and packaging suppliers). Downstream partnerships occur with a select group of large customers (i.e. retailers), with the goal of identifying innovation based on shoppers' insights and having strong consumer relevance."
>
> *Helmut Traitler, former VP innovation partnerships Nestlé (Nestec)*

The new innovation partnership approach[4] was launched in 2006 with upstream partners and it rapidly spread to other activities and downstream partners. At the same time, management launched and promoted its *sharing is winning* philosophy to change internal and external attitudes to partnership. As a result, not-invented-here reflexes have subsided.

Nestlé's CTO supervises all technology partnership activities and the vice president of innovation partnerships reports to him. Besides orchestrating partnership deals, he is responsible for a number of activities like intellectual property management and the development of new systems, which often involve machine suppliers. As for product development with the NPDI, partnership development is a structured process that now works quite smoothly.

Developing Competencies and Attitudes

Nestlé is convinced that management attitudes must support innovation and this is why the CTO is seen as a mentor to his direct reports. Attitudes within R&D must change to support ongoing innovation efforts. This, Nestlé believes, can be achieved at least in part through training. To this end, every marketing course offered by the company keeps two seats open for R&D members, typically senior product managers.

> "The CTO's mission is the continuous improvement of innovation. This means working on strategic alignment, processes, competencies and attitudes. We started ten years ago by trying to make R&D more business-centric. Besides providing extensive training, we work on R&D career management."
>
> Werner Bauer, CTO

Nestlé also offers R&D staff three career management options. Over time, every member of the R&D community can decide to follow one of three possible career paths: (1) become an expert in his/her discipline; (2) follow the project management route; or (3) prepare for a general management job and learn to manage others. Each route leads to a similar level of compensation and recognition for the highest performers.

Building Innovation-supporting Organizational Mechanisms

The CTO is supported by three mechanisms within the R&D community: A network of R&D coordination managers, a network of experts, and an innovation acceleration team.

The *network of R&D coordination managers* consists of R&D managers embedded in each business unit. These managers, who are generally quite experienced business-wise, are supposed to facilitate innovation. They manage the interface between the commercial side of the business and the R&D community. They focus on a number of project aspects dealing with *what* issues, such as quality assurance, regulatory activities and the like, whereas the head of the PTC serving that particular business handles the *how* side of the development. These R&D coordination managers report to their SBU head with a dotted line to the CTO, with whom they spend a fair amount of time. This keeps the CTO fully informed of most project issues. The innovation management function offers senior R&D managers valuable business experience, so it is not surprising that some of them are ultimately chosen to manage a business or a PTC.

Besides R&D coordination managers, Nestlé has set up a *network of experts*, whose task is to develop and share knowledge on topics that are important for the corporation. These experts, numbering about 70, focus on the cutting edge of sciences and technologies that are relevant for Nestlé. They are part of and maintain their job in the R&D community but "meet" regularly in *expertise team rooms*. Alongside these technical experts, business heads have created their own network of business specialists – for example, people who know everything about a product like coffee. Generally, Nestlé's experts are motivated by the recognition they receive from management. Each year, a gala dinner brings all experts together, and awards are presented for exceptional performance in knowledge development and management.

Nestlé's *innovation acceleration team* consists of a relatively small number of young, generally high potential managers, who help business units go from concept to market with the objective of making most innovations transferable. Like many consumer goods companies, Nestlé needs to have a strong focus on local markets. This means that an innovation developed for a given market, if left on its own, may not be compatible with other markets, even though the concept could easily be transferable. It is therefore the role of the innovation acceleration team to intervene at the concept development stage to ensure that the needs and peculiarities of other relevant markets are taken into account. Members of that network act as internal innovation consult-ants. They operate according to a structured handbook that specifies how they should work.

> "It is a great weapon, for a CTO to have a team of tal-ented youngsters working on critical projects! The only problem is that you lose them as they are hired as business managers!"
> *Werner Bauer, CTO*

The innovation acceleration team, which includes about 20 managers working on around 20 projects per year, has now reached its fourth generation of managers. Some of these internal consult-ants have been promoted to important management positions within Nestlé, including head of the NRC.

ADDRESSING NESTLÉ'S CRITICAL INNOVATION CHALLENGES

From a content point of view, Nestlé is readying itself to address major societal issues related to its vision and ambition of becoming known as *the* nutrition, health, and wellness company. These issues deal with global phenomena like the aging population and the problem of obesity. Addressing these systemic problems requires building totally new integrative capabilities, i.e. from scientific knowledge and clinical testing to functional ingredient develop-ment and targeted product development and commercialization. The creation of the Nestlé Institute of Health Sciences on the campus of the Swiss Federal Polytechnic Institute of Lausanne was a step in the right direction, but many more steps need to be taken to meet these objectives.

From an innovation governance point of view, there are two important challenges to be addressed: (1) business managers' temp-tation to decentralize R&D, and (2) the need to maintain an emphasis on disruptive innovations.

Challenges to the Current R&D Organization and Resource Allocation

To an outsider, Nestlé's R&D organization might appear highly decentralized, given that it is based on many labs, research centers, excellence centers, and product and technology development centers – the 32 PTCs scattered around the world. These centers mostly work on projects decided by the businesses – as noted earlier, businesses decide on the *what*. But R&D decides how these centers work and, to a large extent, allocates their resources. Indeed, it is the CTO's responsibility to propose an overall R&D budget to the executive board. In addition, Nestlé's R&D resource allocation rules specify that spending decisions are as follows:

- 50% of the overall R&D spending is decided by the business units;
- 25% is decided by geographic zones and key markets; and
- 25% is decided by R&D, i.e. by the CTO.

Nestlé has to some extent given its R&D organization a considerable amount of freedom on where and on what to spend its money. This freedom is, naturally, challenged by the business organization and Bauer is afraid that some Nestlé business managers might like to control a much bigger share of the company's R&D resources. But he defends the current system that allows top management to initiate strategic projects. The current system ensures that all businesses pay the same amount for R&D to the corporation, even though some of them, by their very nature, require a larger share of resources.

> "The more people believe in innovation as a growth driver, the more they want to control their resources!"
>
> *Werner Bauer, CTO*

A second issue for the current R&D organization is that some of the fastest-growing markets would like to have exclusivity on their R&D labs' activities, which could lead to a fragmentation of R&D. For example, China might want to have 100% control over the R&D lab in Shanghai, a center that now serves all markets in Asia and Oceania. This, Bauer believes, would signal the end of the traditional role of PTCs as excellence centers serving multiple regions and markets.

Challenges to Keep on Introducing Disruptive Innovations

Given the conservative nature of their markets, food companies are not traditionally geared to introducing disruptive innovations. Nestlé is probably a notable exception in the industry considering the many firsts it has scored over the years, such as Nescafé instant coffee, based on revolutionary freeze-drying technology, and more recently Nespresso, which has become the ultimate premium coffee system.

The issue is how Nestlé can maintain its past rhythm of introducing radical innovations or – to use its own vocabulary – how to ensure that its current system leads to true innovations, as opposed to mere renovations. This challenge is on the mind of all executive board members, starting with the CEO, Bulcke. At Nestlé, people who need money to work on a revolutionary idea will probably not get it from the business side, which tends to be too busy with current product pipelines. They will have to find a new source of funding for risky undertakings and they are likely to find it from the CTO, or even from the CEO, who is financing the second generation of Nespresso systems.

In summary, Nestlé appears to have succeeded in implementing a well-functioning innovation governance model. The model works as a comprehensive *system* and its performance can be ascribed to at least five factors:

1. The top management team, starting with the CEO, is very involved in most of the critical facets of innovation, particularly with the promotion of innovation-enhancing values and attitudes and the coaching of new ventures.
2. Thanks to its superb R&D network and its five-generation pipeline process, Nestlé has achieved a good balance between incremental renovations and radical, category-building innovations.

3. The system builds on a smooth partnership between an experienced, business-oriented, and entrepreneurial CTO[5] and business leaders who value technology for its ability to introduce game-changing products.

4. These leaders have managed to involve all organizational and geographical units of the company in planning and implementing innovations through a participative process of strategy and R&D conferences.

5. Everyone in the company, including members of its scientific and engineering community, is encouraged to listen for the consumer's voice and to work toward ensuring that Nestlé deserves its reputation as the world's premier "nutrition, health, and wellness company."

NOTES

[1]This story includes large extracts from the business case "Innovation and Renovation: The Nespresso Story" by Joyce Miller and Kamran Kashani, Ref. IMD-5-0543, distributed by www.thecasecentre.org. It is also based on a conversation with Alfred Yoakim, a member of the Nespresso team since 1986. All the quotes are from the IMD case.

[2]Source: "Innovation and Renovation: The Nespresso Story" by Joyce Miller and Kamran Kashani, ref. IMD-5-0543 distributed by www.thecasecentre.org.

[3]Compiled from a videotaped speech by Paul Bulcke at the 40th St. Gallen Symposium in 2010 and from Nestlé's 2012 annual report.

[4]Refer to "Creating Successful Innovation Partnerships" by Helmut Traitler and I. Sam Saguy of Nestlé in *Food Technology*, March 2009, www.ift.org.

[5]By the time this book is published, Nestlé's executive vice president and chief technology officer, Werner Bauer, quoted in this chapter, will have retired after a long and distinguished career of 23 years with Nestlé. The board of directors has appointed Stefan Catsicas, provost and executive vice president of the King Abdullah University of Science and Technology in Saudi Arabia, to succeed Werner Bauer as executive vice president and chief technology officer of Nestlé SA, effective September 1, 2013.

CHAPTER 10

APPOINTING INDIVIDUAL INNOVATION CHAMPIONS

Example 2 – DSM's Innovation Governance Model: The Entrepreneurial CIO[1]

Royal DSM is a global life sciences and materials sciences company headquartered in the Netherlands. In 2009, it received the Outstanding Corporate Innovator Award from the Product Development and Management Association (PDMA). The award recognizes organizations that demonstrate exceptional skill in continuously creating and capturing value through new products and services. This award, presented to Rob van Leen, DSM's chief innovation officer (CIO), indirectly recognized the quality of the company's innovation governance. The company had indeed made a lot of progress in the way it managed innovation since transforming itself from a commodity chemical company to a high value-added specialty chemical company. Although management entrusted most of its growth and innovation mission to its business group directors, it also counted on its high-profile corporate Innovation Center, under Van Leen's leadership, to stimulate, steer, and sustain the company's innovation drive.

GOING THROUGH DECADES OF TRANSFORMATION AT DSM

Few companies have transformed themselves like DSM (formerly Dutch States Mines), which started as a state-owned coal company in 1902. It successively added fertilizers, industrial chemicals, and raw materials for synthetic fibers to its product portfolio. After the country's last coal mine closed in 1975, petrochemicals became the company's focus, and profits from raw materials for plastics grew by double digits. In 1989, the company was privatized and listed on the Amsterdam Stock Exchange. Since then, and as a direct consequence of an entirely new strategy formulation process, DSM completely refigured its business portfolio and its approach to innovation.

Reconfiguring the Business Portfolio

Feeling an urgent need to improve the quality of its strategic process, which had become merely a number crunching exercise, in 1992 management launched a new collective strategy formulation approach for each business group: the Business Strategy Dialogues (BSDs). The BSD approach was complemented with the Corporate Strategy Dialogues (CSDs) in 1994. The objective of CSDs was to develop a long-term corporate strategy and set priorities for the company. The aim of the new strategic process was to ensure that DSM continued to shift its focus to more value-added products, thus enabling its entry into markets with higher growth and greater profits.

> "I joined DSM because it was the only company I knew that transformed itself and showed its willingness to change deeply for the long term. Its transformation was well planned and executed."
>
> *A DSM business group president*

Under the leadership of the CEO, Simon de Bree, DSM continued to focus its portfolio on life sciences and performance materials. In 1998 it acquired Gist brocades (Gb), a Dutch biotechnology company that had become a leader in penicillin, enzymes, and food ingredients, all derived from microorganisms such as yeast, bacteria, and fungi. This acquisition brought DSM expertise in pharmaceutical intermediates, food specialties, and biotechnology. The culture and open approach to research and innovation at Gb were also attractive to DSM, which was larger and somewhat less flexible.

In 2000 Peter Elverding, who had succeeded Simon de Bree as CEO, led a CSD that resulted in "Vision 2005 – Focus and Value." The vision was to move DSM away from its reliance on petrochemicals and complete its transformation into a specialty chemical company through organic growth and acquisitions. In 2000, the company acquired Catalytica Pharmaceuticals in the USA, and in 2002 it sold its large petrochemical business to the Saudi Basic Industries Corporation (SABIC). It was the largest single transaction in the company's history and provided DSM with enough cash to expand its portfolio. Roche's Vitamins & Fine Chemicals Division was acquired at the end of 2003, allowing DSM to inherit 6000 skilled employees and add more high-quality specialty products to its portfolio. This acquisition helped restore sales and achieve the target of having 80% of sales coming from specialties by 2005. It also resulted in DSM becoming the world's leader in vitamins and achieving its goal of establishing a solid life sciences activity. Neoresins was acquired in 2005 and a number of non-core commodity businesses were divested over the following years, enabling DSM to become a pure-play life sciences and materials sciences company.

In 2005 Elverding and DSM management initiated the company's "Vision 2010" which focused on completing the portfolio restructuring task that had been started a decade earlier. It also introduced a major innovation drive – creating an Innovation Center, appointing a chief innovation officer and setting an ambitious innovation growth target of €1 billion in new sales by 2010.

In 2007 Feike Sijbesma, who had come to DSM through the Gb acquisition, became CEO, and in 2010, management's new vision became "DSM in motion – Driving focused growth." The company had completed its portfolio restructuring and was directing all its efforts on growth, in both its business groups (BGs) and new businesses, referred to as emerging business areas.

In 2011, the company reached sales of €9 billion. By that time it had more than 200 offices and sites in 49 countries and employed over 22,200 employees worldwide, with one-third of the workforce being Dutch. The combination of life sciences and materials sciences provided the company with an interesting position for growth in areas such as biotechnology and biomedical materials.

DSM is organized around five *clusters* and seven *BGs*:

- The Nutrition cluster includes two BGs: DSM Nutritional Products and DSM Food Specialties. It serves customers within the food, feed, beverages, and flavor sector.
- The Pharma cluster consists of the DSM Pharmaceutical Products BG and DSM's 50% interest in the DSM Sinochem Pharmaceuticals joint venture. Both are important suppliers to the pharmaceutical industry.
- The Performance Materials cluster and its three BGs – DSM Engineering Plastics, DSM Dyneema®, and DSM Resins & Functional Materials – supply advanced materials to a broad range of industries.
- The Polymer Intermediates cluster and its BG – DSM Fibre Intermediates – supply among other things caprolactam, the raw material for nylon.
- The Innovation Center is the most recent cluster. It was created and is headed by Van Leen. It comprises, alongside a business incubator, three new entrepreneurial businesses, or emerging business areas: DSM Bio-based Products & Services, DSM Biomedical, and DSM Advanced Surfaces.

Rethinking its Innovation Governance Approach

Until 2005 and management's Vision 2010, DSM managed innovation in a traditional way, through its R&D organization. A large research center – DSM Research – conducted research for all businesses. The director of research and development (R&D) reported to the managing board, at least one of whose members had previously been a director of R&D. The focus was on process improvements and operational excellence. Most projects were about cost reduction, and the word that was used across the organization was "standardization." Systems were standardized and rolled out across all business groups, irrespective of their focus. Despite a number of successful innovation projects, like the one that led to the polyethylene fiber Dyneema – the strongest fiber in the world – DSM remained a rather conservative company.

> "DSM had a good track record of process innovation; yields kept increasing. But there was no daring product or business model innovation!"
>
> *Rob van Leen, CIO*

Through the acquisitions of Gb and Roche Vitamins & Fine Chemicals (and later Neoresins), DSM ended up with a patchwork of R&D centers in addition to the old central R&D lab. Some sites ended up competing for projects. Between 2000 and 2005, the company came up with very few innovations, and by the end of 2005 the innovation portfolio in several business groups was empty. A new model of steering R&D and business innovation was clearly needed.

In 2005, in the context of DSM's new Vision 2010, an Innovation Center (IC) was established at corporate level to accelerate and support innovation. The notion of an Innovation Center had come from the head of corporate planning (now called Corporate Strategy & Acquisitions). The idea was to set up a unit dedicated to managing the innovation process with a strong "central push." The concept was influenced by IBM's emerging business areas model.

Peter Elverding, the CEO at the time, chose 48-year-old Rob van Leen, then the head of DSM Food Specialties, to take on the role of creating, establishing, and running the IC. Van Leen had come with Gb when it was acquired by DSM and he had led both radical and incremental innovation projects. His good reputation and credibility within the company, together with his PhD in sciences and a business degree, made him the perfect candidate.

When Elverding had asked Van Leen to be the company's first CIO, Van Leen was busy with the Nutrition work stream of the Corporate Strategy Dialogue and he was still running his old BG job at the same time, which he was not keen to leave. But he accepted the mission after the CEO declared, "We fully trust you . . . It will be OK. Nobody else is better equipped to do it, so you have to do it!"

> "It was probably unwise to agree to take on a job without insisting that management should first define its role and goals right from the beginning."
>
> *Rob van Leen, CIO*

> "The Innovation Center is organized like any other business group. It has its own HR, controller and review function. At DSM, one of the tasks of the controller is, together with his VP, to build a future that is possible."
>
> *VP Finance & Control, IC*

Van Leen reported to Feike Sijbesma, a member of DSM's managing board. When negotiating the level of his new position, he had insisted on reporting directly to the CEO, but was quickly reassured that Sijbesma was soon (in 2007) to succeed Elverding as CEO. Sijbesma was committed to accelerating DSM's innovation efforts and, like Van Leen, he had brought with him the entrepreneurial spirit of Gb, his former company.

There was no clear assignment when the new post was announced in 2006. So, Van Leen's first task was to draft the job description and to define the boundaries of the new IC, which was entrusted with a number of existing innovation-oriented departments. DSM's IC was defined as comprising, among other departments, a Corporate Technology Office, an Innovation Competence Center, and an Innovation Shared Service Center (including corporate licensing, venturing, and intellectual property activities). It was supposed to develop new businesses for the corporation outside the scope of the existing business groups, and for that purpose Van Leen planned to establish an incubator and an emerging business area program.

Coming from a business group himself, Van Leen established the IC as a business-oriented group, not as a staff support function.

STARTING AN INNOVATION DRIVE TO IMPROVE INNOVATION EXCELLENCE

Setting Innovation Targets

The creation of the IC, the empowerment of a high-caliber CIO, and insistent messages from the managing board all clearly signaled that top management was serious when it proposed adopting innovation as a core value. The managing board set the following six innovation targets:

- Become an intrinsically innovative company
- Adopt excellent innovation practices
- Achieve above average returns on innovation investments
- Reach €1 billion in additional innovation-related sales by 2010
- Make selective acquisitions to contribute to the €1 billion target
- Generate emerging business areas to create new business in the mid to long term.

Conducting an Innovation Diagnostic

Van Leen looked for relevant ways to measure DSM's level of innovation. With the help of an external consultant who proposed an innovation diagnostic tool, the IC performed an innovation audit involving over 700 staff using questionnaires and interviews. The consultant benchmarked DSM against 27 of its industry peers on nine indicators: innovation aspirations; innovation strategy; idea generation and validation; project management; commercialization and launch; portfolio management; external networks; organization; and culture and talent.

On most of these factors, DSM scored below the industry average when it was first evaluated in 2006. The diagnostic has since been conducted by the IC every second year, through 110 questions on the innovation process. In 2012, for the first time, the diagnostic indicated that DSM had reached the top quartile benchmark of its industry.

To follow up on the initial diagnostic, Van Leen and his staff identified the critical new projects in each BG that could contribute to reaching DSM's €1 billion sales objective by 2010. The top 50 projects were then put under the management spotlight. This *Top 50* list is constantly updated and is continually monitored by Van Leen and the managing board.

Promoting Functional Excellence in Innovation

The biggest challenge for the new IC was to help the business groups contribute to the €1 billion target through market-driven, innovative sales. Initially, what was to be included in this figure or how to reach it had not been defined. To assist in meeting the target, a small unit was created to promote functional excellence in innovation. Led by an experienced business manager, it had multiple missions:

- Help the CIO assess and manage innovation
- Gather and share best practices
- Steer improvement programs
- Facilitate the BGs' innovation efforts and initiatives
- Help the BGs address and plan their innovation growth targets
- Support BG heads so they can free up people to work on innovation projects.

Establishing a Reporting System

The outcome of the diagnostic gave Van Leen's financial team a good starting point for developing reports on innovation achievements and performance. The *Quarterly Innovation Reports* (IRs) were launched in the second quarter of 2006 and are still in use today. These reports convey the progress of BGs and the IC in their innovation projects. They describe each BG's innovation sales, launches – new products are included for five years after launch – and the value of the project pipeline. The IC's VP of finance and control goes through the IRs in detail with each BG innovation director and the BG controller in a quarterly conference call. Their role is to identify "white space" opportunities and discuss the BG's innovation management practices. These quarterly reports are widely distributed and reviewed by the managing board, something that was not originally welcomed by the BGs that were performing at the bottom of the list.

> "In the beginning the process was resisted, some called it 'corporate spam.' A few people disagreed but in the end, everyone adopted it and today everybody is loyal. It took the BG directors six months to accept it and to see the value of these IRs. They realize it was the only way to really understand their business."
>
> *VP Finance & Control, IC*

Soon after, a *Top 50 Boost Report* was launched. This complementary report, produced twice a year, allowed Van Leen and the managing board to focus on and evaluate the top 50 projects contributing to the €1 billion target for 2010. This report has now been extended to include the top ventures from the emerging business areas. It is reviewed annually with the managing board.

> "We expect our controllers to be very broad and business driven. They are part of managing the business. They report directly to the BG head but have a strong dotted line to me."
> *VP Finance & Control, IC*

An existing intranet project management tool, called *Project Plaza*, was rolled out throughout the company to support innovation projects and portfolio management. Through this portal, business managers and, for example, their controllers can conduct feasibility studies, analyze business cases, select the right projects, check sales, and quantify the value of projects.

Creating an Idea Box

Over time, more tools and processes were put in place. After a two-year pilot in Switzerland, corporate idea boxes (IBs) were launched in the second half of 2008 to encourage all employees to contribute to an integrated innovation culture. BGs that wished to implement an IB had to set up an infrastructure to manage it, with an IB manager, an IB owner, and idea screeners. The IB itself was not unique to DSM. What was unique was its challenging nature, prompting clear answers to why an idea was needed and what value it would bring to the company.

> "Hundreds of ideas can be generated, but they are not effective if they are not focused. The [IB] process is important because ideas need follow-up. We still need to improve the way we take on ideas, focus and follow-up. Management needs to embrace the organization's idea generation. However, when I look at the number of ideas and the creativity I think we are performing at the top."
> *VP Technology Strategy*

Not all BGs adopted the system immediately, something that the DSM culture allowed, but its use spread gradually and proved highly beneficial.

Distributing Innovation Awards

DSM's innovation awards program recognized and rewarded scientists who had proved excellence in pioneering research that led to innovative products and applications. A Nutrition Award recognized innovative research in human and animal nutrition. A Science & Technology Award encouraged young scientists to conduct creative, groundbreaking research. The Performance Materials Award recognized excellence in innovative research in the field of performance materials. The internal awards program was expanded to recognize both individuals and teams for excellence in science and intellectual property, but most importantly integral innovation. The awards program was generally well accepted and valued.

RESTRUCTURING THE MANAGEMENT OF TECHNOLOGY AND R&D

> "You will always have multidisciplinary project teams managed by marketing people and R&D; but there are no more R&D projects, just business projects!"
>
> Rob van Leen, CIO

As a scientist himself, Van Leen had personal experience of R&D management. His former responsibility as a BG head had also convinced him of the need to introduce a clear focus on market-oriented radical innovation and a much higher degree of business orientation. So he promoted the concept that innovation and the underlying R&D, manufacturing, and business development processes had to be managed by an entrepreneur from start to finish.

Implementing a New R&D Model

Van Leen believed in having an entrepreneurial business manager oversee the market research and the design phase of projects. Input into the pipeline would come from the Business Strategy Dialogues, and the innovation project would be driven by the needs of the business group. A project manager from R&D would head up the technical part of the project, reporting to the entrepreneur. The entrepreneur has two key roles: (1) to drive and oversee the product/business specification phase, and (2) to be the interface manager with all functions involved in the project or program.

According to Van Leen's new model, the concept of a central research lab was abandoned and a hybrid model was adopted, similar to the way research had been managed at Gb, where product and application development were under the business units and funded by them. Competence-oriented groups were created to serve the whole company, but they were located in specific business groups. Thus there was a Biotechnology Center at the former Gb site; a Nutrition Center at the former Roche Vitamins site; and an Organic Chemistry Center and a Materials Science Center at the largest DSM site.

> "The three-axis business model is a good model for big R&D organizations. It is designed for a Dutch culture in which scientists accept responsibilities for certain competences without necessarily being the bosses of others. In other cultures, like in Switzerland, the hierarchical model prevails and you are recognized only if you are the boss of other people."
>
> *Deputy CTO*

R&D activities were organized along three axes, with separate responsibilities for managing people (leading a unit or department), focusing on science (building expertise in a particular discipline), and project management (managing a project team). This functional set-up was designed to clarify the different responsibilities, accountabilities, and authorities. And the three-axis model was intended to simplify career development routes within R&D, as young scientists and engineers could select one of the three axes and follow a career path corresponding to their choice.

By 2012, after a number of acquisitions of small specialty companies in different parts of the world, DSM had 35 R&D sites. The main R&D centers, however, were still located in the Netherlands, Switzerland, China, and the USA. The total R&D

spending was 5% of net sales. R&D centers collaborated closely on fundamental research with the venturing group as well as with outside parties in academia and industry. The technology base was kept state of the art by a Corporate Research Program, directed by the CTO, which consumed about 10% of the total research budget.

Setting up a Corporate Technology Responsibility

The most radical change was to bring the CTO and his office into the IC, reporting to Van Leen. But the CTO remained, together with his boss, part of DSM's leadership council, i.e. the top 30 senior executives in the company.

> "The CTO reports to the CIO. This was an important signal to the organization that innovation is much more than invention: It is the sum of all the steps that enable you to sell products to markets with profitable results. It by no means diminishes the importance of the CTO, since he is responsible for the quality and output of more than 10% of the DSM workforce!"
>
> Rob van Leen, CIO

The CTO has a corporate budget to ensure that new initiatives are included in the R&D pipeline. His role is to drive the corporate R&D competence plan and fill any gaps. However, he has no direct responsibility over DSM labs, which fall under the authority of each BG's R&D director.

> "The DSTC is responsible for the management and sharing of DSM technologies. It is the highest technology conscience of DSM."
>
> Former CTO

The CTO focuses on three major tasks (besides making the new organization work): (1) chairing the DSM Science and Technology Council (DSTC), which consisted of the chairmen of the R&D councils of the clusters, among other people; (2) allocating, funding, and supervising the corporate research budget and programs; and (3) steering and executing the recommendations of the Scientific Advisory Board that worked for the DSTC.

MOBILIZING INNOVATORS IN BUSINESS GROUPS

Originally, the attitude of BG heads toward the Innovation Center and its role varied considerably. Van Leen had full support for his initiatives from some business groups, typically those with a newly arrived BG head. Other BGs were initially reluctant to see the IC becoming too involved in their process, either because they wished to remain independent or because they did not see what added value the IC could bring to their business.

Van Leen was aware that he was treading a fine line. How much should the IC be involved in improving the innovation process in a BG? He wanted them to be better at innovation but he did not want to interfere or take over responsibility.

> "The Innovation Center helps us challenge the mindset of our people. It is a trigger, a catalyst in terms of methodology and a source of information and help. We get help in scanning to find major improvement areas, in product launch and commercialization, and also in licensing technologies. But it is because the whole company focuses on innovation that things become possible and get moving."
>
> *A BG president*

Gathering Innovation Enthusiasts to Spearhead Change

To promote innovation, each BG had to embark on an improvement program. Because there was a clear difference in the enthusiasm, pace, and determination of the various BGs, Van Leen set up a network of so-called innovation enthusiasts under the name the "Billion Bunch." The name derived from the fact that they were supposed to help DSM achieve the €1 billion target in innovation sales by 2010. Their objective was also to exchange best practices across units on managing innovation. However, since BG heads appointed members of the "bunch," their profile and motivation were not always ideal.

This is one reason that the Billion Bunch network was disbanded after a couple of years and replaced by a network of *innovation directors*. Van Leen wanted indeed to have a real and empowered counterpart in each of the BGs. Today, these innovation directors lead teams of business development managers, and some also have the BG R&D head reporting to them (similar to the CIO–CTO relationship). They remain part of their BG but functionally report to Van Leen in their innovation mission.

These innovation directors and the heads of the IC incubator and the functional excellence unit are now part of an *Innovation Council* chaired by Van Leen. The role of this council is to work together to achieve the company's new innovation target. Indeed, the original objective was vastly exceeded – sales from innovation reached €1.3 billion in 2010. The new corporate innovation target is now to achieve 20% of total sales in 2015 from products and solutions introduced within the previous five years – and the definition of new products has been clearly specified, which is critical for this type of measurement. This is a considerable objective for a chemical company.

Collectively, members of the innovation council discuss the composition of the radical innovation project portfolio and make recommendations to the managing board, which makes the final decisions. Individually, each innovation director is assigned an innovation target corresponding to the situation of his/her BG – some higher, others lower – in order to ensure that the average of all BGs reaches the 20% target. This means that the innovation directors personally follow the progress of their projects from the *Top 50* list and serve as the BG representatives of the IC's functional excellence activities. In addition, each innovation director is in charge of a topic or an innovation theme, which he/she leads DSM-wide.

> "It might be good if we had a President's Fund available to support certain projects. But the president needs a wise body to advise him on how to spend it effectively!"
>
> *Rob van Leen, CIO*

As part of its regular meetings, the innovation council also looks at individual BG project portfolios. They might, for example, advise that the BG increase the level of spending on a particular project by a factor of five in order to develop a cluster of new applications. This, however, means reallocating budgets at the DSM level, which is not an easy task.

Creating a Product Launch Team

Traditionally, DSM did not proactively launch products in its markets. The company lacked marketing and sales talent and experience. So, as part of the innovation boost efforts, and in collaboration with the chief marketing officer, Van Leen hired marketing specialists from inside and outside the company and set up a commercialization and realization team to support the BGs' efforts to take innovations to market. Originally, this service was offered to the BGs free of charge, but they now pay for it.

Launching a Culture Change Program

Together with Van Leen, a number of senior managers felt the need for DSM to become more entrepreneurial, but how? It started with supporting risk taking, something the managing board was willing to do. They also saw the need to change in at least two main areas: (1) to move from a product- and technology-driven culture to one focusing equally on business models and product co-creation with customers, and (2) to foster an attitude of curiosity and customer empathy and interest, a must in life sciences.

> "The purpose of our learning program is to broaden the scope of the leaders and owners of our top 50 projects. We need general managers and they need to speak the same business language!"
>
> *Rob van Leen, CIO*

Van Leen was fully aware of the need for change, which is why he had asked HR to design an ambitious Innovation Learning Program with the support of some of the BG and functional excellence staff. Together, they planned a number of different management development programs targeting various hierarchical levels and functions. In 2012, the first round of programs had involved the leaders and owners of the top 50 projects.

BUILDING A NEW BUSINESS CREATION INFRASTRUCTURE

Van Leen inherited a number of existing and important corporate functions like the Intellectual Property department and the Licensing group. These two units were to provide the bulk of the IC permanent staff, but Van Leen saw limited ways for him to add extra value to them, preferring to focus instead on innovation- and business-building activities.

Mapping Strategic Choices

As part of its recent Corporate Strategy Dialogue input, Van Leen adopted a tool to map the company's innovation initiatives (refer to Figure 10.1). The "blue box" quadrants (in light gray on the figure) represented opportunities for incremental product creation, whereas the "red box" (in dark gray) featured more radical areas for business creation. The red box was defined as containing future new platforms consisting of projects, ventures, and acquisition possibilities. The "blue box vs. red box" concept was quickly adopted

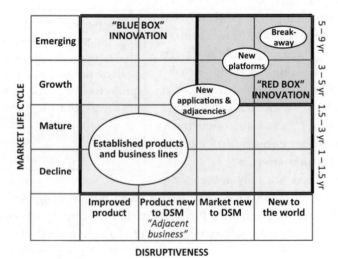

Source: DSM Innovation Center

Figure 10.1: DSM Innovation Matrix

by the organization, all the way up to CEO level, and was used to characterize the company's innovation strategy. Blue box projects generally belonged to the BGs, whereas red box ones – with a few exceptions that were allocated to BGs – entered the realm of the IC, notably the incubator and the emerging business areas.

The composition of the red box portfolio was discussed and agreed upon in the innovation council. Originally, 45 projects were allocated to the red box quadrant. After multiple discussions within the innovation council, the number was reduced to fewer than 15 and the projects were allocated mostly to the incubator and the emerging business areas. A critical factor for the selection of these projects was their potential contribution to building new technology and business platforms, and the potential market size of these platforms. The benchmark retained for these new business platforms set the ideal level at €250 million in sales to be achieved within a 10- to 15-year time span, and with higher margins than DSM's current businesses. Individual stand-alone projects were retained as long as they were part of existing platforms or businesses. Overall, a significant R&D budget envelope (25% of the corporate total) was allocated to the development of red box projects.

Beefing Up Corporate Venturing

Venturing was made part of the IC, and it soon came to play an integral part in the open innovation process. The group teamed up with innovative players all over the world and invested in promising start-ups. The objective was to give DSM access to new technologies and innovative products aligned with the company's growth strategy. Participation in start-ups ranged from 5 to 20% of their capital, giving these companies financial support as well as access to DSM's expertise, resources, and networks.

> "DSM should anchor into areas and not focus on products. Focusing on different projects within an area makes us less vulnerable and more flexible. Management should first fence the boundaries where the business should be, then let the incubator and the business groups work within these fields."
>
> *Former BI director*

The diversity of the venturing portfolio gave DSM a broad window on the world in a wide range of markets including emerging economies.

Creating a Business Incubator

The business incubator (BI) was created – out of the former Corporate New Business Development unit – to be the originator of and platform for large new business opportunities. The BI was to capture larger dynamic shifts in the market and breed more radical, slightly longer-term innovations leading to new business models and higher value products. Its focus was on potential technology and market platforms, not on individual, stand-alone projects.

By 2008, the BI had focused its activities on four innovation areas: climate change and energy; health and wellness; functionality and performance, and emerging economies. A fifth area, the X-factor, was temporarily created in 2008 to leverage the combined knowledge and technology in life sciences and materials sciences. The most promising projects from the BI were expected either to be turned into an emerging business area or to be transferred directly to a business group or even sold off.

The incubator had a small team and a lean infrastructure, which Van Leen was considering how to build further. A first step in that direction was the setting up of local incubators in the emerging markets of India and China.

Seeding Emerging Business Areas

Emerging business areas (EBAs) were created with the mission to look at significant new trends in industries and markets, identify potential *innovation pockets* and relate these to DSM's current market strongholds and technology position. EBAs were defined as broad platforms within which a series of new projects could be launched with the objective of creating entirely new businesses.

DSM's top management wanted entrepreneurial teams, rather than traditional DSM functional teams, to lead these EBAs. Originally, the managing board and Van Leen screened all existing opportunities, reducing the number of possible projects from 14 to four by deciding to allocate some to the BGs and kill others or put them on the back-burner. The four areas of opportunity that were selected were: white biotechnology (biofuels), biomedical materials, personalized nutrition, and specialty packaging.

In fact, the last two EBAs were canceled after four or five years of trying hard. Personalized nutrition – management felt – was a valid concept but came too early for the market. Specialty packaging did not bring spectacularly big solutions to the fore and was terminated in 2010, although an interesting packaging solution for cheese was transferred to DSM Food Specialties, where it is flourishing as part of the dairy portfolio. This allowed management to send a clear signal to the organization – stopping projects is OK.

> "We shouldn't be afraid to start things and stop some of them. We shouldn't be afraid of making mistakes!"
> *Feike Sijbesma, CEO*

> "Our experience with our advanced surfaces EBA shows the power of serendipity! You cannot always plan things completely from the start. You need certain directions for sure, but also some freedom at project funerals, for example to turn it around, introduce a new angle and redirect a project!"
> *Feike Sijbesma, CEO*

Meanwhile, a project from the incubator that had developed an effective anti-glare coating for glass surfaces was turned into an EBA under the name advanced surfaces. Management had been tempted to kill the project for lack of market opportunities – the first application was limited to the glass picture frame market. But the project was re-evaluated and a huge new application identified in coating solar cell panels to increase their productivity. The additional energy produced justified the cost of the coating.

This experience with the early EBAs clearly showed the need for a venture management process. So the IC developed a real stage-gate process for new ventures to provide management with an overall approach to new business creation.

In 2012, the Innovation Center housed three EBAs:

- Bio-based Products & Services – the former white biotechnology platform – which exploits opportunities in advanced biofuels. The unit was transferred to the USA, the largest market for this type of product.
- Biomedical, which conceives, among other applications, biodegradable structures contributing to the development of bones and cartilage in patients. It was also based in the USA.
- Advanced Surfaces, which proposes coating solar panels for greater electricity generation and follows other applications in trapping light. It seems to have considerable potential.

By the end of 2012, all three EBAs were net cash eaters and management was ready to invest huge amounts in their development. Van Leen estimated that all three could become extremely profitable. But they all need to complete 10 to 15 years of maturation before they start delivering.

Growing EBAs and Extending the EBA Portfolio

Given the amount of R&D money invested in the development of EBAs, their progress was a regular item on the managing board's agenda. Van Leen personally devoted 70 to 80% of his time to the three EBAs and the business incubator. This included the time spent in coaching their organic growth strategy as well as in identifying and evaluating partnership and acquisition candidates. Several focused acquisitions had been concluded to boost their expertise and market coverage.

Van Leen was aware that he might be expected to grow new EBAs, since the ones under his leadership were reaching their growth stage. This could create a gap to develop a new EBA. The difficulty was identifying suitable technology and market platforms for these new businesses.

SHOWING THE WAY AT THE TOP

If Van Leen, as CIO, has been entrusted with overall responsibility for innovation at DSM, he can count fully on the support of the

CEO, Feike Sijbesma, who is seen as the ultimate champion of innovation in the company. Sijbesma believes that, for a science- and technology-based company like DSM, innovation is key to corporate growth and profits. He stresses it constantly, in public – he attends all internal and external innovation events – and in private management review sessions. But he also takes concrete and highly symbolic steps to underline management's commitment.

> "When we started the design of our new functional excellence program in 2009, each managing board member was asked to rank the most important objectives for the company and the corresponding functions. To the question: 'How important is innovation for you on a 1 to 5 scale,' our CEO Feike Sijbesma put a tick outside of the boxes, above five."
>
> *Rob van Leen, CIO*

Sijbesma explained: "In the 2008/2009 economic crisis, we initiated a cost-saving program everywhere, but not in technology and innovation! Some of my managers thought that it was unfair that we would not cut costs in R&D. I said to my R&D managers: If you can cut costs in R&D by becoming more efficient, that's fine, but I don't want you to cut costs by doing less. This passed a strong message to the organization!"

Besides regularly reviewing the various innovation reports sent to the managing board, Sijbesma pays particular attention to the top 50 projects, to their staffing and to the resources allocated to them. Given his own technical background and knowledge, he is naturally interested in supervising the whole R&D process but he recognizes that his involvement has advantages and disadvantages for Van Leen and the technical organization. He also maintains a strong relationship with Van Leen and a particular interest in the new business platforms that Van Leen has started in the EBAs.

One of the other important ways in which Sijbesma feels that he can contribute to innovation is by promoting the company's

> "All EBAs report to Rob, but I remain very close to them because I realize that it is always difficult to defend long-term spending. Vis-à-vis Rob, I play a double role. Sometimes, I am his advocate and protector. But sometimes, I play the challenger role."
>
> *Feike Sijbesma, CEO*

values. The four values he emphasizes have a direct bearing on innovation:

- *External orientation:* Sijbesma encourages the "proudly found elsewhere" approach, in contrast to the resistance to ideas "not invented here" that was prevalent in some parts of the organization. He repeats it often: "I don't mind if you didn't invent it!" In this spirit, he has decentralized BG headquarters. Only three BGs have their headquarters in Holland. The others are based in the USA, Singapore, China, and Switzerland.
- *Accountability for performance and learning:* Sijbesma stresses the importance of learning from failed projects. He recognizes that deciding to kill a project is always difficult, but he encourages evaluations to be carried out when there are "project funerals," because these evaluations promote individual and collective learning.
- *Collaboration:* Sijbesma is a strong advocate of the "One DSM" concept and he extols the virtue of looking internally for help within other BGs to solve internal problems, something that was not naturally done before.
- *Inclusion and diversity:* Sijbesma wants to attract a broader mix of people and to encourage different mindsets and behaviors. The managing board includes only two Dutchmen out of five, and two members are based overseas. He promotes this attitude by organizing specific cultural sensitivity training programs, for example on how men and women think differently.

DSM'S OUTLOOK AND CHALLENGES: A CONTINUED FOCUS ON INNOVATION

DSM's Vision 2005 was essentially about business portfolio reconfiguration. The subsequent Vision 2010 focused on creating an innovation governance infrastructure with the appointment of Van Leen as CIO and the creation of the Innovation Center. It also set a first growth target for innovation, i.e. €1 billion of new sales by 2010, an objective that was exceeded. The latest vision, "DSM in motion – Driving focused growth," has established not one, but three deadlines:

- 2013 for a focus on profitability targets: Management wants to create a sense of urgency about profitability.
- 2015 for new sales and growth targets: Management wants innovative products and solutions — developed within the previous five years — to account for 20% of total sales by 2015.
- 2020 for sales aspirations for the three EBAs: These EBAs are designed to contribute an extra €1 billion in profitable sales, while new EBAs might be developed.

These objectives are based on four growth drivers: (1) high growth economies; (2) innovation; (3) sustainability; and (4) acquisitions and partnerships.

> "Economic circumstances have not improved! Nevertheless, I would like to create a new EBA within a two-year time frame, when the current EBAs start requiring a lower level of corporate resources and personal attention."
> *Rob van Leen, CIO*

Van Leen is aware of the importance of the double mission that has been entrusted to him and the IC in order to achieve the company's objective. On the one hand, he needs to grow new high-margin business groups through technological and business model innovation; on the other hand, he has to continue to help the BGs improve their processes, which requires him to be both diplomatic and challenging.

Sijbesma agrees and credits the company's innovation governance model — its CIO and IC — for its achievements so far: "The IC has two roles. First, it is where new growth bubbles are developed; and second, it is needed to supervise where we spend our money! Our model works well and our organization has learned to use this model. If it works, let's not try to do something different. In technology and innovation, we need a long-term approach and we need to make sure that people learn to work in that system."

NOTE

[1]This chapter is derived, in part, from the business case "DSM: Mobilizing the Organization to Grow through Innovation" by Daria Tolstoi and Jean-Philippe Deschamps (2009) Ref. IMD-3-2111, distributed by www.thecasecentre.org.

CHAPTER 11

SETTING UP A COLLECTIVE GOVERNANCE SYSTEM

Example – Tetra Pak's Innovation Governance Model: High-level Cross-functional Steering Groups

Tetra Pak is the world's leading liquid food packaging company. It belongs to the family-owned Tetra Laval Group, headquartered in Switzerland. In 2011, Tetra Pak had filling systems in operation in more than 170 countries. It sold over 167 billion packages world-wide, employed close to 23,000 people, and its sales reached €10.4 billion. Tetra Pak sales consist of three types of products: filler line equipment (called "systems"); packaging materials – these are essentially laminated and printed rolls to be formed, filled, and sealed to become finished packages; and processing equipment for dairy plants and juice packers.

The company's initial growth and success is largely the result of two radical innovations introduced in a row in the late 1950s and early 1960s: (1) the development of highly efficient milk cartons produced continuously on roll-fed, "form-fill-seal" machines; and (2) the development of a process to make its milk cartons aseptic when filled with UHT milk, thus enabling a long shelf-life at ambient temperature.

These innovations took place under the entrepreneurial stewardship of Tetra Pak's Swedish founder and owner, Dr Ruben Rausing. He created the company in 1951 and instilled a passion for innovation which his sons and heirs, Hans and Gad, perpetuated over three decades. The company's product range was at first limited to two milk packages: Tetra Classic® (a tetrahedron-shaped milk carton) and the very popular Tetra Brik® (a rectangular box). Over the years, it evolved into a broad range of packaging solutions of cartons of various sizes and shapes with different types of openings for most categories of pasteurized and ambient liquid food.

Innovation has always been part of Tetra Pak's culture, and the company has been able to leverage the largest R&D resources in its industry. But its innovation governance has evolved through three distinct stages:

- From the 1960s to the mid-1990s, Tetra Pak's innovation was characterized by the predominant role played by its owners, who launched a series of intuitive, more or less successful R&D-driven developments.
- From the mid-1990s to 2006, Tetra Pak's management embarked on a major formal innovation drive. It focused on the innovation process and set up an innovation process board to orchestrate the company's efforts.
- Since 2006 Tetra Pak's management has considerably extended its process orientation beyond innovation, to focus on strategy. It manages its processes through a number of high-level collective decision bodies, or councils.

INNOVATION GOVERNANCE - STAGE 1: PREDOMINANCE OF THE OWNERS

During the first stage in the company's history, Tetra Pak's entrepreneurial founder, Ruben Rausing, and later his sons Hans and Gad, acted as the real innovation supremos. Rausing's vision – to develop efficient carton-based milk packaging solutions for the then emerging supermarket channels – was the main inspiration that led to the development of the company's initial products, which he personally helped design and industrialize. After the success of the first product, a 500 ml tetrahedron-shaped milk carton (Tetra Classic), the company introduced different packaging shapes and sizes. Its greatest success, the Tetra Brik Aseptic, launched in 1969, extended the company's market reach to include fruit juices and other beverages. It became a broad product family as different sizes, shapes, and closures were added over the years.

Rausing's tenet, "A package should save more than it costs," stimulated a constant emphasis on efficiency in terms of package weight, cost, and filling line productivity. While it focused on maintaining quality, minimizing waste, and reducing distribution costs, Tetra Pak quickly built an environmentally friendly image. Much of Tetra Pak's success was linked to (1) its proprietary roll-fed, "form-fill-seal" system technology; (2) the strength of its broad network of entrepreneurial market companies; and (3) a strong emphasis on customer and retailer efficiency. Tetra Pak firmly believed that its excellence in technology and product innovation was a direct result of carefully listening to its customers.

The company had many assets to help it keep innovating after the launch of the Tetra Brik blockbuster. First, its management recognized and valued innovation. Hans and Gad Rausing, following in the footsteps of their innovative father, continued investing in R&D, trusting that at least some of their developments would turn into major market successes. Tetra Pak rapidly built the strongest R&D and sales capabilities in its industry. Over three decades, the owners were involved in − or at least strongly influenced − most new project launch decisions. This R&D-focused period continued after Hans sold his shares to his brother Gad. Thus, many projects were launched in the 1980s and 1990s, but none attained the cost-efficiency or success of the company's breakthrough Tetra Brik Aseptic package.

In hindsight, these disappointing results reflected a number of innovation management weaknesses:

- First, most projects were high-risk, R&D-based projects − not market-focused ones.
- Second, the company lacked an adequate process for translating market needs into specifications.

- Third, project portfolio decisions were often influenced by what management ultimately called "acoustic planning," i.e. whoever shouted the loudest among market company heads got priority.
- Finally, Tetra Pak encountered many execution problems – for example, several products were introduced before they were ready, which antagonized some of the company's customers.

INNOVATION GOVERNANCE – STAGE 2: FOCUS ON PROCESSES

In 1995, Tetra Pak's newly appointed CEO, Gunnar Brock, initiated a move to review and improve the company's innovation effectiveness. Having occupied several senior management positions within the company, he was aware of the deficiencies of its new product development process. One of his first moves was to appoint a small but experienced group of four senior leaders to recommend an improvement program. This small innovation committee consisted of:

- the head of the largest sales region, Europe, Bo Wirsén – a member of the company's top management team – as chairman of the committee;
- the head of the largest business group, the fiber packaging division, Sigge Haraldsson, also a member of the top management team;
- a former country head, Richard Tonkin, with a lot of sales experience and a strong marketing orientation; and
- a very senior R&D manager and planner, B.G. Nilsson, based in the company's main R&D center in Lund, Sweden.

Step 1: Identifying and Addressing Deficient Processes

In 1996, the small innovation committee hired an external consultancy to conduct an innovation audit of the company through an extensive round of interviews with key managers. This audit was then presented to a larger group of 30 or so leaders, representing most functions, in the course of a two-day off-site workshop at the beginning of 1997. Gad Rausing – the company owner – and Gunnar Brock, the CEO, were present together with 25 other senior leaders.

The consultants' diagnosis pointed to a number of deficiencies in most of the processes leading to the definition, development, and launch of new products. They proposed a high-level process map to clearly identify and recognize the interdependencies of these processes. Their recommendations were validated and, in small work groups, the participants quickly agreed on the principle of appointing dedicated managers to start working on the deficient processes. Five experienced *process owners* were subsequently appointed to propose changes to the following processes:

> "We invited our stakeholders to this innovation workshop, particularly the noisy and the influential. The key word was 'mobilization.' At that time, we didn't even understand what questions to ask! There was a latent war between market heads and R&D. This workshop made us understand that innovation is not just the result of the work of smart engineers. A product is the sum of thousands of ideas captured into an organized process. It led to a collective aha! It gave us a mandate and franchise to use words – like process discipline – that were unheard of at Tetra Pak."
>
> *Richard Tonkin, member of the innovation committee*

- business intelligence;
- idea management;
- technology and resource development;
- product and technology strategy and planning; and
- project management.

The process owners were to be freed from their current work responsibilities to focus on their new mission, and they were asked to report regularly on their work to the innovation committee.

Step 2: Benchmarking against Innovative Companies to Fill Functional Gaps

Since the initial diagnostic had identified deficiencies in the strategic management of technology and products, in 1997 Bo Wirsén, the chairman of the innovation committee, decided to personally visit a number of innovative companies to understand how they had structured their innovation governance mechanisms. The companies visited included 3M, Canon, BMW, and Ericsson, among others. These visits, in which other members of management participated, highlighted two high-level functions that seemed to play a major role in the governance of innovation at these companies, namely a chief technology officer (CTO) and a strategic marketing officer (SMO).

Neither of these functions existed at Tetra Pak. The head of R&D, a very experienced manager, did not have the strategic breadth or depth to qualify as a CTO with the mission to help top management make strategic choices regarding technology. And all commercial resources at Tetra Pak were in market companies. These companies – at least the larger ones – generally had strong and competent organizations, but they were exclusively focused on their local market situation. No one in the company seemed to be managing the corporate product portfolio from a strategic perspective.

Following the benchmarking trip, two highly experienced senior leaders were appointed to these two headquarters functions in 1998. Göran Harrysson, a former director of R&D who headed Tetra Pak's emerging plastic business, was named CTO, and Paul Bousser, the head of marketing in France – a leading market company for Tetra Pak – was appointed as SMO. Both were to play a significant role in the further governance of innovation at Tetra Pak.

Step 3: Setting up an Innovation Process Board to Steer Innovation

The appointment of Nick Shreiber, who headed Region Americas, as Tetra Pak's new CEO in 2000 marked an acceleration of the company's emphasis on innovation process improvements. Shreiber was convinced that a disciplined process was the best way to increase the company's innovation output. He was strongly supported by the head of the Tetra Pak Carton Ambient business unit,

Dennis Jönsson, who joined the top management team in 2001, which was then called the Group Leadership Team (GLT). As the first work groups on process development started to recommend changes, the idea dawned on the members of the innovation committee that they ought to enlarge their small steering group to include other relevant functions and gain visibility for their actions. The purpose of this enlargement was to convey the message that innovation was no longer a functional activity of R&D, it was everyone's responsibility. The marketing people, notably in market companies, accepted the message and appreciated it. The concept of an *innovation board* emerged, but right from the start, the word *process* was added to its name to signal its specific emphasis on improving the innovation process. Top management felt that decisions regarding the *content* of innovation, i.e. project portfolio decisions, ought to stay in the hands of the various line managers, namely the business divisions and product line managers.

The original innovation committee was disbanded and its chairman, Bo Wirsén, became the chairman of the new innovation process board; he was soon replaced by Göran Harrysson, the CTO. A number of additional senior and mid-level managers joined the board, representing R&D, marketing, and business management functions.

To support its work on processes, management asked the IT department to create an online, intranet-based innovation management system. The architecture of the system mirrored Tetra Pak's high-level innovation map and its process organization. Thus, process owners now had a portal and platform to explain and outline their process, propose tools to users, and manage their processes on line. For

"Becoming process-oriented and standardizing processes were entirely new concepts for us at that time. The task was more complicated than we originally thought. Every time we held discussions, it led to different conclusions. It took several years to reach an acceptable level. This was a huge shift for management as it reduced the freedom that large market companies had traditionally maintained on product decisions."

Stefan Andersson, former process owner for technology development

example, for the first time, all project information was available on the intranet. Project teams no longer had to spend precious time informing management of their progress. Authorized managers had all data at their disposal within a few clicks on the project portal.

The first task of Tetra Pak's innovation process board consisted of intensifying the process improvement tasks that had started earlier. This proved to be a long and complicated task as no one had done it before, and some of the changes initially attempted were perceived negatively by some functions.

Some of the earlier process owners were replaced and new ones were brought in, for example to handle technology intelligence and product strategy and planning. Process design proposals were regularly reviewed and process owners were encouraged to develop online tools and organize company-wide process sharing and training efforts. This emphasis continued for a couple of years and the company gradually built and documented its new processes.

Step 4: Extending the Mission of the Innovation Process Board

> "The first time we talked about an innovation process – a disciplined process – to many of our innovation executives or employees, their first reaction was: 'You can't put a straitjacket on creativity.' So, explaining and selling the concept that an innovation process actually results in more ideas, in a better prioritization and a greater success ratio in the market was difficult!"
>
> *Nick Shreiber, former CEO*

The initial work of the innovation process board led to a certain amount of skepticism in several parts of the organization. The larger market companies, which were not yet seeing concrete results in terms of product availability and speed of new product introductions, were concerned by what they saw as central attempts to manage product priorities. It meant that they would no longer be able to dictate what would be developed. R&D engineers were also worried to see their traditional freedom being curbed. For many, the sudden emphasis on process was perceived as a dysfunctional threat.

To overcome the skepticism and create shared awareness of the benefits of a focus on process, Tetra Pak's management enlisted the company's internal management development organization, the Tetra Pak Academy. It asked them to organize, with the advice of the innovation process board, a series of seminars on the innovation process for the top 350 leaders of the company who had some involvement in innovation. These one-week seminars, run at IMD business school in Lausanne, presented the innovation process management philosophy and allowed process owners to describe the new processes they had developed. In an "action-learning" spirit, each participant committed to a process implementation project of his/her choice. These seminars proved effective in developing and sharing a common understanding and vocabulary of the process.

In 2003, having completed most of its initial work on processes, management started focusing on product and technology strategy and planning, a critical issue since it determined which products and technologies would be developed. A cross-functional project was launched by R&D and marketing, under the name Link, to ensure that long-term product and technology strategies would be closely aligned. This project led to the development of a very detailed methodology for identifying, classifying, and ranking desirable product attributes and connecting them with specific technologies to be developed.

> "We realized that the difficulties we had experienced in the '90s and early 2000s in the implementation of an enterprise resource planning system were due to our lack of process orientation. Our leadership and management had not mobilized the organization enough behind processes. This realization reinforced their commitment behind new process thinking."
>
> *Richard Tonkin, member of the innovation committee*

Step 5: Intensifying the Company's Process Orientation

Over the years, top management's level of interest in processes increased. The innovation process was well established and had

> "You have to lead from the center when it comes to global processes, whether it is innovation or the delivery of filling equipment or any other major process. You have a lot of value by doing it from the center."
>
> *Nick Shreiber, former CEO*

begun to deliver results. But senior leaders, starting with Dennis Jönsson, the head of the Tetra Pak Carton Ambient business unit – by far the biggest part of Tetra Pak – thought that other global processes would benefit from a more systematic approach.

Jönsson invited American process management guru, Michael Hammer, for a conference on process redesign and management at headquarters, and this led to the start of a major new focus on managing global corporate processes.

A process map was developed to identify Tetra Pak's core operational processes – not just innovation processes. These global operational processes included:

* customer management;
* product creation (the front end of innovation);
* product life cycle (the back end of innovation);
* order fulfillment of capital equipment;
* order fulfillment of packaging materials;
* order fulfillment of service products; and
* supplier management.

Other corporate processes were added so that each main corporate activity was handled as a process. From that point onward, Tetra Pak's top management team became directly and deeply involved in the overall global process governance task.

INNOVATION GOVERNANCE – STAGE 3: EMPOWERING MANAGEMENT THROUGH COUNCILS

Broadening the Scope of Tetra Pak's Governance Mission beyond Innovation

In 2005, Tetra Pak went through a significant change as a new top management team came to the fore. Dennis Jönsson, who had run

Tetra Pak Carton Ambient, was appointed as the new CEO of the whole company, replacing Nick Shreiber. He brought with him his head of development, Michael Grosse, an experienced development engineer whom he appointed as the corporate head of development to replace the CTO, Göran Harrysson, who transferred back to the Swedish organization.

Unlike Harrysson, who was not directly involved in operations, Grosse was responsible for all product development operations and all related processes. He was later put in charge of all technical service operations, a very important function within Tetra Pak and a major profit contributor.

The top management team was now streamlined into four major operational areas and four corporate staff functions. The former included commercial operations; development and service operations; supply chain operations; and processing systems. The latter covered human resources; legal; finance and business transformation; and corporate communications.

> "When I was in charge of Tetra Brik, I wanted to hire a head of development with different professional experience. I hired Michael Grosse, who brought with him the discipline of the automotive industry – he came from BMW – and together we started accelerating our work on processes. We wanted people not just to speak about processes, but to 'live' them."
>
> *Dennis Jönsson, CEO*

> "Dennis came with an ambitious agenda on processes. He built maps of all the governance mechanisms he wanted to create, together with their mission and their membership, which further accelerated process implementation."
>
> *Stefan Andersson, secretary of the Product & Technology Council*

The arrival of Jönsson at the top of the company brought changes in at least three areas:

- Commercial operations were reorganized into *market company clusters*. Together with the head of commercial operations, Jönsson changed Tetra Pak's regional organization into 10 geographic *market clusters*, each run by a *cluster head*.
- There was a renewed focus on product introduction and roll-out, a process that had previously been neglected. The major

change in this area was the nomination of a product management head, under the head of commercial operations, and the
appointment of product managers.

- The company's process orientation was accelerated. This
  renewed focus on global processes meant that innovation was
  no longer singled out. All the global processes listed earlier
  were put on the same level and attracted top management
  attention. Success, management believed, would come from full
  integration and high-level management of all these corporate
  processes. The company invested heavily in tools and competences to support its processes.

Establishing a New Process Management Structure

On the process side, each of the company's seven global operational
processes was split into its different constituents or levels, from
high-level global processes to sub-processes, down to individual
task levels – and this applied to product creation and product life
cycle, the two innovation processes. Each level was officially
assigned to one or several managers as indicated in Figure 11.1. At
the highest level, each global process was assigned to a member of
the GLT who acted as global process leader.

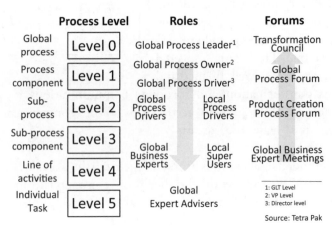

Figure 11.1:   Governance for Process Changes

To guide and support these process leaders in their work, management established a number of forums composed of teams responsible for discussing and addressing process management issues. These forums were staffed and formally structured to make process improvement recommendations to the various owners or drivers who had the decision power.

> "To manage the company, I want to be part of the various forums and councils, but I want them to have their specific mission. There should be no overlap!"
> *Dennis Jönsson, CEO*

The company thus became very professional in managing its innovation process, and also in all the business processes that support and leverage its innovation capabilities, like product management, a new function created in 2006. Today, Tetra Pak has a well-developed product management architecture with a senior leader and product managers assigned by platforms, materials, closures, and packages. They drive the assessment of product needs, advise on product prioritization and complexity reduction, and handle product introductions.

Governing All Processes Collectively through Focused Councils

To break the functional silos that still existed within the company, Jönsson set up a number of high-level *councils* as illustrated in Figure 11.2. These councils constitute the framework for decisions on all corporate processes and issues. Each council has a clear charter defining its mission, a specific and well-defined cross-functional membership, and an established meeting frequency. Each council is chaired by a member of the GLT and includes other selected members of the GLT as well as leaders from the second line of command. These councils are executive, i.e. they make decisions on the various issues that are within their remit.

The decisions of these councils are prepared and documented by a second group of *forums*. These are small, dedicated groups of specialists with their own mission and charter, an official membership

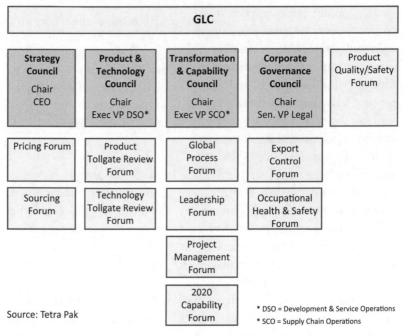

Figure 11.2:   Tetra Pak Council and Forum Structure

and chair, and a set of meetings aligned with the meetings of the councils they are supposed to support.

Establishing Two New Innovation Governance Mechanisms

In the course of this change toward a more collective and comprehensive management system, Tetra Pak's previous *innovation process board*, the company's first real innovation governance mechanism during the period from 2000 to 2005, disappeared as such. It was replaced by the Transformation & Capability Council, under the chairmanship of the executive vice president for supply chain operations. This council maintained its strong emphasis on the *how* of innovation – i.e. on process management initiatives including product creation – but also broadened its coverage to all corporate processes. It expanded its scope to deal with IT-related investments and company restructuring involving changes in IT and processes. Finally, it was empowered to address softer issues like leadership and capability development.

The newly created Product & Technology Council, chaired by Michael Grosse, the executive vice president for development and service operations, became the high-level "control tower" of innovation at Tetra Pak. Today, this council oversees all major product and technology development programs from start to finish, including decisions on resources and project execution. It has set up a project tollgate review system for each platform for which it is directly responsible, but is also charged with approving the tollgates of all critical projects, formerly called *pace plus* projects and now referred to as Level 1 projects. This important council meets six times a year and its charter specifies that it should be involved in the following types of decisions (quoting from a company document):

One-off items (in October):
Approve overall development program and project portfolio.
Approve overall resource allocation and development budget.
On-going items (level 1 projects):
Approve toll-gate transitions.
Terminate development projects.
Review key technology roadmaps and solution approaches.
Review development related issues impacting operations significantly.

> "How do you involve top management in R&D? Certainly not through polished R&D presentations! We want to involve top management in projects . . . for them to understand and contribute to tricky project decisions. These meetings, which last four hours, are not for show. They include real decision points in which they participate."
> *Stefan Andersson, secretary of the Product & Technology Council*

> "We have really seen a tremendous improvement in becoming efficient and effective, and we now make collective decisions. I felt that we had some extremely important people who were involved only when something went wrong. Today, I want Nils [the head of commercial operations] to take a role in decisions on the products he will sell. That makes it easier to correct things when they go wrong."
> *Dennis Jönsson, CEO*

Act as final escalation forum for product-related issues from product toll-gate reviews (PTR) and technology toll-gate reviews (TTR).

Reaping the Benefits of Tetra Pak's Process Orientation

> "In the past, we valued mostly creativity. Now we value the discipline as well. Why have a very entrepreneurial system if you cannot deliver? Now I have a strong belief that our organization will deliver when we start new projects!"
>
> *Stefan Andersson, secretary of the Product & Technology Council*

Today, the general feeling within Tetra Pak is that its process orientation, so strongly promoted by Jönsson and his top management colleagues, has delivered great results. The company had a tremendous backlog of new product introductions which has now been addressed. Its product portfolio is impressive and covers almost all of the basic needs of its 170 markets worldwide.

Besides, management has access to roadmaps on technology and products that are entirely linked, and it has established a process for strategy that seems to work effectively. Management can now look to the company's innovation future from a broader perspective. Nobody seems to question management's emphasis on process any more.

Nevertheless, Jönsson still feels that the culture change towards a deeper process orientation needs to be constantly reinforced. He comments: "It's not easy to change a culture. We need to make everyone understand that the new way of working with process is here to stay; it's not a fad! We want people speaking about it, living it every day, in marketing and sales, not just in technical operations. We also need to show results and be consistent."

FINDING A NEW BALANCE BETWEEN CREATIVITY AND DISCIPLINE

People from technical operations nevertheless have expressed some uneasiness about the possible impact on creativity and entrepreneurship of an excessive emphasis on processes. Concerns have been voiced over the dearth of radical innovations, particularly in technology, but not only there. Since the company was previously in catch-up mode, it had indeed favored incremental technology and product development projects that were urgent, either because of market need or to fight substitution threats in the market, for example in the aseptic plastic bottle segment. As a consequence, few revolutionary product concepts have been introduced in the past few years.

A number of voices have therefore noted the need to adjust somewhat the balance between creativity and discipline. As executive VP for development and service operations, Michael Grosse is one of them.

> "We went from a full focus on creativity to an emphasis on discipline. We have developed a product creation factory with a high degree of roadmap reliability, as opposed to an innovation center! If we continue only in that direction, we might lose our entrepreneurship mindset. Now we are trying to re-create our focus on disruptive innovation! We will always be on the discipline side, though, given the fact that we are not a research organization."
>
> *Michael Grosse, executive VP development and service operationss*

To swing the pendulum back toward creativity and fill the company's project pipeline with a higher level of technology input, Grosse has created and leads both an *innovation forum* and a *network of innovators*. He has also allocated a small part of the company's large R&D budget to exploring and supporting new ideas.

Grosse's *innovation forum* is quite different from all the other process-supporting forums. It consists of six members chosen from among Tetra Pak's most senior and visionary scientists and some heavy hitters representing the key business and product platforms. These members were personally selected by Grosse, who chairs the forum, based on their propensity to explore disruptive technologies and revolutionary product concepts. The way this forum, which meets several times per year, works is less formal and more participative than the other forums that prepare the decisions of the various councils. Topics that this forum explores include, among others, digital printing – an area of great potential for Tetra Pak – frugal innovation, and radical new approaches to reducing product costs. The innovation forum has a budget for starting new projects in promising areas that bypass the main process for project definition and programming.

The *network of innovators*, Grosse's second innovation-stimulating mechanism, gathers about 20 people from the main R&D centers in Lund, Modena, and Japan, all selected for their ability to consider new approaches to current problems. They know one another and value their diverse backgrounds. Grosse brings them together in a *project house* when a specific project requires their expertise and collaboration.

Finally, an award for innovation excellence has been created, alongside the three other company awards for leadership, operational excellence, and customer management.

EXPLORING NEW BUSINESS DEVELOPMENT OPPORTUNITIES

Tetra Pak's freedom to build innovative new activities alongside its carton packaging business is limited by the mission assigned to it by the Tetra Laval Group to which it belongs. It cannot backward integrate its processing system business, for example into dairy farming, which is the domain of the DeLaval Group, a sister company. Similarly, it cannot move into the machinery business for PET plastic bottles – a major competitor of carton packages – because Sidel, the leader for this type of equipment, is part of the Group's portfolio. So, Tetra Pak is bound to grow within its carton packaging and processing industry, and since it will not be allowed to acquire competitors due to its strong market position, all its growth opportunities need to be created organically, through innovation. On the packaging side, this means introducing new products to cater to new or growing market segments. On the processing side, this means developing equipment for the milk powder and cheese industries.

> "It is not our mission within the Tetra Laval Group to create a new leg to our business. We should be creative within our field. Let's optimize what we have!"
>
> *Dennis Jönsson, CEO*

Originally, and this is still true today, growing organically meant principally growing geographically, a strategy that was pursued aggressively, particularly in emerging economies. Tetra Pak has also developed and is growing a solid food packaging business with its Tetra Recart package line, which competes against tin cans.

But the sector with the highest innovation potential may be in services, an area under Grosse's responsibility. With thousands of complex processing and filling systems in the field, maintenance, parts, and repairs have always been an important source of revenues. But both Jönsson and Grosse believe that the company could easily multiply its service revenues and profits by a factor of three. This requires making its systems more "service-friendly," and to do so R&D has already introduced sensors and communication features in its systems.

> "Our advantage over many competitors is the fact that we have contacts with customers every day. Our problem is not a lack of customer intimacy . . . it is getting paid! Customers expect a lot of services from Tetra Pak . . . but for free!"
> *Michael Grosse, executive VP development and service operations*

Service growth will have to be achieved first by capturing a larger share of services performed by customers themselves. It will also come from developing new types of lucrative services beyond traditional maintenance and repair, i.e. services that customers will be ready to pay for because they add value to their operations. This is why Grosse has established a small team to identify innovative new services to offer to customers. Various opportunities have already been identified, for example the sale of consumables, training for customers on plant productivity, consulting services on operational performance, upgrade kits, and the like.

ADDRESSING FUTURE INNOVATION CHALLENGES

Reflecting on Organizational and Cultural Issues

Jönsson is aware that he faces three challenges that, if not addressed, could limit Tetra Pak's innovation performance.

The first is linked to the complexity of the governance system he has put in place. Managers spend a lot of time in a variety of councils and in the many forums to prepare council decisions. No one seems to challenge, at least openly, the new organization since these councils have introduced an effective collective governance system. But the layered system and the many forums are to a certain extent cumbersome – something that Jönsson recognizes – and this slows decisions somewhat.

Innovation speed is a second issue in light of the growing challenge from emerging competitors, even though considerable progress has been achieved through disciplined processes. Jönsson is convinced, however, that quality should not be compromised to reduce time to market. Customers who, in the past, were eager to have new systems installed in their plant, even before they were working 100% reliably, would be much less tolerant of system failures today.

The third challenge facing Tetra Pak's management is common to most innovative companies – where should management draw the line between its demand for performance in all areas and its advocacy of a right to fail. Jönsson is convinced that Tetra Pak's owners accept innovation risk, today as in the past. They support innovation; but they do not want big surprises.

Mobilizing the Organization behind Strategic Threats

From a strategic perspective, Jönsson sees an increased threat coming from two ongoing market evolutions. Both require an even higher level of innovation.

The first threat is the risk of substitution of carton packages by PET bottles, mostly in the non-carbonated beverage area. This threat, which has been present for years, led Tetra Pak to develop an innovative "bottle look-alike" carton package – Tetra Evero Aseptic™ – with a plastic top and a unique approach, for both production and package recycling. Thanks to innovations in its "carton-bottle" product and system platforms, Jönsson believes that Tetra Pak has stabilized its market position, but the threat remains.

The second threat is from copy-cats – referred to as "non-system suppliers" in the company's jargon. These are suppliers of carton materials, originally from China but potentially from other geographical areas, that offer cheaper carton rolls to Tetra Pak's system customers. They manage by cherry picking customers with high volumes and relatively simple product lines. Their lower unit margin is compensated for by their lower cost structure and high volumes. Some of these suppliers are now venturing into the European market. This threat is challenging Tetra Pak's traditional business model which consists of making its margin principally on packaging materials. To address this competition effectively, management knows that it has to drive costs down aggressively, through both technological innovation and a drastic reduction in unnecessary complexity in the company.

> "How can we combine two conflicting needs, i.e. the need to keep offering more differentiation to our customers and the need to standardize and go for volume to lower our costs?"
>
> *Dennis Jönsson, CEO*

Rethinking Development Focus and Operations

From an R&D perspective, Grosse sees two additional challenges that will need to be addressed in the near future.

The first is to rebalance somewhat the company's development efforts in favor of new highly productive and cost-efficient architectures. In a way, Tetra Pak's strong customer orientation has meant that the company has always put commercial demands and considerations before rethinking its fundamental architectures. This – Grosse believes – has maintained systems that are not as efficient as they could be. Changing focus may require the support of marketing and sales people who often take the lead in product decisions. Their active participation in the Product & Technology Council is therefore critical.

The second challenge is to extend the company's global R&D position by shifting the traditional R&D focus on Europe to create new centers of excellence in emerging markets. This will require a significant mindset change in a company that has always counted on its European R&D centers.

DRAWING THE LESSONS

Tetra Pak has been working on and perfecting its innovation governance system over the past 15 years with great results in terms of innovation performance. Analyzing its evolution over the years allows us to identify at least six success factors:

1. A strong commitment to innovation and personal engagement from the top management team including, but not only, the past three CEOs, without forgetting permanent reinforcement by the board of directors and the owners.
2. A progressive but steady enlargement of the scope of governance, initially focused on *process* but gradually extending to decisions on the *content* of innovation – project portfolios – through the various councils.
3. A strong focus on concrete implementation activities through a comprehensive process organization and management system and a clear hierarchy of missions and responsibilities from the very top level (GLT) down to the individual task level.
4. A broad sharing of the new process philosophy by the responsible owners and drivers through various intranet-based tools and the organization of extensive management development programs.
5. A willingness to bring fresh perspectives from outside the organization by recruiting senior leaders from relevant industries, such as the automotive industry, and effectively setting them up in their new responsibilities.
6. A high degree of patience and persistence over many years, since the systems in place had to be perfected step by step and extended progressively, and people had to be trained to make them work.

PART IV

DESIGNING YOUR OWN GOVERNANCE SYSTEM AND MAKING IT WORK

CHAPTER 12

GETTING STARTED

How Michelin has Rethought its Governance Model

Throughout this book, we have advocated the need for innovative companies to regularly review their approach to governing innovation in order to make it more effective. Some companies do it on an incremental basis, perfecting their system while keeping the same organizational model. Others adopt a more radical approach by exchanging their traditional model for a totally new way of allocating responsibilities and governing innovation. This is what Michelin, arguably the world's most innovative tire company, has done.

There are, generally, several drivers of this more radical type of change. It frequently starts with a management desire to broaden the company's scope of innovation and/or boost its performance given new market and competitive developments. But it is also frequently triggered by a change in top management and the arrival of a CEO with ambitious growth objectives and the will to leverage innovation as the main driver of that growth. This is what happened at DSM around 2005 and this is the process that Michelin has embarked on recently.

We believe that the path Michelin has followed in questioning its past practices, streamlining its innovation process, and coming up with a new innovation ecosystem – all of it achieved in a couple of years – should inspire many companies and show them one way to go. Michelin has reinvented its innovation governance model, and it has done so through deep personal engagement at the very top of the company. The management team does not claim that the system is perfect, yet, but they remain fully committed to keep improving it.

A LONG HISTORY OF INNOVATION IN TRANSPORTATION

Pioneering Rubber Tires

The roots of Michelin go back to 1832 in Clermont-Ferrand, in the Auvergne region of France, when two entrepreneurs applied a British invention[1] to produce a variety of rubber products. They built a small manufacturing plant and set up a partnership limited by shares in 1863. The company became Michelin & Co. in 1889 when two brothers from the founding family, Edouard and André Michelin, started to exploit a new rubber brake pad for horse-drawn carriages, "The Silent." This marked the beginning of the company's activities in rubber-based products for facilitating transportation and mobility, a mission that continues to guide the company today.

Most Michelin observers attribute the company's ability to sustain innovation to the strong and visionary influence of the successive members of the family who steered the company for more than a century. The two Michelin brothers were fertile inventors and marketers, applying their rubber knowledge to the emerging bicycle tire market. They introduced the first detachable and hence easily repairable bicycle tire, before beginning to produce tires for automobiles, trucks, and even airplanes. They manufactured airplanes during World War I and introduced the first trains on tires in 1929. To encourage mobility, they developed the first tourist guides and roadmaps, and they promoted road numbering and road signs. Edouard ran the company; his brother, André, was an astute commercial communicator and marketer. He launched and promoted bicycle and automobile races to demonstrate the superiority of the company's products. The Michelin Man logo, created in 1898, became universally recognized by motorists and, in 2000, a panel of professionals voted it the world's best logo.

Michelin's historical focus on innovation continued with the two brothers' successors within the family. Over time, they introduced most of the new modern developments in tires. In 1935, Michelin took over the automobile manufacturer Citroën and started developing the legendary Deux Chevaux which became a hit with young baby boomers after World War II. But what made Michelin the recognized innovation leader in the tire industry was the introduction of the revolutionary X radial casing tire in 1946. The concept brought such great benefits in terms of safety and tire life that, despite its higher cost, it was adopted by all tire manufacturers and became a world standard.

Building a Global Technology-intensive Company

The globalization and growth of the company from the post-World War II period until the late 1990s was led by François Michelin, Edouard's grandson. He was at the helm from 1955 to 1999 and passed the top job on to his own son, Edouard, who took over until the tragic accident that caused his death in 2006. From 2006 until 2012, Michel Rollier, another family member and Michelin's managing general partner, continued the family's historic focus on globalization and innovation, until he was replaced by Jean-Dominique Senard, the first non-family member CEO.

François Michelin was credited with refocusing the company on tires,[2] keeping only the maps and guides business as part of the original family jewels. He acquired a number of competitors, including Uniroyal/Goodrich and a few smaller companies. He also initiated the company's globalization drive by establishing factories and subsidiaries in both North America and Latin America as well as in Asia. That move was continued and amplified under his son Edouard Michelin and Edouard's successor, Michel Rollier.

A fervent believer in technology, François set up the most advanced R&D and testing capability in the industry, which led to the development of tires for all kinds of applications, including Formula One cars, the space shuttle, and the Airbus A380 super jumbo. Michelin progressively applied its radial tire concept to all road and off-road vehicles as well as airplanes, and it developed a range of improved variants of that X tire casing. But François was not fully satisfied with incremental developments. So he urged his research department to pursue disruptive innovations.

Encouraged by their CEO, Michelin's engineers came up with several radically new ideas, some of which were cleverly engineered but ended up having limited application potential. Large amounts were invested in these developments, which caught the imagination of the company for a while but proved disappointing in terms of performance or costs, and thus had to be discontinued.

> "These failures to deploy certain radical new concepts reflected a lack of lucidity on the part of Research, and an absence of challenge on the economic and market impact of these technologies on the part of management. We learned a lot from these mistakes!"
>
> *Philippe Denimal,*
> *former head of research*

The most famous of these developments was PAX, an innovative but expensive tire and wheel system with an internal support ring that allowed drivers to continue their journey on a flat tire. The non-standard nature of the wheel, its assembly and specific service equipment, and the cost proved to be barriers to the generalization of the system.

> "When Edouard Michelin took over from his father François, he found these developments in his basket. Out of loyalty, he backed them up to the limit before finally stopping them!"
>
> *Patrick Oliva, VP strategic*
> *anticipation and sustainable*
> *development*

Another disruptive manufacturing process innovation, called C3M, made it possible to build tires on a very compact machine from individual materials (rather than traditional pre-assembled components). It was not adopted on a large scale due to its disappointing cost/performance ratio. Its merit proved to be in stimulating manufacturing engineers to improve their traditional process to attain the performance level of the C3M, while continuing to use their current manufacturing set-up. Additionally, the bold approach for such a compact, modular process did lead to a breakthrough in manufacturing technology. This fundamental process technology now has numerous applications on new tire assembly machines, including high performance tire production.

Promoting Sustainable Mobility and Electric Propulsion

François Michelin was also a visionary regarding the future of mobility. As a company, Michelin always tried to contribute to vehicles' energy efficiency, but the concern for sustainable mobility really became part of its vision and mission in the 1990s. Management was aware that road transportation would have to dramatically change in terms of practices and technologies to reduce greenhouse gas (GHG) emissions, primarily carbon dioxide (CO_2). The contribution of tires to this overall CO_2 and GHG reduction objective was significant. Indeed, tires have a major impact on vehicles' rolling resistance and thus directly on energy efficiency and emissions. This observation led Michelin's scientists and engineers to work persistently to reduce the rolling resistance of the company's tires. The Green X tire, introduced in 1992, was a significant advancement compared with Michelin's traditional radial tires. Improvements continued regularly over the years, leading in 2007 to the Energy Saver tire with its record-breaking low resistance.

In the truck category, the X One truck tire replaced standard dual tires with a single tire, providing significant improvements in rolling resistance and reductions in mass. Both the Energy Saver and the X One innovations have been recognized as industry transformers in a period when the contribution of tires to reductions in CO_2 emissions is highly valued.

The launch of Challenge Bibendum in 1998, described as a "global clean vehicle and sustainable mobility forum," was a tangible sign of the company's environmental commitment. Players from the automotive industry and the energy sector were invited to work on reconciling the automotive world and the environment by demonstrating new technologies and vehicle concepts for sustainable mobility.

Since electric vehicles (EVs) were expected to have lower mechanical resistance because of the removal of the internal

> "The CDM was to make us aware of what could come next in the area of electric vehicles, which is absolutely crucial for us in our core business of tires. At the same time, there may be some interesting business opportunities for us in these areas. So we decided to have a look, to be totally open and totally creative in identifying potential partners to produce and market CDM's new systems."
>
> *Patrick Oliva, VP strategic anticipation and sustainable development*

combustion engine, the relative importance of tire rolling resistance in the total loss of energy would be significantly higher. Based on this consideration, Michelin's tire research and development organization had developed new low rolling resistance targets for EVs and a totally new concept tire for EVs.

Convinced that the future of the car industry would be strongly impacted by solutions in electric propulsion, in 1996 François Michelin decided to set up a small research center, called CDM (Conception-Development Michelin), near Fribourg in Switzerland. The center was totally devoted to the development of zero emission automotive technologies that had a real chance of being used in the future. This was one of François Michelin's last decisions before handing over to his son Edouard. Because of its different scope and time horizon, this small research center[3] was deliberately set up some distance from Michelin's main tire technical center in France, which viewed it with a certain amount of skepticism.

Twelve years after its creation, Michelin's CDM research center had developed and successfully demonstrated the feasibility and performance of a broad range of innovative systems and components for electric and hybrid-electric vehicles, all covered by numerous patents. They included electric drives, fuel cells, and hydrogen storage systems.

Exploiting Opportunities in the Digital Era

In 1989, Michelin – world leader in road maps and tourism guides[4] – pioneered the first computerized system[5] allowing travelers to create roadmaps with detailed instructions. The company was therefore uniquely positioned to exploit opportunities in digital navigation systems. It started to work on its own GPS system, in competition with companies such as Garmin and TomTom. But in the early 2000s, management stopped all hardware developments, which were becoming extremely expensive, to focus instead on software. The company introduced a web-based navigation system – ViaMichelin – and is now developing GPS mapping and traffic information software to be embedded in high-end car navigation systems, a fast-growing segment. Michelin insiders believe that the company's relatively prudent move into digital navigation systems reflects (1) management's predominant focus on tires, and (2) a historical lack of management mechanism for venturing and new business development. Indeed, the creation of CDM and its focus on electric vehicles was the result of a personal visionary decision by François Michelin, not the outcome of a well thought through corporate development decision.

REFOCUSING ON INCREMENTAL INNOVATION, EMERGING MARKETS, AND PROFITABILITY

In the 1990s and early 2000s, the whole organization was so R&D led that this created voids in other management areas, which did not help in addressing its competitiveness and financial health challenges. Besides, unsuccessful engineering-led

> "François Michelin was in love with science and technology. He spent most of his time in the research labs!"
> *Philippe Denimal,*
> *former head of research*

developments affected the morale of R&D. They also created some skepticism in the organization and management toward radical R&D.

So, when he took over after Edouard Michelin's untimely death, Michel Rollier faced a threefold challenge. He felt that he needed (1) to better link the company's creative research group with the market; (2) to build manufacturing capacity in the emerging markets of Asia and Latin America; and (3) to rapidly improve the company's level of cost competitiveness and profitability.

In pursuit of renewed financial health for the company, Rollier refocused the organization on productivity and manufacturing rationalization. He was helped in this by Jean-Dominique Senard, one of his two managing partners[6] in charge of finance and strategy.

Streamlining R&D

Having noticed that the company had not benefited enough from its disruptive innovations, Rollier passed a new message to staff: "Let's reorient Research so that it focuses on products that the market wants!" Didier Miraton – the second managing partner – acted as CTO in charge of Michelin's Technical Center. Together with his number 2, Terry Gettys, they launched an analysis of the company's past technological successes and failures. This assessment was used to introduce a number of changes to streamline and standardize the development process. These changes, introduced between 2007 and 2011, dealt with R&D ambition, speed, resources, and processes. They included:

> "Our I2M approach was designed to contain the traditional *push* side of Research. In the past, researchers made hypotheses on our objectives, developed new concepts, built 'demonstrators' [prototypes] and presented them to the product line organizations that were generally surprised. The innovations could be technically brilliant, but their implementation could significantly add to the product cost or reduce the capacity of the plants. This led to new development cycles in research and a loss of time and resources!"
>
> *Terry Gettys, executive VP RD&I*

- Better recognition of the three distinct phases in product development: Advanced research to develop new concepts and new materials; pre-development – called *markers* in Michelin's R&D terminology – to elaborate some of the concepts from Research into producible tires; and development, industrialization, and commercialization.
- A more ambitious development program regarding the evolution of Michelin's future tire features. Given the increasing quality in the tire industry as a

whole, Michelin had to perform 20 to 30% better on key tire features to gain significant differentiation and justify its price premium. But such changes could have a disruptive impact on manufacturing.

• A gate review system and a better way to link the research organization with the market through what was called an *Innovation to Market* (I2M) process. It was entrusted to the product line organizations, which were the ultimate receivers, developers, and industrializers of the new product concepts developed and prototyped by Research.

The new I2M approach was steered by the product line groups (passenger cars and light trucks; trucks; specialties, i.e. aircraft, earthmover, agricultural and motorcycle tires; and materials). It consisted of selecting from the research organization's output the most compatible and attractive concepts for the product lines on the basis of their business case. The pre-development group would then take the retained concepts and design the precursors of future product ranges to be developed and industrialized by the market organizations. The task of the I2M teams – a combination of technical, financial, and industrial people from the product line organizations – was therefore to establish a better link between Research and the market.

Figure 12.1 presents a simplified picture of Michelin's research, development, and industrialization structure (RD&I) toward the end of Rollier's tenure as CEO, and of its main output.

This refocusing on the market meant that the product line groups started to play a leading role in selecting and positioning key innovations in their new product portfolios. In a context of undercapacity in manufacturing and the need to reach a higher level of profitability, the product line groups started to apply stringent filters to radical ideas from Research. Thus, several of the latest disruptive developments conceived by the research organization were kept on hold due to a lack of resources for their market validation and industrialization. The bulk of Michelin's capital investments were indeed earmarked for new plant capacity in emerging markets like India, leaving radical concepts without adequate resources for rapid deployment.

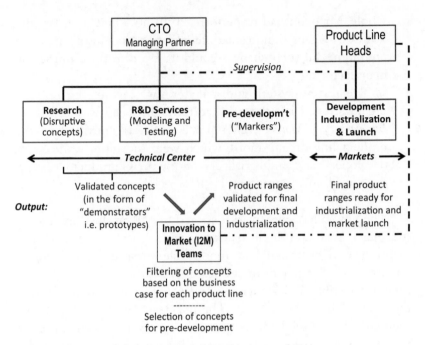

Figure 12.1:   Michelin's RD&I Organization and Process

This shift in emphasis, away from disruptive technology-pushed innovation toward market value-driven developments, and the resulting empowerment of the product line groups regarding new products, created some concerns within Research that had always benefited from special attention from the former CEOs François and Edouard Michelin.

TAKING THE HELM AND REFOCUSING ON PRODUCT AND MARKET LEADERSHIP

Leveraging the Strengths of a Global Organization

A change of CEO – from Rollier to Senard – was announced in the spring of 2011 to become effective in May 2012. It was accompanied by the departure of the CTO and his replacement by his number 2 – Terry Gettys – an experienced American engineer who became executive vice president in charge of RD&I.

With a 14.6% share of the global market for tires, in second place behind Bridgestone, Michelin continued to vie for global market leadership and increased growth. By the end of 2012, the company had 113,500 employees; it had produced 166 million tires in 69 production facilities in 18 countries, and conducted marketing operations in more than 170 countries. Its 2012 consolidated net sales amounted to €21.5 billion, broken down as follows:

- Fifty-two percent came from passenger car and light truck tires and related distribution. The company was number 1 worldwide in both high-performance tires for cars and fuel-efficient tires. It was also strong in tire distribution thanks to its own networks of distributors – Euromaster in Europe and TCI in the USA. [7]

- Thirty-one percent resulted from truck tires and related regrooving, retreading, and distribution. Michelin was number 1 in the world in radial truck tires and in retreading.

- Seventeen percent came from its specialty businesses. This category covered tires for the agricultural, two-wheel, off-road, and aerospace markets. It also included Michelin Travel Partner (the maps and guides business and the organizer of the Via-Michelin website and of the navigation software activity), as well as Michelin Lifestyle, its accessories business.

Michelin's strength was in the replacement tire market, where its reputation for quality allowed it to command a price premium of 5 to 10% over its competitors. Replacement sales represented close to 80% of volume in the market for passenger cars and light trucks and the same proportion in the truck market.

Keeping a Strong RD&I Organization

When Gettys took over the management of the RD&I organization, Michelin's technological advance over its competitors was based on a strong organization with over 6000 engineers, technicians, and testers. They spread across a network of laboratories and test centers in Europe, North America, and Asia (China, Thailand, and Japan). The group spent almost 3% of its sales on RD&I, with two primary objectives:

- To achieve the best performance balance for each type of tire use, in terms of safety, durability, fuel efficiency, and carbon emissions, as well as quietness and comfort.
- To reduce total lifetime cost of ownership for its customers.

Michelin prided itself on being the preferred supplier of tires for the motorsport industry and it had developed a special department specifically for that purpose. The company also collaborated closely with most of the world's vehicle manufacturers and bodywork designers, helping them in their innovation processes. Its partnership extended to the design and development of futuristic concept tires for cars to be exhibited in the main car shows around the world.

Building a New Top Management Team

Under Rollier, Michelin had been led by a triumvirate with a managing general partner (Rollier) as CEO and two managing partners. When he took over the CEO role, Senard did not retain the triumvirate. He reinforced the Group's former executive council, which had served as an advisory council to the managing partners, and turned it into a Comité Exécutif Groupe (CEG), with more accountability when it came to steering the company's performance. The CEG included 11 members:

- the four product line directors;
- the director of all the geographic zones;
- the director of RD&I;
- the director of commercial performance; and
- four corporate directors (in charge of finance; corporate communications and brands; personnel; and corporate development).

An "extended CEG" was created including functions such as individual geographic zone directors, heads of research, strategic anticipation and sustainable development, purchasing, and a few other key central functions.

Refocusing on Product Leadership

Having made a lot of progress on productivity and costs and expanded its capacity in emerging markets, Michelin was now in the perfect position to reinforce and accelerate its innovation focus. Senard fully appreciated the challenges the company would have to face and the role that effective innovations would need to play.

Michelin was in danger of seeing its superiority in tire performance threatened by competitors. To keep its price premium in the market, the company had to boost superior product performance in areas most valued by customers. Since the premium segment of the tire market was limited in size, Michelin also needed to pursue cost-effective innovations and leverage them in broad market segments under its multiple brands.

Senard was also concerned by what he saw as the danger of loss of innovation spirit in his business organization. The company's product line management teams were busy with much-needed capacity building programs and jockeying for position in the market with their leading competitors. Radical innovation was no longer their first priority. As for Michelin's scientists and engineers, they remained uncertain about the best way to get the market organizations to adopt their new product concepts.

Finally, Senard was convinced that his management team, by being focused on tires, was missing growth opportunities in adjacent or totally new product or service areas. Based on these considerations, Senard set the objective to reinforce Michelin's product and market leadership with a rapid action plan.

> "Jean-Dominique Senard clearly considered that Michelin needed to boost the company's innovation performance to guarantee its future. His ambition was to energize the entire organization, not just the RD&I group."
>
> *Terry Gettys, executive VP RD&I*

Addressing the Product Leadership Challenge through a Dedicated Project Group

In June 2011, Senard held a series of meetings with Gettys, the new head of the RD&I organization, on how to accelerate the time to market for key innovations. Gettys immediately started a work

> "Together with Gettys, we selected the members of our Lead project group on two criteria:
> - their personal experience and legitimacy with regard to innovation; and
> - their mental openness and preparedness to challenge the status quo and propose radical solutions.
>
> We also thought that our group would benefit from the perspective of a couple of 'outsiders!'"
>
> *Pascal Thibault, head of organization, consulting, and transformation*

group to evaluate the existing company-wide innovation process and identify its strengths and deficiencies. He also consulted Pascal Thibault, head of organization, consulting, and transformation within Michelin's HR department, to explore how to boost innovation in the company.

The shift in focus from managing research to managing the whole innovation process came up naturally and it was quickly endorsed by Senard. Gettys and Thibault subsequently suggested creating a small task group – called the Lead project group – to address the challenge, under Gettys' leadership.

Ultimately, the Lead group was set up with members from different areas, as follows:

- the head of Research, the department traditionally responsible for inventing new concepts;
- the two leaders of the US and Japanese research centers;
- the head of the manufacturing process research group;
- a marketing specialist from the passenger car product line, experienced in the front end of innovation;
- a former boss of the agricultural product line, now responsible for Michelin Solutions, the company's new service arm;
- the head of the strategic anticipation and sustainable development group; and
- two "guests" – a consultant and a former Michelin senior manager who had assumed responsibility for the company's sports association.[8]

The Lead project group was up and running by July 2011. Senard insisted that it had to come up with recommendations to Rollier and Senard by early November. Quickly, Thibault realized that what was at stake was an entirely new innovation governance model and process for Michelin. The limited time frame available for formulating concrete recommendations meant that the group would need to be coached by another external consultant who specialized in helping teams in the conception and implementation of radical change.

With the help of their consultant, the Lead team organized two intense workshops spread over two months. Each workshop was attended by about 20 or 30 participants and preparation involved a number of meetings in small groups. The first workshop focused on a diagnostic of the situation and the second on formulating a broad set of recommendations. The final report, "Innovation Performance and Dynamics," including what they called a new *innovation governance ecosystem* – was presented in early November 2011 and approved.

> "To meet our deadline, we decided to adopt a 'land and learn' approach, i.e. to go very fast and learn while moving ahead, without shooting for perfection. We decided to make a broad assessment of the situation in small groups, then to move rapidly toward framing solutions. The level of enthusiasm for the solutions in the team was very high."
>
> *Terry Gettys, executive VP RD&I*

The architecture of the new governance model is shown in Figure 12.2.

The Lead team's conclusions were very detailed and contained preliminary missions for each part of the innovation governance ecosystem, together with tentative suggestions of people to be in charge. It covered the following tasks:

- Assigning responsibility for the CDM center – the Swiss advanced research group which developed systems for electric cars – to the worldwide research director.
- Revisiting and improving the Innovation to Market (I2M) process that links concept research with the product development organization.
- Reviewing the way the research organization works, with the objective of broadening its scope.
- Improving the identification and inclusion of previously unarticulated customer needs in product specifications.

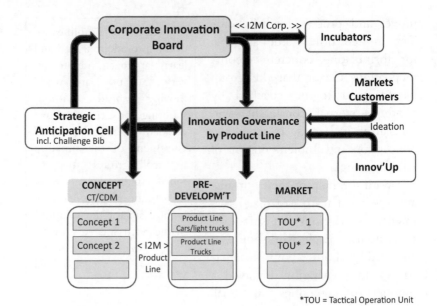

Figure 12.2: Michelin's New Innovation Governance Ecosystem

- Broadening the collection of ideas to the entire Michelin organization and not only the RD&I group.
- Reinforcing and structuring Michelin's ability to track and exploit weak signals announcing important future developments.
- Building an incubator for innovations offering potential new business opportunities that do not fall directly within the domains covered by the tire product lines.

SETTING UP A CORPORATE INNOVATION BOARD (CIB)

> "The direct and personal commitment and involvement of the CEO in innovation . . . that's what has just changed with the creation of the CIB!"
>
> *Jean-Dominique Senard,*
> *CEO*

The Lead project team's main recommendation, which was enthusiastically endorsed by Senard, was to establish a high-level corporate innovation board (CIB). This board would take strategic decisions on innovation priorities and orchestrate company-wide efforts to boost innovation performance. This new mechanism de facto replaced the functional roles and organizations that had hitherto tried to pilot innovation.

Staffing the CIB

Senard welcomed the Lead project team's proposal that he should formally chair the CIB, with Gettys serving as "animator." The membership of the CIB reflected the strategic importance of the decisions to be made, because the CIB would deal not only with the *process* of innovation but also with the *content* of the company's innovation portfolio.

Besides the CEO (Senard) and the executive vice president RD&I (Gettys), the CIB included several members of the Comité Exécutif Groupe, namely the four product line heads. It also included the director of commerce, the head of corporate development, and the head of strategic anticipation and sustainable development, acting as CIB secretary. Finally, it was decided that two external, non-Michelin executives would be invited to participate – a French executive bringing competencies in services innovations, and a highly reputed innovation management professor from India.

> "To avoid our traditional loops between Research and the market and to go faster, I suggested to Senard that the product line heads could be associated with prioritizing the objectives of Research and setting its boundaries. Today, in the CIB, we determine the themes to be pursued by Research and we give them the constraints that can be anticipated for feasible large-scale deployment."
>
> *Terry Gettys, executive VP RD&I*

Operating the CIB

The first CIB meeting took place in March 2012, a mere four months after the Lead project group presented its recommendations to the Michelin partners. At that first meeting, Senard and Gettys, as chairman and animator respectively of the CIB,

> "We never have CIB meetings in the boardroom. We hold them in rooms with individual tables, posters on the walls and prototype 'demonstrator-wheels' all over the place. Members must remember that they are there to manage innovation concretely; they are not at the CIB in a traditional corporate governance role!"
>
> *Terry Gettys, executive VP RD&I*

reminded its members of their two missions to:

- take strategic decisions on needs and research priorities; and
- manage the dynamics of innovation company-wide.

By March 2013, the CIB had already met four times and it had reached its cruising speed of three meetings per year, in March, June, and October. Gettys now believes that he needs to introduce a more regular scheduling of topics to optimize the timing.

To ensure that all CIB members are clear about the points that have been discussed and decided, each meeting ends with a formal reading of the decisions. These decisions are collectively reformulated to avoid misunderstandings and surprises when members go back to their business.

The main strategic role of the CIB is now to steer the development process, particularly the front end, by determining the strategic objectives and priorities of the research group. Research will no longer work in a pure *technology push* mode; it will follow the priorities defined by the CIB on the basis of their market potential. The CIB has thus become a cross-functional locus for identifying and enforcing ambition-driven product/market objectives. It will be helped in its mission by the strategic anticipation unit, which is expected to contribute insight and foresight.

Management recognizes, though, that decisions on new products made in the CIB need to strike a balance between satisfying the immediate, incremental needs of the product lines and being ready for the future by funding more radical concepts. Given the presence of the four product line heads on the CIB, who are evaluated annually on sales and profits, such a balance might be difficult to strike . . . unless the other more neutral members, and particularly the CIB chairman and the animator, weigh in heavily to defend the more radical projects.

In its first year of operation, the CIB established two new domains that had not previously been treated as priorities by Research. This demonstrated the effectiveness of the broad CIB membership in identifying significant societal and market trends in order to anticipate new technology domains needed for future products and services.

SETTING UP OTHER ELEMENTS OF THE INNOVATION ECOSYSTEM

Encouraging a Bottom-up Ideation Process

The Lead project team had recommended the promotion of two sources of new bottom-up ideas. The first one, which still needs to be further developed and implemented, is the search for unarticulated customer and market needs.

The second, called Innov'Up, entails the implementation of a formal bottom-up ideation process to act as a strong counterbalance to the top-down impetus embedded in the CIB. A leader has been appointed and experiments have already been launched in the form of "challenges." Indeed, to make this bottom-up quest for ideas concrete and mobilize the organization, a number of questions have been asked to the entire Michelin Group, which should enable people to work together on these challenges and recommend responses. These challenges have already led to promising results.

The use of social media is also being promoted to allow people worldwide to react to and enrich the ideas generated. The task of filtering ideas has been entrusted to the incubator office (see below), and the CIB is determined to act on the best ideas generated.

> "People have innovation in their genes at Michelin, but we need to unleash it. It can remain dormant for three reasons: (1) lack of time to innovate due to excessive operational constraints; (2) Incongruent performance measurement system; (3) Our perfectionism! We expect everything to be perfect the first time. As soon as we open the door and authorize people to innovate, it gives great results!"
>
> *Pascal Thibault, head of organization, consulting, and transformation*

Putting New Business Building Activities in Incubators under the CIB Spotlight

Before the creation of the CIB, Senard had already promoted a separate service business, Michelin Solutions, with the objective of developing and selling a broad range of service offerings for cars and truck fleets, later to be extended to fleets of aircraft and off-road vehicles. This business was staffed by some of the company's best marketing minds, who were encouraged to work with a broad range of hardware, software, industrial, IT, and financial "complementors" to offer comprehensive and integrated fleet transportation and mobility solutions.

As a way of managing these new activities – hardware, systems, software, and services – that do not fit with Michelin's existing product lines, the incubator concept was adopted. The most obvious incubator candidates were those technologies that had been developed to a good maturity level, yet fell outside the priority scope of the tire product lines. Everyone at Michelin is aware that the outlook for these activities is uncertain, given that they resulted from a pure "inside-out" perspective. They were not products requested by the market. They ought to be complemented by other "outside-in" business ideas, emanating from a systematic search for unarticulated or latent customer needs. The two ideation processes mentioned above and put in place as part of Michelin's innovation governance ecosystem (refer to Figure 12.2) will undoubtedly contribute such ideas once they are fully operational.

The incubators created by the CIB are under the supervision of an incubator office headed by an entrepreneurial manager. His mission is fourfold:

- Put in place a process and tools to evaluate, screen, and rank ideas coming from both the markets/customers and internal sources – through the Innov'Up process – based on their attractiveness for Michelin and their feasibility/risk.
- Develop and implement a formal venturing process with specific development phases, linked with progressive investment gates, and a way to reduce technical and market uncertainties.

- Coach these new project teams as they proceed, particularly in their partnership discussions and business development efforts.
- Recommend to the CIB, which will remain the main decision body, the new projects worth incubating, as well as those whose outlook does not justify continuing investment and hence need to be stopped.

The CIB will maintain overall supervision of these new businesses and will be ready to create an operating company for them if their market outlook is positive and they are viable from a business point of view.

> "We told the heads of our incubators: 'You have a budget to explore a business, be open, go and find your-selves external partners, but keep Michelin's high quality standards'!"
>
> *Jean-Dominique Senard,*
> *CEO*

One of the missions of these incubators is to change Michelin's attitude to innovation. Traditionally, market failures on radical innovation concepts were regarded as abnormalities, and they remained tainted with frustration. Nobody talked about them. With the incubator concept, management is passing a very different message, i.e. not all projects are expected to lead to success. In a way, incubators should rid Michelin of its guilt feelings about high-risk innovations and they are expected to liberate the generation of new ideas.

But Senard and his CIB colleagues are aware that the profiles required to lead and work on incubating projects – intrapreneurs and risk takers – may not be widely available within the company. Michelin has traditionally sought solid professionals, focused on quality and operational performance, to progress its mature tire business, rather than explorers and go-getters. These profiles are critical for successive incubators and in some cases may have to be sourced outside the company.

Cascading the CIB Idea to the Product Line Level

To manage innovation at the product line level, two parallel organizational mechanisms were created: the Passenger Car Innovation

Committee and the Trucks Innovation Committee. These committees are headed by the product line director and key staff responsible for marketing, technical development, industrial development and quality, plus the heads of the corporate research and pre-development groups. Their major role is to steer the I2M filtering process, i.e. to select the major innovations from Research to be introduced in their product line, work with pre-development to build a strategy and business case, and then steer the industrialization phase to go to market as fast as possible. Industrialization and commercialization are handled at the regional level by tactical operational units which have the same product line functions but in a given market area, like North America or Asia.

ANTICIPATING THE NEXT STEPS

Members of the CIB appreciate that they have a long road ahead to overcome some of the limitations of their new innovation governance system and to extend and complement it with new features.

Correcting Current Deficiencies

Three potential challenges have been identified and are being remedied.

The first one has to do with the risk of excessive short-termism. This fear is linked to the fact that the product lines currently strongly influence the broad orientation of research, i.e. the themes to be explored and decisions on product priorities. This could reinforce the danger of developing a silo mentality in which each product line narrowly concentrates on its immediate, incremental development objectives. At the CIB meetings, the members must represent the overall best interests of the company, with a strong priority on getting the most impactful innovations to market rapidly. The issue of whether disruptive tire concepts, once invented and validated, can be handled within the current approach – i.e. within the I2M process – or whether they need to be nursed by a specially funded tire incubator has not yet been evaluated.

The second challenge is linked to the first one. Product line heads, particularly of the leading ones, i.e. passenger cars and trucks, may be tempted to pull too many research and pre-development resources toward their own domain. As head of the RD&I organization, Gettys feels that his role is to stop excessive requests by these product lines to the detriment of some of the smaller, less vocal ones. He is helped in this task by the fact that the CIB includes a number of leaders with a broad corporate perspective, e.g. the heads of commerce, corporate development, and the strategic anticipation unit, as well as the two "outsiders." Besides, the product line heads have been chosen for their ability to act for the good of the company, not only of their business.

The third challenge is that the I2M process – which is in place to validate the concepts developed by Research and filter them on behalf of individual product lines – is perceived to be too slow. Indeed, it generally involves a number of time-consuming activities, such as market research to identify potential customer targets and price ranges. For some innovations it also includes joint testing of *demonstrators* (prototypes developed by Research) with OEM customers or fleet operators to check how well they are accepted. These activities can take 12 to 18 months of work before go/no-go decisions can be made. The solution that has been adopted is to start this I2M investigation process six months before the demonstrators are totally validated. But Gettys believes that the overall lead time is still too long and will have to be shortened in the future.

Extending the Scope of the CIB

After only four meetings and a number of substantive changes in strategy and process, CIB members know that they must extend the scope of their innovation governance activities.

Setting Up Innovation Indicators

One of the first tasks on Gettys' to-do list is to propose a number of innovation-related indicators. Michelin has a disciplined culture, and when people are given indicators, for example on safety, they tend to act effectively to improve the factors being measured, in this case the rate of accidents. Product line heads each have 15 indicators on their scorecard and every organizational entity has a scorecard, so applying a measuring philosophy to innovation input and output would not be difficult. But Gettys is concerned not to overdo it and to add only the most important indicators to the current pyramids.

Promoting Innovation Excellence

This focus on innovation performance indicators and on benchmarking, according to Gettys, should be entrusted to a new corporate function which aids the CIB by tracking innovation performance. This function is viewed as a necessary resource to constantly assess the dynamics of innovation, i.e. corporate-wide innovation excellence, beyond RD&I activities.

Looking for Business Model Innovations

Another concern, shared by most members of the CIB, is to broaden the scope of innovation to cover more than technologies and products, for example toward new business models. Michelin has traditionally innovated in its revenue model to take full advantage of the superiority of its radial tires in terms of longevity and retreadability. For example, instead of selling truck tires or off-road equipment tires to fleet operators, the company has pioneered the concept of invoicing operators on the basis of ton-kilometers. Similarly, its aircraft unit invoices airlines on the number of take-offs and landings accomplished with a given set of tires. But these revenue model innovations are already proven, and the company will need to establish a process to systematically pursue new business model innovations.

Searching for Innovation Opportunities in Internal Operations

Senard is interested in applying innovation concepts to the field of services, as exemplified by his strong involvement in Michelin Solutions, the company's full service arm for private customers and fleet operators. But he is also quite keen to introduce innovative new concepts in the company's internal service functions. One of his most visible moves was to create Michelin Business Services, an internal department for efficiently consolidating all kinds of administrative

> "I want to show that the boss is fully engaged behind innovation. As CEO of the company, I will definitely continue to chair the CIB!"
> *Jean-Dominique Senard,*
> *CEO*

and logistics functions. This, he believes, should bring efficiency gains via highly focused centers of excellence that support a number of company functions. Indeed, Michelin's organizational entities around the world are currently run independently and have their own administrative infrastructure, which leads to a number of cost redundancies that could be eliminated.

Building a True Culture of Innovation Company-wide

Finally, Senard and his CIB colleagues are aware that the company's culture may have to evolve if innovation is going to extend beyond RD&I specialists to reach all corners of the organization. This may require a major change program to encourage attitudes of openness, initiative, collaboration, risk taking, and entrepreneurship, among other qualities.

One of the guidelines for such a change program might be the Michelin Performance and Responsibility (PRM) approach, which was launched in 2002 to help everyone in the Group remain focused on the long-term consequences of their decisions. As indicated on the website: "In addition to expressing Michelin's sustainable development commitment, PRM also shows that achieving performance and responsibility is the best way to move Michelin forward. In 2012, PRM's 10-year anniversary was widely celebrated across the Group." The PRM approach has stressed and measured a number of the company's achievements in areas like sustainable development, customer orientation, and corporate social responsibility. As the highest-ranking champion of the PRM philosophy, Senard may be tempted to leverage PRM's traction by finding a way to integrate an innovation agenda into the PRM list of great internal and external causes.

GOING PUBLIC AND MAINTAINING
THE EFFORT

After testing the new governance model and checking that it helped to address Michelin's innovation challenges effectively, Senard felt the need to inform the Michelin organization more broadly. He communicated the news about the new innovation governance model at his first general assembly of shareholders as CEO. The participants had not expected Michelin's management to tackle the company's challenges through innovation. They were thrilled to learn that innovation was, once again, at the center of management's priorities.

But Senard and his CIB colleagues know that they now have to mobilize the entire organization behind their new innovation agenda. The first information round covered the 90 or so most senior managers. The next step was to reach 3000 company managers around the world in a conference called The International Bib Forum. The conference, which was held in Paris, allowed Michelin's executive committee to present the company's new innovation governance ecosystem. But it also stressed that innovation, in addition to its strong top-down dimension, requires a massive bottom-up effort to mobilize the entire organization in the quest for market insights and innovative ideas. Management expects that everyone in that forum will have understood that he/ she can participate in this effort.

At that conference, besides announcing that management would organize a corporate innovation award, Senard publicly stressed that his personal commitment at the head of the CIB is not a temporary phenomenon. It is there to stay . . . because innovation never ends!

NOTES

[1] One of the two French entrepreneurs, Edouard Daubrée, married the niece of Scottish scientist Charles Macintosh, who discovered that rubber was soluble in benzene.
[2] Michelin sold Citroën to the Peugeot Group in 1974 in order to concentrate on its core tire business. Later it sold all its non-tire activities (suspensions, wheels, batteries, etc.) except the maps and guides business.

[3]In 2010, it employed 70 or so engineers and technicians.
[4]The company sold 10 million maps and guides in 2011.
[5]The 3615 Michelin system was made available on Minitel, a French Videotex online service accessible via telephone lines (it is considered one of the world's most successful pre-World Wide Web online services).
[6]Michelin is incorporated as a partnership limited by shares. It is led by a managing general partner (CEO), assisted if needed by one or two managing partners.
[7]Michelin had taken over some of its European distributors and created a broad Europe-wide network of tire service stations called Euromaster. Its agencies sold competitive products in addition to Michelin tires.
[8]Since its creation, Michelin has always believed in the values of sport as a management philosophy. The company has been a strong promoter of sports in its organization, and the sports association it sponsors in Clermont-Ferrand is one of Europe's largest and most dynamic sports clubs.

CHAPTER 13

RECOGNIZING THE IMPERATIVES FOR AN EFFECTIVE GOVERNANCE SYSTEM

The previous case stories illustrate the fact that companies often adopt very different innovation governance models, even when these models belong to the same generic typology as the one we introduced in Chapter 5. For example, companies that have chosen to entrust their CTO or CIO with overall responsibility for innovation may differ significantly in the scope and/or the level of empowerment that they assign. To a large extent, these differences reflect specific industry, company, and management conditions, as well as historical experiences with one model or another. Top management preferences – for example, for strong personal involvement or for delegating responsibilities to others – often determine the model that will be chosen. Other influencing factors are the innovation maturity of the company and the personality of the innovation leaders available. The absence of recognized best practices – innovation governance models are seldom discussed and compared in the innovation literature – means that each company finds it necessary to develop its own customized design and to make it evolve over time.

The same case stories, combined with our empirical experience with a number of other companies, emphasized the fact that innovation performance is often not directly dependent on the type of governance model used. Rather, innovation performance reflects the strength of top management's commitment and engagement, and the credibility, skills, and energy of the actors who undertake the governance mission. Does this imply that all the governance models listed in Chapter 5 are equivalent in terms of effectiveness? The answer is obviously no, and Chapter 6 highlighted significant differences in levels of satisfaction with them. The question that remains open is whether these differences in satisfaction reflect the nature of the model – would some be more effective than others? – or rather the way the model has been implemented. We generally favor the second alternative: Each model can be made to work well; it just depends on the attention and care with which it is put in place and managed.

To help top management teams reflect on the effectiveness of their governance models – a prerequisite for improving them – we propose a number of evaluation criteria, or imperatives. These criteria represent generic success factors for any type of governance model. The conditions are not model dependent – they reflect instead how a model has been specifically implemented in a company. We have identified and will discuss eight of these success factors:

1. The level of commitment and engagement of the top management team – particularly the CEO – behind the chosen model.
2. The breadth and depth in the scope or coverage of the implemented model, in terms of process and content, as well as hard and soft issues.
3. The relative independence of the model with regard to the unique personality and skills of a single individual, i.e. its robustness vis-à-vis a change of actors.
4. The ability of the model and its key actors to gather broad and proactive support from the rest of the organization.
5. The inclusion of adequate checks and balances in the model, as well as processes and tools for continuous performance evaluation and improvement.
6. The robustness of the model vis-à-vis external pressures and crises, in terms of allowing the company to "stay the course" and meet its long-term innovation performance objectives.

7. The capacity of the model to evolve, enlarge its scope and grow with the company, particularly when operations and market coverage are being globalized.
8. The clarity and accessibility of the governance model for the board of directors, for information and auditing purposes.

After discussing each imperative, we give a checklist of questions that members of the C-suite can use to evaluate the position of their company and identify potential areas for improvement.

COMMITMENT AND ENGAGEMENT OF THE CEO AND TOP MANAGEMENT TEAM

The companies that we interviewed for our case examples have this feature in common − their top management team, starting with the CEO, is genuinely committed to turning innovation into a core competence of the corporation. This is in contrast with quite a few other companies we know, whose management seems only to pay lip service to innovation.

Interestingly, most of the companies covered in our case examples can be characterized as having gone through a succession of innovation-fervent CEOs over at least a couple of decades. This is certainly the case with IBM and its long series of CEOs who progressively reinvented the corporation, in contrast with some of the company's now defunct competitors. It is also true of Nestlé, Tetra Pak, Corning, and DSM, which have each adopted a different innovation governance model but featured several innovation-oriented CEOs. In each of these companies, we speculate, so strong is the CEO's mark on the company's innovation psyche that it would be almost unthinkable to see a new CEO coming into the top job without sharing the same passion for innovation as his/her predecessor. Companies that have not experienced a succession of innovation-oriented CEOs in the past can still "join the club" with a new CEO, but this will require a particular effort on the part of the newcomer to break with the past and create a new and lasting innovation legacy.

The personal commitment of the CEO to governing innovation proactively – whether directly or indirectly through an appointed leader or group of leaders – is generally shared by several members of the executive team, typically those dealing with technology, products, and new business development. These senior leaders usually play an essential role as "relayers and amplifiers" of the CEO's engagement. Other leaders in charge of operations, financial management, and corporate administration may not participate directly in innovation activities but they should be expected to be, at least, sympathetic toward its overall direction and to support it. Special mention should be made of the chief human resources officer (CHRO), generally a key member of the executive committee. In many companies, these leaders are left out of innovation discussions and initiatives. Yet, they are essential in ensuring that there is an adequate supply of innovation leaders within the organization through recruitment, performance evaluation and rewards, and career planning. They are also the most likely candidates to launch an assessment of the innovation culture or climate of the company before trying to improve it. In some particularly motivated companies, CHROs can also become involved in coaching people and projects – just like their business colleagues – and in organizing corporate-wide innovation events and award celebrations.

Even if they are not the prime drivers of innovation, CEOs and senior leaders express their commitment and support of the company's innovation agenda in many different and complementary ways.

First, they can set the broad context in which innovation will take place, and this means establishing bold innovation and growth objectives for the company, as well as defining innovation targets and priorities. This also includes measuring progress and tracking results. At Nestlé, for example, Paul Bulcke emphasizes the importance of his company's one-page roadmap for aligning his very large organization on a few critical missions, performance measures, competitive axes, growth priorities, and operational imperatives.

Second, they can propose a number of values to guide the behavior of both leaders and staff and communicate extensively about these values. Innovation is often part of these values, of course, but many other values not directly linked to innovation in fact support the company's innovation agenda, at least indirectly. P&G's famous "5E" leadership model does not mention the word innovation per se. However, its five leadership priorities – envisioning; engaging; energizing; enabling; and executing – can clearly be seen as indirect innovation leadership values. The same can be said of DSM's four values: external orientation; accountability for performance and learning; collaboration; and inclusion and diversity. The CEOs of these two companies constantly reinforce these values in their words and deeds, i.e. in their concrete decisions and performance reviews.

Third, CEOs and members of the top management team can convey their support for innovation by allocating resources to it. One of the most visible signs of their commitment to innovation is choosing the best people to lead innovation activities. When a star performer is chosen, for example Rob van Leen as DSM's CIO, then a clear message is sent to the organization about the importance of innovation. Another visible sign of commitment is through innovation budgets and the funding of high-risk/high-reward projects.

Last but not least, CEOs and C-suite members can show their commitment to innovation through a number of highly visible moves, some concrete, others more symbolic. In the concrete category, senior leaders, including the CEO, can volunteer to coach important and risky projects or new businesses, for example by chairing their board. They can also make it clear that they will stay the course and maintain R&D spending levels even in difficult times, as Corning, Nestlé, and DSM do. On the more symbolic front, CEOs can make a point of visiting their R&D labs regularly to talk to scientists and engineers about the nature of their work and show interest. Corning CEO Amo Houghton's visit to Sullivan Park after the downturn and Corning's board's visits to the company's scientists illustrate the importance of such contacts.

Personal participation in innovation events like award ceremonies conveys the same message – management cares!

Checklist: Commitment and Engagement of the CEO and Top Management Team

1. How deeply engaged is our CEO in innovation matters? Does he/she spend enough time on innovation?
2. How strongly is this commitment shared within the C-suite? How many executive committee members can we count as true "innovation champions"?
3. What are the tangible and symbolic signs of our CEO's engagement? Are these signs perceived and understood by the organization?
4. Do the leaders to whom we have allocated specific innovation missions trust us? Do they feel that they are able to ask for advice or help when they need it?
5. Do we try to help and support our appointed innovation leaders without interfering directly with their responsibilities?

BREADTH AND DEPTH IN THE SCOPE OR COVERAGE OF THE MODEL

An effective innovation governance system should be geared to handle all facets of the company's innovation agenda. It starts with a top management vision and attitude regarding innovation – reflecting the commitment and engagement mentioned earlier – and the setting of broad innovation objectives and priorities. It should also cover: (1) the company's strategies and plans regarding new products and technologies; (2) its processes, for both the creation and the launch of new products and services, as well as for venturing into new businesses; (3) its culture and values; and finally (4) its resources in terms of people, skills, and budgets. These innovation dimensions must be mutually compatible and reinforcing. The list of these innovation dimensions, which is summarized in Figure 13.1, can be used by management for a quick check, i.e. which of these innovation dimensions do we cover in our innovation governance system, and which ones have we somehow left

Figure 13.1: Multiple Dimensions of an Innovation Governance System

aside? Frequently, the innovation governance reality in many companies does not cover such a broad scope.

In fact, most companies evolve through these various dimensions as they progressively try to unleash and master innovation as a management discipline. We have observed and mentioned in previous chapters that newly founded companies – think of Amazon, Google, and Facebook – do not have, or seem not to have, a need for an explicit governance process. It is as they mature that it becomes imperative to make the model explicit. So, in the evolution of governance practices there are maturity phases, and we have observed three broad ones.

The first phase is evident when companies start addressing their innovation challenges through a focus on processes. This is generally when innovation deficiencies are the most visible because they translate into poor project selection, chaotic project management, long lead times, and mediocre new product launches. The first changes management tends to make involve implementing a phased review process with a number of "project gates" and a formal approval mechanism for proceeding from one gate to the other. These shifts toward more process discipline are often introduced by the head of technical operations, for example the CTO, backed by the business sponsors of the projects. Then comes the appointment of fully empowered project leaders and the mobilization of relatively autonomous innovation teams. Once projects are being properly managed, other processes start moving up the priority list, typically at the front end of innovation, e.g. customer understanding and preference mapping, inventory of technologies and competencies, and idea management; at the back end, commercialization comes to the fore. Tetra Pak offers one of the richest examples of such a strong historical focus on processes.

The second phase occurs when management, after streamlining deficient processes, starts formally addressing the content of its innovation efforts, generally through strategy questions and portfolio management considerations. This can of course be done in parallel with the first phase. From an innovation governance point of view, this phase is quite different in terms of management attention and involvement because innovation portfolios are supposed to be aligned with business objectives and strategies. This requires the strong personal involvement of the top management team and the creation of different organizational mechanisms to manage the choices. At Tetra Pak, it meant moving from an innovation process board, in charge of all processes, to a number of councils with heavy management participation. It also involved aligning product and technology strategies and plans. Many companies, unless they experience major problems in respect of competencies, resources, or organizational behavior, remain focused on the second maturity stage, which may be sufficient to increase their innovation yield substantially.

The third stage of maturity is reached when the top management team expands the scope of its innovation governance system to take a more holistic view of innovation and the creation of new businesses. This only happens when the top team – often with the CEO as the main innovation driver – considers innovation as a *must have* competitiveness factor and growth driver, not just a *nice to have*. In the quest for enhanced innovation performance, management will consider all factors – hard and soft – and will give innovation the highest priority when it comes to resource allocation. The third phase also includes the ability to enter into partnerships that open up new fields of innovation. This is clearly what marks Corning's and IBM's innovation history, and what is happening at DSM today.

**Checklist: Breadth and Depth in the Scope or Coverage
of the Model**

6. How extensive and effective is our coverage of our innovation
    processes? How well are we doing at the front end? At the
    back end? Do we keep improving?
7. How comprehensive and effective is our handling of our
    portfolio strategy? Are our product and technology strategies
    aligned, with each other and with our business strategy?
8. Have we included venturing and new business creation in our
    innovation governance model? Have we established a specific
    process and recruitment for these activities?
9. Are we taking a proactive and transparent approach to innova-
    tion resource allocation, in terms of people, competencies, and
    budgets?
10. Have we defined innovation-enhancing values as part of our
    corporate values? How well do we broadcast and enforce
    them? Are we working on our innovation climate?

INDEPENDENCE OF THE MODEL WITH REGARD TO THE UNIQUE TALENTS OF ONE INDIVIDUAL

Some of the governance models introduced in Chapter 5 – for
example, the subset of the top management team, or the high-level
cross-functional steering group – are built around the principle of
collective innovation management. In these models, a number of
senior leaders either allocate specific missions to one another or
collectively share the overall responsibility for innovation. In that
sense, these models are much less dependent on any single individual than models that have entrusted the whole mission to a
single champion, be it the CEO, the CTO, or the CIO, or to a
couple of leaders, e.g. a CTO and a senior business unit head.

To stay robust over time and withstand unavoidable organizational changes and staff moves, an innovation governance model
should indeed avoid being overly dependent on the unique personality
and skills of one person. The paradox comes from the fact that

exceptional talents are always necessary to steer and govern innovation. When the chosen model relies on a single high-level leader, it is indeed critical to choose someone with a great character, personal charisma, and a high level of energy, as well as a unique combination of skills, i.e. strong technical understanding, an acute sense of the market, and a good dose of social, political, and emotional intelligence. These are the kinds of people who can move mountains. At the same time, making everything dependent on a gifted leader can be dangerous. Highly talented individuals are often targeted by head hunters and can leave their job or be promoted. The risk is particularly high when these innovation leaders – particularly the more junior ones, innovation managers rather than CIOs – feel a lack support from the top management team and become frustrated with their mission.

At the opposite end of the scale, depending on a single individual to drive all innovation activities in the company for too long may introduce another risk, that of losing the cutting edge. People who stay in their job too long may slowly become less motivated, not to say stale. Innovation requires regular breaths of fresh air and new blood. It is therefore the responsibility of the CEO and the C-suite to be aware of those two risks, which can be reduced in several ways. In the case of companies like IBM where the CEO is in ultimate charge, it is especially important for the board to be aware of these risks and to play a role of oversight and management when necessary.

The most obvious way to counter the risk of overdependence is to ask the leader in question to identify and coach one or several "understudies," typically by allocating several of the leader's tasks to them. It is standard practice in most highly developed HR departments to earmark high-potential substitutes to replace existing leaders in case of need. This is particularly important for critical positions like CEOs, CTOs, and CIOs. But management may also ensure that the leader in question has built a number of organizational mechanisms to leverage his/her strengths and handle part of his/her mission.

The DSM example offers a good illustration of both the risk of overdependence on a leader and of the ways to alleviate it. DSM's CIO is an exceptionally talented and charismatic leader, and much of the company's success on the innovation front can be, at least in part, attributed to Van Leen. However, Van Leen and his managing board have worked hard at making other talents emerge and take responsibility. As the head of DSM's Innovation Center, Van Leen is now surrounded by leaders who play a critical role in innovation. The innovation council he has set up includes a number of promising innovation directors, who act as the CIOs of their business group. And the head of DSM's current business incubator – a former business group head – is of the caliber to play a major role in innovation.

Checklist: Independence of the Model with Regard to the Unique Talents of One Individual

11. To what extent is our innovation governance model dependent on the charisma and talents of a single individual or a couple of people?
12. If it is highly dependent, do we make sure as members of the C-suite that our lead innovation champion(s) have permanent access to the top management team for support?
13. Have we asked our innovation leader(s), with the help of the HR department, to earmark potential successors and to coach them?
14. Are we monitoring the behavior of our innovation leader(s) to prevent any temptation on their part to run innovation as a purely "personal" mission?
15. Are we prepared to replace our innovation champions before they lose their sparkle or grow frustrated?

ABILITY OF THE MODEL TO GATHER SUPPORT FROM THE ORGANIZATION

Whichever governance model management chooses, it will be effective only if the people responsible for implementing the change – individually or collectively – obtain the cooperation and support of the rest of the organization for their innovation initiatives. Gathering support for change initiatives is not easy, as all leaders who have struggled to introduce a real change agenda in their company will testify. Several factors typically contribute to obtaining broad and proactive organizational support.

First, the attitude of business units and functions vis-à-vis new directions will be determined by the level of empowerment and credibility of those people entrusted with the innovation governance mission. The higher their hierarchical level and authority, the more likely they are to gain support from the rest of the organization. The highest level of cooperation will obviously be reached when the CEO is personally involved in the process. The Tetra Pak example provides a good illustration of such a situation. Even though the company's CTO is officially the man in charge of product and service innovation, the company's CEO is widely perceived as the ultimate process champion and innovation prescriptor, and he sits on all the key councils that deal with innovation. As one of the senior leaders put it, who can oppose the direction adopted by the company when it is so strongly advocated by the CEO? Generally, all models that involve the direct participation of members of the top management team will benefit from broad support throughout the organization.

At the opposite end of the spectrum, it will be very difficult for lower-level managers to mobilize businesses and functions behind an innovation change agenda, unless they are strongly endorsed by the top team. In Chapter 6, for example, we discussed differences in empowerment between dedicated innovation managers – typically upper-middle managers reporting two levels below the executive committee – and chief innovation officers reporting directly to the CEO, like Van Leen in the case of DSM. The mediocre level of satisfaction with the innovation manager model in our survey can probably be ascribed to innovation managers' relatively low hierarchical position, which prevents them from obtaining support for their initiatives.

The second factor that is required to trigger a broad following throughout the organization is the quality of management communications regarding innovation. The message should always come from top management and it should be clear and convincing in explaining why the company needs to focus on innovation and what this means in practice. It should also be frequently repeated so that it stands out in people's minds.

The third imperative for mobilizing the organization is management's assurance that the focus on innovation is there to stay, i.e. that it is not a "management flavor of the month" but will be the way to go for years to come. This is not only a matter of communication, although it is critical. In real life, and particularly if they have been "burned" before, people judge what they see, not just what they hear. They will seriously side with management if they see that concrete decisions are congruent with the original message. In this sense, the fact that DSM's management did not cut R&D during the last crisis made everyone understand that the company was serious about innovation.

A last condition for gathering organizational support is to ensure that managers at all levels are not caught up personally in conflicts linked with potential discrepancies between what they are told to do and the way they are evaluated. This is a classic pitfall of many change programs – performance evaluation criteria do not correspond to the company's new priorities. Such discrepancies are often rapidly noted and discredit the change message.

Checklist: Ability of the Model to Gather Support from the Organization

16. Does our organization perceive that our innovation agenda is ultimately in the hands of the CEO and his/her top management team?

17. If we have delegated our innovation mission to lower-level managers, does the organization perceive that they are strongly supported by top management?

18. How clear and convincing are our corporate communications on innovation? Are they repeated often enough to stand out in people's minds?

19. Do our people understand that our innovation focus is here to stay, and do they see that our management decisions are congruent with our innovation objective?

20. Have we adapted our performance evaluation system to ensure that it is in line with our innovation priorities and objectives?

INCLUSION OF CHECKS AND BALANCES AND A FOCUS ON CONTINUOUS IMPROVEMENT

We defined innovation governance in Chapter 1 as a sort of "corporate constitution" for innovation because it provides a frame for all innovation activities by defining the roles, powers, and limits of the various players and by organizing the way all innovation-related processes work. Any constitution should provide its stakeholders with the correct level of checks and balances between the various power holders. And innovation governance is no different because it involves entrusting leaders or groups of leaders with special powers outside normal hierarchical relationships. This, of course, depends on the organizational model the company has selected for allocating innovation responsibilities and the extent of the powers allocated to the chosen innovation leaders. For example, if CTOs or CIOs have been given a company-wide innovation governance mission, to what extent are they empowered to intervene in the business sphere of their corporate colleagues with whom they have no hierarchical relationships?

Checks and balances, in the case of innovation governance, deal with defining the roles and responsibilities of the innovation chiefs, their expected ways of operating in relation to their senior colleagues, and the right of recourse of these colleagues if they feel their leadership rights have been unduly encroached upon. At DSM, the CIO is entitled to conduct a regular innovation performance audit of his colleagues' business groups. But this review is jointly conducted by the Innovation Center controller and the business group controller. The idea is that both parties should reach a consensus. If there is disagreement, the issue is referred to the managing board, which receives every audit. The role of the top management team in that domain remains essential. C-suite members are the ones who ensure the proper level of checks and balances.

No company we know, even the most innovative, feels entirely satisfied with its innovation system. In fact, the more "advanced" they are in their innovation management practices, the more demanding companies seem to be. This is why good innovation governance systems provide for a process of continuous improvement. This presupposes that:

1. the company has started its innovation drive with a comprehensive audit of its various innovation activities and processes;
2. this audit is repeated in an objective manner at regular intervals, ideally using industry-wide benchmarks; and
3. the audit is communicated to top management and triggers a series of change programs by the responsible leaders.

This process is in place at DSM and seems to be giving encouraging results if we consider how rapidly the company has reached the top performance quartile of its industry.

Checklist: Inclusion of Checks and Balances and a Focus on Continuous Improvement

21. Does our innovation governance system allow for an adequate set of checks and balances to offset the powers entrusted to our innovation leaders?

22. Is our top management team fully playing its role as the ultimate recourse in case of conflicts between our innovation leaders and the line organization?

23. Did we start our innovation journey with a comprehensive diagnostic of our strengths and weaknesses? Did we use industry benchmarks for that audit?

24. Do we have a process for regularly updating this innovation performance audit, and is it widely communicated for maximum impact?

25. Do our regular updates trigger change programs and does our top management team follow up on these improvement commitments?

ROBUSTNESS OF THE MODEL VIS-À-VIS EXTERNAL PRESSURES AND CRISES

It is not uncommon to see companies embarking on a major innovation effort for a while, then to witness a substantial weakening of their focus and drive as soon as the first market or economic crisis appears. Under such circumstances, when it is not reducing the whole R&D program, management may typically cut innovation budgets and cancel longer-term or risky projects. These kinds of reactions are extremely detrimental to innovation activities that require steady, long-term investment and effort. They also send the message that, for top management, innovation is merely nice to have, not a must-have. This prevents people down the organization from making strong personal commitments to innovation and from taking risks. It is therefore essential to ensure that the innovation governance system is able to resist most of these short-term knee-jerk reactions when the company is confronted with crises.

Management can take at least three measures to help the company's innovation governance system resist this roller-coaster risk, in the face of ups and downs in markets and economic cycles.

The first one is to ensure that the innovation system and budget are kept reasonably lean, even in favorable times, to avoid having to cut projects in bad times. This means, of course, paying a lot of attention to R&D budgets and the selection of new projects. It also implies avoiding devoting a lot of resources to full-time innovation management staff. Maintaining a lean central innovation staff is possible when the line organization is fully mobilized and participates actively in all innovation activities.

The second measure is to have one, or ideally several, high-level innovation advocates at the top management level. Of course, when the CEO is personally viewed as the ultimate corporate innovation champion – as is the case in all the companies we surveyed – it helps in maintaining the focus on innovation in times of crisis. Strong CTOs or CIOs can also protect the company from drastic budget cuts; it all depends on their relative weight in the top management team, particularly vis-à-vis CFOs who, naturally, will call for cost-cutting.

The third measure is to isolate somewhat the innovation budgets of business units from the rest of their budgets to avoid across-the-board cuts in bad times. Business leaders who are often judged on their overall budget may be tempted to cancel longer-term activities to maintain short-term profits. Isolating innovation budgets – generally R&D expenditures – can be achieved by lumping true innovation projects into "multi-year programs" that can be approved in that form by top management and separated officially from all other expenditures that are subject to classical performance evaluations. For example, Corning's innovation councils allocate the innovation resources and manage the innovation portfolio precisely to avoid the problem of "parochial" decision making on the part of the businesses.

Checklist: Robustness of the Model vis-à-vis External Pressures and Crises

26. Have we ever had to significantly reduce our innovation efforts because of a market or economic crisis? What has been the impact of such a move on our credibility?
27. Do we pay attention to maintaining a lean approach in R&D and in our innovation activities? Is our full-time, dedicated innovation staff kept to a minimum?
28. Do we have high-level innovation advocates in the top management team, capable of defending our innovation focus in periods of crisis?
29. Are we able to be selective when we have to cut budgets across the board? Can our business leaders decide independently where they want to cut costs?
30. Do we practice the approval and resourcing of "multi-year programs" for important innovation endeavors, thus protecting them from cyclical fluctuations?

CAPACITY OF THE MODEL TO EVOLVE, ENLARGE ITS SCOPE, AND GROW WITH THE COMPANY

Most if not all companies grow and evolve over time. Some do it rapidly, reaching billions of dollars in sales in a decade or less, others change more slowly. Some of them expand in terms of product range or diversify by entering completely new fields and creating new industries; others maintain the same product range but expand their geographical market coverage. Many change their structure over time as they create new business units and globalize their operations. Most have to adapt to the radical changes introduced through digital technology, internet, and the emergence of social networks. All these changes naturally affect the way innovation needs to be carried out, and hence governed. This means that an innovation governance model that is well suited to a particular company condition may not be adapted to the next stage in its development. This explains, at least in part – because changes in management also play a role – why many companies change their innovation governance model over time.

There are many different ways to adapt innovation governance to changes in the company's condition and environment. Some companies may change models altogether, for example passing from a centralized model to a distributed one, or from relatively loose to much more structured governance. Other companies – and this is the case with most of the examples in this book – keep the same basic governance model but make it evolve to address their current challenge.

Nestlé, for example, has gone through a subtle change in the personal involvement style of its CEO, as the former outspoken and visionary CEO has become board chairman, leaving his position to a new CEO with a more hands-on approach to innovation management. Tetra Pak has maintained its focus on the process aspect of innovation over the past decade, even amplifying it over the past six years. It has also continued to rely on the cross-functional steering group model to steer its innovation efforts. But the company added a new angle by giving greater consideration to the content of innovation, i.e. product and technology strategies and priorities. This has led to the more proactive participation of the most senior managers in a number of corporate councils, some of them totally devoted to innovation. DSM, by contrast, has kept its sophisticated innovation governance infrastructure relatively unchanged over the past few years, but is now "going east" with it as it is opening small innovation incubators in India and China. Corning has introduced ways of finding uses for its core technologies rather than waiting for others to ask for new uses.

It is therefore important for management, as it regularly reviews its governance model, to assess whether the model it has chosen is expandable in terms of scope, product, or geographical coverage, and to prepare for this evolution.

**Checklist: Capacity of the Model to Evolve, Enlarge its
Scope, and Grow with the Company**

31. Do we regularly review the mission, scope, and resources of
     our innovation governance system and model in light of our
     evolving challenges?
32. Do we have the right balance between new product creation
     and new business creation (the outcome of our incubator)
     given our growth challenge?
33. Should we change the balance between our focus on process
     and our focus on content (strategies and project portfolios)
     and what does that mean in practice?
34. How likely is it that we will have to further centralize or
     decentralize our innovation activities? What impact will this
     change make on our governance system?
35. What changes in our innovation governance system and
     model do we need to make to prepare ourselves for true
     business and R&D globalization?

CLARITY AND ACCESSIBILITY OF THE GOVERNANCE MODEL FOR THE BOARD OF DIRECTORS

In Chapter 2, we advocated the need to keep the board of directors well informed of the company's innovation governance philosophy, of its approach, and of its chosen model to implement it. This is critical, particularly in companies for which innovation is a key growth driver. The board needs to understand how the company has organized its innovation efforts and what issues it is facing in order to exercise its dual management supervision role of supporting and challenging.

As part of his/her regular communication remit, the CEO should explain to the board the approach that he/she has chosen for innovation governance and the reasons for such a choice. This assumes of course that the model chosen by the company is clear in the minds of its top team, something that is not always the case. The board will naturally expect to hear how the CEO intends to be personally engaged behind the company's innovation drive, even if overall responsibility has been entrusted to another senior leader or group of leaders.

Most boards have occasional access to the company's senior leaders to hear about progress achieved in a number of important domains. It is therefore good practice to ask the innovation governance head(s) – the innovation-dedicated members of the top management team, the CTO, the CIO, or the head of the innovation board, etc. – to present the results of the company's innovation audit to the board at least once a year and discuss future issues. Board members are often deprived of such information and it would help them better understand the company's strategy and outlook. As mentioned in Chapter 2, they will naturally want to be reassured that management is properly aware of the strategic risks linked with either innovation myopia or misguided investments. The board could also challenge the CEO to upgrade the company's innovation governance system if results do not meet its expectations.

In short, innovation performance and its drivers, as well as the company's innovation governance organization, are items that should be put on the board's agenda for information and regular discussions, alongside the other important strategic and organizational issues.

Checklist: Clarity and Accessibility of the Governance Model for the Board of Directors

36. Is our governance system clear enough in our minds – in terms of who is ultimately in charge of innovation – to be presented to the board of directors?
37. Has the CEO presented our innovation governance model to the board, and are subsequent changes in this model discussed with the board?
38. Does the board have access to our senior innovation leaders on a regular basis, as they have access to other senior company officers?
39. Do we discuss the different types of innovation risks, both internal and external, with the board to ensure they endorse our innovation strategy?
40. Have we adopted the habit of presenting an annual audit of our innovation activities and performance to the board?

AUDITING THE COMPANY'S INNOVATION GOVERNANCE ACTIVITIES

In discussing the role of top management with regard to innovation governance in Chapter 3, we suggested that the C-suite should regularly review the effectiveness of the company's innovation system and model to improve it on a continuing basis. In the course of such regular reviews, members of the C-suite should take the time to explore together – honestly – how the company's governance model meets these eight success factors before taking any corrective action that may be needed. The checklist questions after each of these eight imperatives could help in this review. We would suggest that each member of the top team should do this evaluation individually before sharing the results with one another. A form, similar to the one shown in Figure 13.2, could be used to collect individual evaluations and launch discussions on the most commonly shared deficiencies and corresponding improvement opportunities.

Criteria of governance model effectiveness	Not met at all				Fully met	Comments
	1	2	3	4	5	
Commitment & engagement of the CEO and top management team						
Breadth and depth in the scope or coverage of the model						
Independence of the model with regards to the unique talents of one individual						
Ability of the model to gather support from the organization						
Inclusion of checks and balances and a focus on continuous improvement						
Robustness of the model vis-à-vis external pressures and crises						
Capacity of the model to evolve, enlarge its scope and grow with the company						
Clarity and accessibility of the governance model for the board of directors						

Figure 13.2:   Evaluating the Company's Governance Model

CHAPTER 14

ALIGNING INDIVIDUAL AND COLLECTIVE INNOVATION LEADERSHIP

This book is based on a core belief, namely that sustained innovation performance is conditioned by the quality of the company's innovation governance. Management teams that are not fully satisfied with their innovation governance system – and Chapter 6 showed that they are numerous – need to start by building and sharing a vision of the desirable improvement path ahead. As with all major change efforts, a leap in innovation governance effectiveness requires a three-phase approach:

1. Creating a *shared awareness* of the current situation and issues. This implies agreeing on the deficiencies of the current governance system vis-à-vis best practice, on the benefits to be expected from the desired change, and, in addition, on penalties to be incurred if there is no change.
2. Building a *shared vision* of the desired governance end state and of the path to get there. This requires agreement on the specific attributes of an effective governance model, on the root causes of current problems, on likely obstacles on the route forward, and on options and roadmaps for the change process.
3. Obtaining a *shared commitment to action* from the whole team. This includes agreeing on a set of priorities, on a migration project structure, on performance indicators to track innovation

progress, and on adequate support programs, for example to improve the culture or change behaviors.

Chapter 13 recommended reviewing and assessing your innovation governance system on the basis of eight factors. The first and most important is an attitudinal element that everyone in a company can observe, namely the level of commitment and engagement by the top management team, and particularly the CEO, behind innovation and the chosen governance model. Such an attitude reflects a combination of *individual and collective innovation leadership*.

Indeed, to thrive, innovation requires two things: First, members of the top management team should share the same set of beliefs and values regarding their role, and behave consistently as innovation leaders, every day and in every situation. Second, C-suite members should work together as a cohesive team, complementing one another in terms of talents and styles.

For this to happen, everyone in the management team must start with a personal reflection and self-examination to assess:

1. The extent to which they meet, individually and collectively, the main leadership imperatives for innovation, i.e. are you truly behaving like innovation leaders?
2. Their individual model of leadership, i.e. what motivates, predisposes, and equips you, individually, and the C-suite, collectively, to play an active role in innovation governance?
3. Their innate, instinctive leadership style and that of their management colleagues, i.e. what will naturally orient you toward certain innovation activities?
4. How they can ensure innovation teams comprise leaders with complementary styles, i.e. how can you leverage individual talents to govern innovation effectively?

The results of these individual self-assessments ought to be shared openly and constructively within the top management team, for example during a vision-building workshop to devise a better innovation governance system. The best way to initiate a new vision is to start by taking stock of the current situation, aspirations and predispositions of everyone in the team. Note that this leadership appraisal process has fruitful applications for all kinds of corporate change initiatives, not just for innovation governance.

Let's review each of these four leadership elements.

DO YOU MEET THE MAIN LEADERSHIP IMPERATIVES OF INNOVATION?

The book *Innovation Leaders* mentioned in Chapter 1 addressed an important question: Is there a special type of leadership for innovation – the answer was clearly yes – and, if so, what are its main characteristics?[1] The book proposed six behavioral traits of innovation leaders. In addition, it suggested that innovation leaders do not necessarily share the same interests and talents. Some are more attracted by and predisposed to become involved in the creative front end of innovation – typically dealing with technologies, ideas, and concept portfolios. We call them *front-end innovation leaders*. Others, or *back-end innovation leaders*, naturally focus on the operational side of innovation and managing projects from concept approval to market launch and roll-out. It is therefore advisable for each member of the C-suite (1) to review these six behavioral traits and assess whether they are being met, individually and collectively, and (2) to identify who in the team falls naturally at the front end or back end of innovation.

Do You Generally Behave Like an Innovation Leader?

Trait #1 – Do You Show Signs of Both Emotion and Realism?

Using a description proposed by Daniel Borel, the entrepreneurial founder of Logitech, the first leadership trait of innovation leaders is their ability to combine a genuine interest in creativity with close attention to process discipline. Of course, innovation leaders encourage and support innovators and are open to their ideas; they also ensure that their staff design and use a process to generate, acknowledge, screen, and rank ideas before they can be validated and turned into potential projects. At the same time, they are pragmatic and involved in all the critical project execution tasks that require a lot of implementation discipline. Of course, some leaders lean more to one side than the other, but the two aspects – creativity *and* discipline – need to be well represented within the top management team. Given the usual cross-functional composition of most executive groups, which consist of creative marketing and technical leaders as well as more operational ones, this first innovation leadership trait is likely to be well met as a group.

Trait #2 – Do You Accept Risk and Failure and Promote a Passion for Learning?

This second trait, or at least the first part of it – acceptance of risk and failure – is generally recognized as the main attribute of innovation leaders. In fact, the important aspect is the second element: a passion for learning from experiments and mistakes. The only benefit of a bungle is that it makes people reflect, learn, and become wiser. This is why innovation leaders make a point of exhorting project teams to systematically organize honest debriefing sessions at the end of each project – particularly if it fails – to understand the mistakes that were made and draw lessons. In assessing the extent to which they meet this requirement, leaders have to be candid with themselves and look at the reality, which means being conscious of their actions, not only their words. Questions to ask include: Do we seriously analyze our failures and try to understand their root causes? What really happens in our company with the teams and project leaders that fail? Will the people involved be penalized in their career? If the justifica-

> **Learning from Mistakes. What Do These Authors Say?**
>
> "Why make the same mistake twice when there are so many mistakes to choose from!"
>
> *Oscar Wilde*
>
> "If you are going to fail, at least have the courtesy to do it in a new and interesting manner!"
>
> *Geoffrey Moore*

tion for failure is learning, then innovation leaders must also make it clear that repeating the same mistake is unacceptable.

Trait #3 – Do You Have the Courage to Stop Projects, Not Just to Start Them?

Innovation has to do with starting new things, so new project ideas tend to abound in innovative companies. One of the critical leadership roles of top management is to ensure that the portfolio of projects meets the company's objectives and strategies and bears a reasonable chance of success. This implies the need to prune projects that either do not fit with the strategy or show a dubious outlook in terms of market impact. This mission, which is often unpopular with project initiators, assumes that management is able to exercise discernment about the future of a project if it is continued. It raises the difficult question of when to persist or when to pull the plug. Innovation leaders tend to rely on two elements to make such a decision. The first is a deep gut feeling about the superior customer value that the project will create if it is successful. The example of Nespresso, described in Chapter 9, illustrates this point convincingly.

> **Canceling a Project is Not Failing!**
>
> "Sometimes, during the phase review process management cancels projects. When this happens to a project, you shouldn't necessarily consider it a failure. What *is* a failure is when a project keeps going when it deserves to be cancelled. Not every project that starts down the pipeline should reach the market. In fact, in many companies fewer than 50 percent of the projects that start ever reach the market. Your new product development resources are too valuable to squander on projects that, on the way to market – or, even worse, *in* the market – turn out to be mediocre."
>
> *New Product Development for Dummies, p. 159*

Some members of Nestlé's executive group were indeed so convinced of the superiority of the espresso produced by their new system that they agreed to keep funding the project for 16 years. The second argument in favor of persisting with an uncertain project is when customers express a strong interest in the project outcome.

Trait #4 – Are You Good at Building and Steering Teams and Attracting Innovators?

> **Teamwork According to Catmull**
>
> "If you give a good idea to a mediocre team, they will screw it up! If you give a mediocre idea to a great team, they will either fix it, or throw it away and come up with something that works!"
>
> *Ed Catmull, Pixar Studios*

If invention can be an individual phenomenon, innovation is always the result of a team effort, as noted by Ed Catmull, co-founder of Pixar and president of Pixar & Disney Studios.[2] It is therefore not surprising that innovation leaders pay a lot of attention to the teams they have assembled for an innovation project. The first thing they do is to select team members carefully in order to balance skills, experience, and personalities in an optimal way. This implies that they do not pick team members on the basis of who is available, but on who will bring the best contribution to the project. In some companies, like Sony, this goes as far as giving the leaders of critical projects a free hand to raid the entire organization to find the talents they need, irrespective of departmental turf lines. Once teams are brought together, innovation leaders take care of their resource and coaching needs, and they open their door for advice, as needed, but without interfering in the team's work. Innovation leaders value and trust teams, and they know how to recognize and reward them, which makes them popular with innovators.

Trait #5 – Are You Open to External Technologies and Ideas?

Innovation leaders promote openness across all functions and they encourage their staff to go out, broaden their horizons, and build external networks. Once again, as for tolerance of failure, there is a gap between preaching the open innovation gospel and practicing it in reality. Some leaders talk officially about the need to go out and be open, but in fact resent seeing their staff take time away from their normal work to build external relationships and explore idea and technology sources. In most companies, marketing people are expected to go out and meet information sources in the market to identify new trends and detect ill-met, unmet, or latent customer needs. Similarly, technology specialists in R&D are encouraged to establish networks in their scientific community to build intelligence and identify promising new technologies. What is less common is to see marketers and technologists engage in common exploratory market trips. And yet, a cross-functional exposition to the market and a confrontation of ideas are often the most fruitful ways to develop innovative concepts. So, innovation leaders need to encourage these experiments.

Trait #6 – Do You Show Passion for Innovation and Share it Widely?

A common element in the personality of innovation leaders is the high level of energy and enthusiasm for innovation that they convey to their staff. This passion can generally be communicated because passionate leaders tend to attract passionate followers. Daniel Borel was known for his passion, and he insisted that it be one of the important elements to be detected through personality tests for new job candidates.[3] Of course, being passionate about innovation does not mean being blind to the risks involved. It means being determined to conduct projects, to make them successful, and also, as mentioned above, to know when to stop them.

> **Passion Required to Join Logitech**
>
> "We make a living, we exist, we survive because of innovation. So, if someone would not share that passion at every level, he would not join Logitech!"
>
> *Daniel Borel, co-founder and former chairman of Logitech*

Are You a Front-end or Back-end Innovation Leader?

Innovative companies generally have a number of innovation leaders in the organization, including of course in the C-suite. To succeed and sustain innovation, they need the right combination of front-end and back-end leaders, since the two types are complementary. In pharmaceutical firms, front-end leaders are typically found among the heads of discovery, under the leadership of the chief research officer, whereas back-end leaders tend to be in charge of clinical development, manufacturing, and marketing and sales. It is generally relatively easy to identify these two types of leaders because of their functional orientation and also their general management interests and attitude.

Steve Jobs was undoubtedly a front-end innovation leader at Apple and he exemplifies the profile of these promoters of radical creativity:

- Passion for new ideas, new products, and new designs to meet customers' unarticulated needs or improve their experience.
- A bias toward questioning the status quo and challenging staff with all kinds of questions: why? what if? what else? why not? who? who else? how much? how? how else?
- Adoption of a VC-like philosophy regarding returns, i.e. knowing full well that only a fraction of new ideas and projects will succeed, and thus focusing on those with a big win promise.
- Willingness to experiment and open new paths, which means accepting risk and tolerating failure.
- Ability to promote individual and team freedom and create a climate of mental adventure and excitement that will naturally attract innovators.

Tim Cook, who replaced Jobs at the head of Apple, is an archetypal back-end innovation leader. He is known for having superbly handled Apple's supply chain, manufacturing outsourcing and logistics, thus freeing Jobs to focus on his front-end interests. Cook probably meets several if not all of the characteristics of back-end innovation leaders, who are the proponents of operational discipline:

- Focus on getting products to market flawlessly and cost-effectively by mastering all the operational foundations necessary to go smoothly from concept to launch and roll-out.
- Insistence on planning quality as well as on process discipline and standardization to make innovation replicable.
- Demand for speed to market through a high level of cross-functional integration and a first-time-right philosophy in implementation.
- Flexibility in execution decisions, based on operational knowledge and pragmatic risk management.
- Ability to motivate staff for product battles and promotion of a "launch and learn" approach, possibly leading to product improvements and relaunch cycles.

Besides identifying front- and back-end leaders, their position in the organization and their respective clout, management needs to ensure that the handover between them is smooth, which may not be easy given their very different personalities and leadership styles. In appointing an innovation leader as CEO, boards should be aware of the implications of their choice. If they appoint a front-end innovation leader like Jobs at the helm of the company, who will take care of the disciplined operational side? And if they choose a back-end leader as CEO, like Cook, who will defend an aggressive front-end agenda?

> **Leadership in a Nutshell**
> "Leaders do or cause to be done all that needs to be done and is not being done to achieve what we say is important.
> They propose a sense of purpose, a sense of direction and a sense of focus.
> They build alignment and get commitment."
> *Preston Bottger, IMD professor of leadership and management development*

WHAT IS YOUR OWN LEADERSHIP MODEL?

Besides reviewing the leadership imperatives for innovation, members of the top team – and more generally all senior leaders –

Source: Preston Bottger

Figure 14.1:   Characterizing Your Own Model of Leadership

need to reflect on what drives them as individual leaders. Preston
Bottger, who teaches leadership and management development at
IMD business school in Lausanne, believes in Lao Tzu's famous
observation: "He who knows others is wise; he who knows himself
is enlightened." This is why he advocates that every manager who
aspires to a leadership position should reflect on his/her own
model of leadership. This, he suggests, implies assessing four elements and understanding how these elements support, or sometimes conflict with, the company's position and its innovation
challenge (refer to Figure 14.1).

At the center is the first element, *your personal position as a
leader*, including your hierarchy of motivations and drivers – both
intrinsic (i.e. personal and deep-seated) and extrinsic (i.e. influenced by your external environment). Recognizing your individual
motivations and making them explicit is important as a first self-
assessment step for innovation governance:

- Why do you want to promote an innovation agenda?
- What would you like to achieve, individually and collectively?
- How much energy are you ready to invest to meet your
  objective?
- What's in it for you, personally?
- What do you like and dislike about steering innovation?
- What are your beliefs about what it will take to succeed?

- What are you ready to do to show your commitment?
- What are you ready to give up? (If anything.)
- How long you are ready to go on for?

The second element, according to Bottger, is *your knowledge bank* or your personal assets for governing innovation. This includes:

- your individual talents and skills, i.e. what you are good at;
- your past experience with innovation and change management;
- your knowledge of how the company works and of the location of its untapped potential;
- your internal and external networks; and
- your access to information, concepts and tools relevant for innovation.

The third element is *your preferred methods* for gaining and exerting influence and introducing change:

- Do you believe in personally showing the way through your acts and decisions?
- Are you an adept of persuasion through rational argument?
- Do you prefer to call on people's emotional intelligence and followership?
- Are you afraid of a confrontation of ideas?
- Do you feel comfortable building coalitions toward a common objective?

Finally, the last element of your personal model of leadership is *your vision of your workplace*. This includes:

- your perception of your management team effectiveness and of its inner workings;
- your understanding of your company and of its strengths and weaknesses;
- your assessment of your industry and where it is heading; and
- your vision of the broad environment in which your company is operating.

This first self-assessment can be complemented by characterizing your leadership style and understanding how your type of leadership matches some of the imperatives for an effective governance system.

WHAT IS YOUR OWN INNATE LEADERSHIP STYLE?

Being aware of your own leadership style and that of your management colleagues is a difficult but useful undertaking. A number of models have been developed over the years for this purpose. The most widely used – the Myers-Briggs personality typology – is useful for defining the psychological underpinnings of a leadership profile. But it is not easy to make it operational as a leadership model because of its complexity, notably because of its 16 types. As a consequence, and for our purposes, we prefer to use a simpler model, developed by management author Robert Tomasko[4] for his consulting clients. Experience shows that this model is very intuitive, i.e. people can easily recognize themselves and their colleagues in this typology, just by reviewing the descriptors of each style.

Leaders – suggests Tomasko – need to develop four complementary abilities:

- To be aggressive, like a *warrior*.
- To be conserving, like a *judge*.
- To adapt to situations and people, like a *diplomat*.
- To support people and ideas, like a *mentor*.

Every leader has a combination of these four characteristics in different proportions, and the combinations vary from one leader to another. In most cases, leaders feature one (and sometimes two) of these four traits as their *major*, i.e. they instinctively behave according to their major trait, even though they can proactively bring their other traits to bear as *minors* in different proportions and situations (refer to Figure 14.2 for an illustration).

This simple typology of leadership styles is relatively easy to use. Our experience shows that the descriptors of qualities and excesses for each of these four leadership styles, which are listed in the following paragraphs, are sufficient for anyone to detect the *major* and *minors* of everyone in the management team.

Let's review each of these four archetypes, characterize them in terms of philosophy and behavior, and indicate where, on the innovation governance front, they can be either particularly effective or, in some cases, dysfunctional.

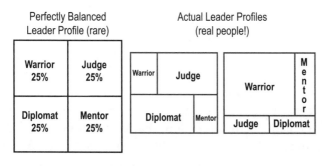

Source: Robert Tomasko

Figure 14.2:   Every Leader Features a Combination of Four Traits

Are You Primarily a *Warrior*?

Warriors are action-oriented, dynamic leaders. Their philosophy is: To be successful, you have to make things happen! *Warriors* are proponents of a "just do it" approach, rather than of thorough analysis and planning. They also naturally tend to promote outside-in perspectives and approaches. Because of their qualities – they are typically masterful, confident, persuasive, risk taking, and forceful – they are at their best when the name of the game is taking charge and showing initiative. But these qualities can be pushed to an extreme, thus leading to questionable behavior. They can indeed be domineering in dictating assignments and approaches, instead of being masterful; their confidence can turn to arrogance; they may be coercive with staff instead of persuasive; they may favor gambling rather than risk taking; and they can be seen as pushy rather than simply forceful. So, extreme *warriors* may not be effective when a situation requires the art of delegating and winning cooperation.

Leaders whose major trait is the *warrior* are competent in all innovation governance tasks that deal with adopting a bold vision and game plan, spotting new business opportunities, sponsoring high-risk, high-reward projects, launching new products, and creating new ventures. They are also forceful in pursuing acquisitions to complement their company's technology profile or reinforce its market base. On a people motivation side, they typically attract and motivate business-oriented innovators and self-starting entrepreneurs through their dynamism and "go get it" approach.

However, uncontrolled *warriors* may feel, and give in to, the urge to work against the principles of governance, which at its most basic level demands cooperation and dialogue – and, of course, following the rules. They may trigger resistance and frustration, particularly within functions and units outside their organizational turf, e.g. marketing if they come from the R&D side; R&D if they are from marketing; market companies if they are at headquarters, etc. They may also act more on instinct or gut feeling than through thorough analysis of the facts and careful planning. They may establish key performance indicators but may not always base their actions on indicator trends if these go against their perception of reality. *Warriors* accept data that confirm their opinion, but they might dismiss facts that go against their vision and mental model. Some of them do not hesitate to artificially generate the kind of data that justify their undertakings. Additionally, they may be inappropriate for leading complex negotiation deals related to innovation partnerships, given their impatience, forcefulness, and lack of diplomacy.

Some of the shortcomings of full-blooded *warriors* can in fact be reduced by their other, secondary traits. For example, if *warriors* have a *judge* element as secondary leadership trait, their reluctance to engage in data analysis and planning may be subdued. If they have a *diplomat* tendency as a second trait – an infrequent occurrence, though, because the two profiles tend to be incompatible – they are definitely in a good position to lead partnership discussions. If they have a significant *mentor* overtone in their profile, they may be in a better position to marshal the energies of their staff to achieve their objective and obtain cooperation.

Are You Fundamentally a *Judge*?

Judges are "no-nonsense" leaders with a bias for solid analysis. Their philosophy is: To be successful, let's base our decisions on facts! In this sense, they are the opposite of the more instinctive *warriors*. Their qualities – they are practical, economical, tenacious, reserved, thorough, and detail oriented – make them indispensable when important decisions need to be based on thorough analysis, and when pros and cons must be carefully evaluated before acting. But, as for *warriors*, the qualities of *judges*, if taken too far, can become detrimental. Their practical sense may lead to unimaginative behavior; their economical bias, if excessive, may make them stingy; their tenacity can turn into rigidity; their reserved behavior may lead to their being perceived as dull; being thorough may cause them to be overelaborate; and their detail orientation could mean they are seen as being data-bound. All of this may prevent them from reacting quickly and improvising in an emergency. In the worst case, *judges* are at risk of falling prey to the famous analysis–paralysis syndrome.

Leaders with a definite *judge* style can play an important role in innovation governance. Their bias toward rigorous analysis ensures that important decisions, for example on make-or-break projects, are carefully evaluated, thus limiting the risk of failure. They are also capable of establishing and standardizing complex processes. They are good at organizing functions, defining roles and responsibilities, and streamlining decision procedures. As proponents of the classical saying "Things that cannot be measured cannot be improved," they naturally tend to establish and monitor performance indicators. Because of their trustworthiness, *judges* are typically appreciated by the company's controller and CFO – archetypal *judges* themselves – and they can play a major advisory role vis-à-vis the CEO.

However, their attention to detail may make them unpopular with the more instinctive innovators and entrepreneurs. Over-zealous *judges* may indeed slow things down, particularly in the action-intensive product development and launch phases of the innovation process, which require quick decisions and reactive management. They may also restrain management from taking innovation risks, for example in pioneering a new technology, introducing a totally new product category, and being first in the market.

The above descriptions characterize full-blooded *judges*. In reality, however, as with the other three styles, leaders operate on the basis of their major trait, but its excesses are most frequently offset by their minor traits. This applies to *judges* particularly when their minor trait is *diplomat* or *mentor*. Either of these dispositions can make them more sensitive to the personal views of their subordinates, thus more effective when challenging projects and decisions. A *judge* with a *warrior* minor – an association often found in CEOs, although the reverse is more frequent – combines the best of both worlds, i.e. a realistic approach to risk taking.

Do You Behave Like a *Diplomat*?

Diplomats are leaders who believe that a harmonious organization performs better than a dissenting one, so they listen to the opinions of their teammates and staff before making decisions. Their philosophy is: To be successful, let's ensure everyone gets a fair deal and is able to contribute his or her best talents. This predisposition makes them more inside-out oriented than *warriors*. Given their qualities – *diplomats* can be flexible, willing to experiment, tactful and patient, socially skillful, and to certain extent shrewd – they are at their best when making trade-offs and handling cross-functional conflicts. But, as with the other traits, these qualities can turn into limitations when applied with excessive zeal. Their flexibility, when carried to an extreme, may make them inconsistent; their bias toward experimentation may make them reluctant to commit to a course of action; their tact and patience may make them overcautious; their attention to social skills may turn into indecisiveness; and their shrewd approach to human relations may be perceived as a desire to manipulate people. In short, *diplomats* may not be good at forcing a decision and sticking their neck out on a given course of action.

On the innovation governance front, *diplomats* are likely to be effective in establishing what we referred to in Chapter 1 as an *innovation constitution*, defining unambiguously the roles and responsibilities of various functions and units in innovation. They are talented at solving turf conflicts and ensuring everyone paddles in the same direction. As members of top management, they can facilitate the emergence of a consensus on important decisions on strategy, projects, and funding. Their role is also important in managing open innovation initiatives and partnerships, since they strive to achieve win–win deals.

But overcautious *diplomats*, particularly if they water down imaginative concepts to please everyone, may lead the company to develop dull products. An urge for consensus can indeed be dysfunctional in innovation. *Diplomats* may be reluctant to see conflicts emerge on innovation ideas, particularly if these ideas have reached the top management team.

> Rebecca Henderson, who taught innovation management at MIT before joining Harvard Business School, described the spirit that characterizes the best performing innovation teams as *high conflict–high respect*. She exhorted innovation teams to engage forcefully in conflicts on ideas and approaches, but to respect one another as team members.

As with the previous profiles, leaders with a *diplomat* character trait may see the risk of dysfunctional behavior reduced by their secondary leadership style. We have already mentioned that leaders with a strong *diplomat* style are infrequently associated with *warrior* characteristics. They can, however, combine common traits with *judges* and this may make them more practical and decisive. When they combine a *diplomat* and *mentor* profile, a frequent occurrence, they are likely to be excellent developers of human resources, notably of future innovation leaders.

Do Your Staff Consider You as a *Mentor*?

Mentors pay close attention to the personal development of their staff, coach them, and sponsor their initiatives. Their philosophy is: To be successful, we need a team of motivated people whose talents are being used in a right way. Their qualities – they are considerate, somewhat idealistic with regard to the potential of their staff, modest, supporting, and responsive – make them accomplished at working with others and developing team members. They are often seen as the wise leaders whom people go to when they have a problem to which they see no solution, or when they enter into a personal or professional conflict with colleagues. But *mentors'* qualities, if pushed too far, can have a negative impact on their effectiveness as born leaders. An overly considerate attitude may be perceived by some colleagues as softness; their idealistic view of people's qualities can be interpreted as gullibility; their modesty may make them unimposing; their supporting attitude can be seen as paternalism; their responsiveness may verge on passivity. These excesses make them ill-adapted to promoting an outside-in attitude in their organization and in gearing up their staff to fight tough competitive battles.

Leaders with a definite *mentor* profile can play an important role in innovation governance, for instance by aligning people behind the company's innovation agenda and promoting corresponding values. Their strong people orientation makes them indispensable to the top management team as advisers when allocating innovation responsibilities or appointing innovation teams. They can also detect opportunities for improvements in the company's innovation climate and identify obstacles that management needs to overcome. They tend to be keen to launch management development programs to fill gaps in innovation-related skills. Finally, they are useful in handling interpersonal conflicts within innovation teams or between functions.

But because of their innate bias toward looking inside the organization, *mentors* may not be effective in leading their staff into product battles. By focusing their energy on handling internal interfaces rather than becoming immersed in the market, they may miss innovation opportunities. They are therefore dependent on the motivation, external orientation, and self-starting attitude of their colleagues.

If *mentors* feature a *warrior* minor, which introduces an outside orientation and a bias for action, many of their shortcomings will be mitigated. In fact, a *warrior/mentor* combination can be extremely appropriate for leading an innovative organization. *Mentors* can also have *judge* overtones, which give them a more analytical − less emotional − approach to managing people, teams, and processes. When combined with a *diplomat* minor, *mentors* can be competent at handling complex negotiations, for example with partners.

HOW DO YOU LEVERAGE INDIVIDUAL TALENTS TO CREATE EFFECTIVE INNOVATION TEAMS?

Tomasko's typology of leadership styles can prove useful when deciding about allocating responsibilities for innovation. It is worth stressing that there is no hierarchy among these four styles. Each has its strengths and can contribute to steering innovation and aligning people behind an innovation effort. Each also includes a number of biases and weaknesses, which must be recognized. This underscores the importance of combining complementary profiles within management and innovation teams to achieve balance.

New product development projects are often, intuitively, assigned to *warrior* leaders because they tend to be professionally aggressive, proactive, risk taking and market oriented. But at the same time, teams need rigor in analysis, methods for minimizing uncertainty and risk, and a disciplined process for navigating through the project gates. This may require a second in command with a strong *judge* inclination, i.e. a thorough and prudent leader.

If the project team is not balanced across all profiles, this can be achieved by paying special attention to the composition of the project review team – the higher level committee in charge of challenging the project team and approving its completion of the requirements of each gate. If there is no *warrior* profile in the project team, for example, then the chair of the review committee should be a *warrior* type to invigorate the team, create a sense of urgency, and stress the need to be market oriented. If the project team is in the hands of a strong *warrior* leader, then the review committee should be composed of *judges* and *diplomats*, the latter to smooth interfunction relationships, notably regarding turf sensitivities and conflicts over resource allocation.

Similarly, the top management team can apply this typology within the innovation governance model. For example, if the primary responsibility for innovation is allocated to a single person, e.g. to the CTO or the CIO, then the natural leadership style of that person needs to be recognized. If this leader is perceived by peers as a true *warrior* – as happens frequently because companies like to appoint *doers* in this position – management would do well to recommend that the *warrior* appoints people to work with him/ her who have a complementary profile. Whether consciously or subconsciously, leaders often look for a second in command or assistants who have the same major leadership trait as they do. *Warriors*, for example, may be tempted to surround themselves with other *warriors*, simply because they feel more comfortable dealing with people like themselves. However, a *warrior* CTO or CIO needs a *judge* as his/her assistant to handle the disciplined part of the job, for example the standardization, improvement, and supervision of processes, and the implementation and tracking of innovation performance indicators.

The challenge is obviously easier to address when the governance model allocates innovation responsibilities to a group of leaders, such as the subset of the top management team, or the high-level innovation steering group or board – which has managers spanning different hierarchical levels. In these cases, it is desirable for the leaders in question to possess different styles, thus ensuring that the group is reasonably balanced in terms of leadership profile.

ALIGNING LEADERSHIP AND INNOVATION GOVERNANCE

To close this reflection on leadership and governance, it may be useful to briefly review why *innovation leadership* provides a foundation from which *effective governance* will emerge.

Why Does Innovation Need to be Governed?

As we have pointed out, innovation is a highly complex corporate activity, which crosses many of the boundaries that exist in most companies.

The kind of governance that emerges naturally in a complex system with many groups that have differing goals, expertise, and interests is typically *tribal* – each group possesses its own rules and its own judgment of what is important. As sociobiologist Edward

O. Wilson put it in a chapter entitled "Tribalism is a Fundamental Human Trait": "to form groups, drawing visceral comfort and pride from familiar fellowship, and to defend the group enthusiastically against rival groups – these are among the absolute universals of human nature and hence of culture."[5]

Anyone who has been in the position of managing or leading innovation has no doubt come across the functional tribalism that can defeat innovation – whereby innovators want the most radical breakthrough solution they can imagine, engineers want to spend years perfecting one aspect of the innovation, manufacturers want to preserve the efficiency of their processes, sales just wants something that will please their current customers (e.g. something faster or cheaper or prettier), and so on. These are not simply differences of opinion – these are core beliefs about what is essentially important. This is why innovation needs to be governed.

Why Should Innovation Governance Models be Made Explicit?

As we have just seen, tribalism is one form of governance that emerges in complex companies in the absence of an explicit model. In addition to tribalism, companies may exhibit governance models that resemble democracies, republics, monarchies, aristocracies, plutocracies, dictatorships, and of course the lack of government, or anarchy.

The tacit models of government that large and complex systems adopt do not usually provide the best possible methods of coordination and execution. Corporate democracies are often extremely inefficient. Aristocracies or monarchies, where the senior leadership is automatically chosen from among the elite – be they members of the founding family or of some other inner circle – do not look widely for appropriate leaders and are often subject to conservative and tradition-bound thinking. Dictatorships may become tied to the inspiration, personality, operational style, and judgments of a particular leader, with disastrous consequences when that person retires. Any tacit form of government is likely to be held captive by a limited scope of knowledge, information, and relationships as leaders assume that their knowledge, their world view, is the best one – or perhaps the only one. This is true for corporate governance in general; it applies also to innovation governance.

The alternative, then, as we have argued throughout this book, is to make the company's model of innovation governance explicit, for example in an *innovation constitution*.

Governing Relates to Knowing What You are Doing

Sometime in the later decades of the 20th century, innovators (then called new product developers) began to ask what would make their work more successful. Would it be useful to gather together teams with members who represented the tribal functions early in the process? Was there a way to outline the decisions that needed to be made and the tasks that needed to be undertaken in order to get an idea to market? How could the likely success or failure of a project be assessed before too many resources were allocated to it, and how might the company be able to align its product strategy with the actual projects that were being resourced?

As these and other fundamental questions were raised, and as companies discovered ways of addressing them that created a discipline around the enterprise of innovating, the boundaries of the activity expanded to include both purposeful exploration of new opportunities and the introduction of innovation partners. The digitization of information and globalization added to the complexity, but also to companies' ability to draw on vast resources while at the same time being able to coordinate means and information.

Corporate leaders and innovators now have access to the world at the click of a mouse. They can gather and communicate critical information in the form of maps and diagrams that reveal not only data but also context. They have designed and implemented processes and practices that foster genuine communication and understanding among their "tribal groups" as well as with partners and customers. And yet, even with all of this in its favor, in many instances innovation seems not to be working as well as we might expect.

Now is the Time to Start Governing Innovation

Happily, there *is* a better way. First of all, innovation has become governable. That is, top management now has many tools to enable it to set innovation goals and objectives, to measure progress – or the lack thereof – towards these goals, and to assess what is contributing to success or failure. Second, innovation has become, for most companies, an inescapable issue of basic survival in this fast-moving and networked world. Third, *innovation*, unlike *new product development*, regularly requires the company to make decisions that challenge its core identity – for example, moving to new business models, partnerships, and new businesses – and this requires the explicit participation of empowered individuals or groups in the company.

Many of the companies we have written about derived their governance model from an understanding of their history and culture – the basis of their innate or tacit models. Some drew on models they were familiar with at other companies. All took into consideration their strengths and weaknesses, and we believe that none of them thought that the model it implemented would necessarily work forever – i.e. they are open to, even committed to, changing and improving the model.

We predict that as governance increasingly becomes an explicit matter of concern, management's ability to set innovation goals and agendas and to move effectively toward accomplishing them will improve markedly. We also suspect that success in governing innovation will open up new areas that cannot now be predicted. But we know that the key ingredients for participating in whatever the new world brings will still be effective governance, leadership, and collaboration.

NOTES

[1] Deschamps, J.-P. (2008). *Innovation Leaders: How Senior Executives Stimulate, Steer and Sustain Innovation*. Chichester, Wiley/Jossey-Bass.

[2] Catmull, E. (2008). How Pixar Fosters Collective Creativity. *Harvard Business Review*, September: 64–72.

[3] Videotaped interview with Daniel Borel, former chairman of Logitech, on "Innovation & Leadership," IMD, 2003.

[4] Robert M. Tomasko is a management author and consultant who has written four best-selling books: *Downsizing: Reshaping the Corporation for the Future*, New York, Amacom, 1987; *Rethinking the Corporation*, New York, Amacom, 1993; *Go for Growth*, Hoboken, John Wiley & Sons Inc., 1996; and *Bigger Isn't Always Better*, New York, Amacom, 2006. He directs the Social Enterprise Program and holds a faculty appointment at American University, where he teaches graduate courses in corporate social responsibility, effective activism, leadership, NGO management, and social entrepreneurship.

[5] Wilson, E.O. (2012). *The Social Conquest of Earth*. New York, Liveright Publishing Company, p. 57.

APPENDIX: EXAMPLES OF TASKS AND INITIATIVES TO SUPPORT INNOVATION

Any audit of a company's innovation governance system, whatever the model chosen, must include a management review of the range of tasks that should be carried out by those people (or governance mechanisms) responsible for innovation. The questions management should ask are twofold:

- Do the people (or collective mechanisms) to whom we have allocated the responsibility for innovation carry out *all* the tasks that are part of a comprehensive innovation governance system, i.e. is the scope of our governance system comprehensive?
- How have these tasks been allocated between the person(s) or mechanism with primary responsibility for innovation and those with a support function, and has this allocation been clearly communicated to everyone in the company?

To help in this review, we propose a broad checklist of typical initiatives that support innovation. The checklist consists of eight parts:

1. Diagnostic and continuous improvement
2. Innovation vision and strategy
3. Innovation content management
4. Innovation process management
5. Organization and infrastructure
6. Competencies and attitudes

7. Climate and culture
8. Allocation of specific management responsibilities

1. DIAGNOSTIC AND CONTINUOUS IMPROVEMENT

Have we:

*   Defined the scope and the specific topics to be covered in our initial innovation performance diagnostic?
*   Conducted – internally or with external help – a benchmarking study on the chosen performance factors and processes?
*   Elaborated and conducted an internal questionnaire survey and carried out selected interviews to collect opinions from our managers on innovation issues and deficiencies?
*   Established – as a result of this survey – a first diagnostic and inventory of innovation issues, and identified priorities for improvements?
*   Adopted a process and annual cycle for revising/updating this diagnostic and tracking improvements?

2. INNOVATION VISION AND STRATEGY

Have we:

*   Launched a collective process to formulate a new innovation vision or to update it (for example, through small work groups with our senior leaders)?
*   Identified – as a result of the above exercise – our objectives for innovation in the next five to 10 years and the main thrusts to be adopted as a priority?
*   Discussed and validated this new vision (and its consequences) within our group leadership team?
*   Translated this vision into resource allocation objectives (for R&D, operations, and commercialization) by main type of innovation?
*   Launched a project to define a long-term technology strategy aligned with the strategic priorities of each of our product lines or types of activities?

3. INNOVATION CONTENT MANAGEMENT

Have we:

- Clearly defined the extent to which the responsibilities that we have allocated to a leader (or group of leaders) as part of our governance model cover the *content* of innovation?
- Ensured that our leaders responsible for innovation operate permanently in a cross-functional mode, i.e. with balanced input from the technology and the business sides?
- Established a formal process to formulate and align our technology and product strategies on a regular basis?
- Defined product and project portfolio management responsibilities, i.e. who proposes, advises, and decides on new projects, as well as a process for project reviews?
- Set up a policy and process for the development and deployment of new ventures beyond our existing lines of activities?

4. INNOVATION PROCESS MANAGEMENT

Have we:

- Adopted a general, high-level innovation model outlining the main sub-processes within innovation (incremental and radical), and have we broadcast that model widely?
- Collectively selected the critical processes to be improved first (typically the most important and the most deficient)?
- Assigned specific responsibilities (e.g. to *process owners*) for the development or revitalization of these processes?
- Established an approach and calendar for a collective review of the plans and results of these process improvement initiatives?
- Defined and selected a set of performance indicators (from the initial diagnostic) for each of the processes selected?

5. ORGANIZATION AND INFRASTRUCTURE

Have we:

- Recommended concrete mechanisms to ensure an effective link between R&D, marketing, and operations at the project level?

- Analyzed and recommended an organizational structure for the development of new activities (e.g. formalization of an incubator)?
- Proposed a predefined path for the management of new activities and their future allocation (to product lines or to new entities yet to be created)?
- Created a new full-time function for *innovation excellence* to support the innovation initiatives and projects of the various business groups and track results?
- Created an intranet platform and portal for the online diffusion and management of the various processes and projects?

6. COMPETENCIES AND ATTITUDES

Have we:

- Identified – from the initial diagnostic – the main deficiencies in competencies associated with managing innovation projects?
- Started a process to identify and exchange best practices, both internal and external, to be managed by the *innovation excellence* function?
- Proposed an innovation management development program targeted at all managers of innovation projects and new activities?
- Proposed a system to set individual objectives and performance measures regarding innovation?
- Organized and launched collective motivation events: innovation days, innovation competitions and prizes (for different categories), and others?

7. CLIMATE AND CULTURE

Have we:

- Characterized – through a survey and individual interviews – the innovation climate within the company and the main obstacles identified?

- Worked in small groups on the most important obstacles, and recommended changes to remedy them?
- Included this measure of the *innovation climate* in the regular cycle of opinion surveys on employee engagement?
- Made concrete recommendations to all managers on how to promote – through words and deeds – a mindset that supports innovation?
- Made sure that the company's internal publications share innovation experiences and progress?

8. ALLOCATION OF SPECIFIC MANAGEMENT RESPONSIBILITIES

Have we:

- Officially appointed the leader – or group of leaders – to whom we have entrusted overall responsibility for innovation, and clarified roles and empowerment levels?
- Selected and nominated the different *process owners* and *process coaches*, or *sponsors*, for each process critical to innovation success?
- Recruited – internally, if available with a compatible entrepreneurship profile, or externally – the leaders for the new emerging business areas (if any)?
- Staffed an *innovation excellence* function, responsible for leading a network of *innovation champions* (if this is part of the chosen governance model)?
- Considered appointing *innovation champions* within each line of activity and main function to stimulate and support innovation?

INDEX

Index compiled by Annette Musker